GRANDES HORIZONTALES

GRANDES HORIZONTALES

The Lives and Legends of Four
Nineteenth-Century Courtesans

Virginia Rounding

BLOOMSBURY

First published in Great Britain 2003
This paperback edition published 2004

Copyright © 2003 by Virginia Rounding

The moral right of the author has been asserted

Bloomsbury Publishing Plc, 38 Soho Square, London W1D 3HB

A CIP catalogue record for this book
is available from the British Library

ISBN 0 7475 6859 6

10 9 8 7 6 5 4 3 2 1

Typeset by Hewer Text Ltd, Edinburgh
Printed in Great Britain by Clays Limited, St Ives plc

www.bloomsbury.com/virginiarounding

For my companion of the
rue du Chemin Vert

Of such women, you know, the mould is broken. We will not see their like again.

Zed, *La Société Parisienne,*
La Librairie Illustrée, Paris, 1888

CONTENTS

Acknowledgments

I would particularly like to record my thanks to Thierry Savatier, great-great-nephew of Apollonie Sabatier (La Présidente), for his willingness to share his knowledge and insights about his great-great-aunt, and for furnishing me with proof copies of the relevant pages of his edition of Gautier's *Lettres à la Présidente* before publication, as well as sending me details of some documents pertaining to Marie Duplessis, auctioned in 1984. Monsieur Savatier also put me in touch with Dr Wendy Nolan Joyce, who devoted part of her PhD thesis to Madame Sabatier. Professor John Klier, Head of the Hebrew and Jewish Studies Department at University College London, gave me useful information about Jews living in Moscow in the early nineteenth century. Thanks are also due to the librarian of the Wallace Collection for access to the Collection's file on Madame Sabatier, to the Travellers' Club in Paris for access to the Hôtel Païva, and to the staff of the British Library, the London Library and the Bibliothèque Nationale. (Mention also has to be made of the man who feeds the cats in the Cimetière de Montmartre and who, for a small contribution to his cat project, will direct visitors to any grave they wish to find.)

Unless otherwise indicated in the notes, all translations from the French are my own, including those of the correspondence between Apollonie Sabatier and Charles Baudelaire and of extracts from poems by Alexandre Dumas *fils* and Théophile Gautier. I have also made a point of translating passages of the *Mémoires de Cora Pearl*, only using the 'authorised' version of *The Memoirs of Cora Pearl* when the original translation (or, rather, version) seems particularly felicitous (or at least not inaccurate).

The *Demi-monde*

T HE FOUR COURTESANS or *grandes horizontales* whose lives and legends are examined in this book were all, in differing ways, representative of the *demi-monde* in nineteenth-century Paris – that is, of that half-world midway between respectable high society and the low life of the common prostitute. *Demi-monde* is a term suggestive of twilight, of a world of shifting appearances and shadow, where nothing is quite what it seems, a world between worlds. Alexandre Dumas *fils* was the first to give the term wide currency in his play *Le Demi-monde*, first performed in March 1855, and his strictures in the introduction to a later printed edition suggest that it, and its associated *demi-mondaine* (a woman belonging to the *demi-monde*), had soon come to be used rather more widely that he had himself intended. Dumas *fils* is at pains to establish 'for dictionaries of the future'[1] that the *demi-monde* is not synonymous with the 'mob of courtesans',[2] despite the fact that this is how the term has been habitually deployed. Rather, it is the class of the *déclassé*, a word denoting a person who had fallen in social status and thus become 'declassed'. Declassed women included victims of scandal, divorcees, women separated from or abandoned by husband or lover, 'merry widows', or foreign women whom the authorities might deport when it suited them. According to Dumas *fils*, a woman could not simply choose to join the *demi-monde*; rather, the circumstances of life may mean that she arrives in it without appearing to have exercised any choice, or as a result of the choices she had made having more far-reaching consequences than she ever imagined. He asserts that the *demi-monde* is in fact made up of 'women of honourable stock who, as daughters, wives or mothers, were received and cherished as of right in the best families, and who deserted'.[3] But even Dumas *fils* does not wish to restrict the designation to such women, and so he concedes that the *demi-monde*

> also welcomes girls who started out in life with an error, women who live with a man whose name they adopt, elegant and beautiful foreigners recommended and protected by an intimate friend, under his personal responsibility, and finally all those women who had roots in legitimate society, and whose fall has love as its excuse, as its sole excuse . . .[4]

A *demi-mondaine* could not necessarily be identified by her appearance, and this could prove a difficulty for visitors to Paris. Even that most expert of Parisians, the writer Maxime Du Camp, could declare 'one does not know today whether honest women are dressing like prostitutes, or prostitutes are dressed like honest women.'[5] The *demi-monde* knew how to copy the *haut monde* (the world of high society) and yet at the same time the *haut monde* was not above copying the half-world, particularly where fashionable dress was concerned. But though the two worlds might on the surface seem indistinguishable, there was nevertheless a chasm fixed between them. There was a bridge over this chasm, but it led in one direction only: it was easy enough for a woman from the *haut monde* to fall and find herself in the *demi-monde* but no return journey was possible, no way for a *demi-mondaine* to climb her way into high society, no matter what riches she might amass or works of charity she might undertake.

Where the definition proffered by Dumas *fils* departs most significantly from the general usage of the term is in his insistence that the *demi-mondaine* does not accept money for her favours, that she 'clings to this basic premise: "We give, we do not sell"',[6] and she is thus distinguished from the courtesan, for whom love is a financial transaction. In fact, despite Dumas *fils'* best efforts, the *demi-mondaine* and the courtesan have always been virtually indistinguishable, and whatever else may remain in doubt about the women known as Marie Duplessis, Cora Pearl, La Païva and La Présidente, their willingness to accept money from the men in their lives (though in varying degrees, La Présidente presenting a markedly different case from the other three) is not in question.

Of these four women Marie Duplessis was the first to die, in 1847 at only twenty-three years old. She thus missed out on the golden age of the French courtesan, though can perhaps be seen as its most significant forerunner. That age was the era of the Second Empire, the eighteen years from 1852 to 1870 when France was ruled by Louis Napoleon Bonaparte, the Emperor Napoleon III, who was both the step-grandson and the nephew of the first Napoleon. (Napoleon III's mother, Hortense Beauharnais, was both the daughter of the Empress Josephine by her first husband, and the wife of Napoleon I's brother, Louis.) The ostentation and delight in show of that era, along with the at least apparent prosperity, provided a perfect setting and encouragement for the opulent lifestyle of the pampered and gla- morous courtesan, a type of which Cora Pearl and La Païva were notorious and highly successful examples. There was also always an element of the ersatz, the not-quite-real, about the world of Napoleon III and his court. The Second Empire drew its legitimacy from the First, itself resulting from the extraordinary personal power and charisma of Napoleon I, and much of the court ceremonial and protocol of the Second Empire was merely an imitation of that of the First. The supportive, if supercilious and patronising, comment of the *Illustrated London News* in August 1852 set the tone for what was to be the prevailing judgment of the Second Empire and its 'showiness':

When Louis Napoleon was first heard of we had little respect for the man, and no expectation that he would succeed. Five years ago an outcast and an adventurer, forbidden even to tread the soil of France and now the controller of its fate, his success is the greatest marvel in the modern political world, full as that is of strange occurrences . . . If France can be guided to peace and kept tranquil by shows, shows may in the end be as useful to them as Parliaments . . . A theatrical Empire in France will be a pleasant show for the rest of Europe, if the French be satisfied by the representation, and their Emperor seek popularity and power only in pyrotechnical victories.[7]

Thus the imperial court could be seen as mirroring and sharing some of the essence of the *demi-monde*, not only in its ostentation but also in its shadowiness, its sense of unreality and its flair for imitation, and the women, like La Païva, who rose to startling prominence through an accumulation of wealth about whose origins it was best not to enquire too closely shared some of the characteristics of the Emperor who had arisen out of a lifetime of exile and relative anonymity to claim what he considered to be the inheritance of his uncle and step-grandfather.

This book is not only about the lives of four courtesans but also about the legends surrounding them, the images made of them largely through the writings of others, both their contemporaries and subsequent commentators and historians. It is a truism that much of what we know, or think we know, about nineteenth-century women comes from the writings of men, and the case of these four women is no exception. The most well-known of the memoir writers of this period of French history were the Goncourt brothers, Edmond and Jules, who every night wrote up in their Journal their impressions of the people they had encountered and the events they had witnessed during the day. They occasionally attended the soirées of La Païva and La Présidente, and their comments, with their habitual attendant elements of misogyny, anti-semitism and general disapproval of everyone apart from themselves, have coloured the way these women have been seen ever since. An equally vituperative diarist was Count Horace de Viel Castel, an official at the Louvre and a regular visitor at the soirées given by Princess Mathilde, cousin of Napoleon III, where he picked up all the gossip. He added to the construction of the negative image of La Païva in particular. Other memoirists usually had their own axes to grind, especially those writing in the aftermath of the collapse of the Second Empire and looking round for someone to blame. Those society women who wrote diaries for publication used them partly as a vehicle to express their disapproval of the *demi-mondaines*, in an attempt to clarify the distinction between this half-world and their own respectable sphere, while the few *demi-mondaines* who produced their memoirs were concerned not only to justify themselves but to see off the competition of their fellow courtesans. In all these accounts objective truth, if there is indeed such a thing, was in short supply. And then there were the novelists, playwrights and poets who used what they knew, or imagined, of the life of this or that courtesan in the service of their art.

I have chosen these particular four women to write about as they were subject more than most to the image-making of others, and of themselves. They each became the stuff of legend, both within their own lifetimes and subsequently, and their stories demonstrate the addiction to myth-making which is a part of human life and discourse. Any account of a life is a story, affected by the interpretation, style and point of view of the teller and all previous tellers, and the accounts given of the lives of these women demonstrate this fictionalising process particularly clearly, and none more so than those devoted to Marie Duplessis who became the prototype of the virtuous courtesan through her portrayal as Marguerite Gautier in the novel by Alexandre Dumas *fils, La Dame aux camélias*. Her identification with this romantic heroine affected all subsequent judgments and even physical descriptions of her, with the result that the 'real' Marie (who was also in part a fabrication of her own making) slipped into the shadows. The image she has become is almost entirely constructed of the words of others, the only words we have direct from her consisting of one or two brief letters, the main evidence of her way of life being a stash of invoices found after her death.

La Païva, born Thérèse Lachmann, is surrounded by a horde of unlikely legends through which she has attained the status of a fairy-tale character, the evil witch luring young men to part with their wealth by casting a spell of incomprehensible sexual magic upon them. The stories that were told about her attest both to her unusual power and to the prejudices of the storytellers, prejudices against women, Jews and foreigners, all of which Thérèse embodied, along with an infuriating (to the onlooker) ability to make money and a delight in showing it off. Again, words which have come down to us from her own pen are very few and mainly concern practical arrangements, but she did make a very clear statement of her own in the design and building of her opulent *hôtel* in the avenue des Champs Elysées, which still stands and continues to convey a strong impression of this remarkable woman.

Apollonie Sabatier, also known as La Présidente, was the subject of two particular image-making exercises, first as *La Femme piquée par un serpent* (The Woman Bitten by a Snake), a sculpture based on a cast of her body by Auguste Clésinger, and then as *la très-Chère, la très belle* (the Dearest, the most beautiful) of the poet Charles Baudelaire's *Les Fleurs du mal*. Both of these artistic endeavours had a profound effect on Apollonie's life and on the way she has been viewed by her own and subsequent generations. Again, we have little to go on as far as her own words are concerned, though the fragments which remain of her letters to Baudelaire convey a clear sense of her generosity of character and something of the spirit which drew so many men of letters and the other arts to her.

Cora Pearl is the only one of these four women to have written her own account of her life, to take the power of fabrication completely into her own hands, for Cora's memoirs present the version of her life which she wants us to have. Yet she too was subject to the myth-making of others, a myth-making again contaminated by prejudice, particularly against foreign women who profited from the foibles of Parisian men. The descriptions, both physical and moral, given by their contemporaries of all four women were also heavily influenced by prevailing stereotypes of prostitutes, as codified by Dr Parent-Duchâtelet in his highly influential text, first published in 1836, *De la Prostitution dans la ville de Paris considérée sous le rapport de l'hygiène publique, de la morale et de l'administration* (On prostitution in the city of Paris from the point of view of public hygiene, morality and administration).

In looking at the lives and legends of Marie Duplessis, Cora Pearl, La Païva and La Présidente, I will attempt to distinguish each life from the legend, while being aware that this may not always be possible, that to strip away the legend completely may be to leave little of the life. The two have become so thoroughly intertwined, so hard to tell apart, that these women truly inhabit a *demi-monde*, a twilit half-world where the image is frequently taken for the reality and nothing is quite what it seems.

---

1 Alexandre Dumas *fils*, *Théâtre complet, avec Préfaces inédites*, Vol.II, Calmann Lévy, Paris, 1895, p.11

2 Ibid.

3 Ibid.

4 Ibid.

5 Maxime Du Camp, *Paris: ses organes, ses fonctions et sa vie jusqu'en 1870*, G. Rondeau, Monaco, 1993, p.351 (first published between 1869 and 1875)

6 Alexandre Dumas *fils*, *Théâtre complet, avec Préfaces inédites*, Vol.II, p.12

7 *Illustrated London News*, No.575, Vol.XXI, Supplement, Saturday, 21 August 1852

CHAPTER ONE

Prostitutes and Prostitution in Nineteenth-century Paris

T HE HIGHLY PAID courtesan of the *demi-monde* represented the pinnacle of a continuum of women who traded their bodies and their company for financial reward in mid-nineteenth century France. Throughout much of that century Paris enjoyed one of the most regulated systems of prostitution in the world, a system envied by the authorities of many other capital cities. Dr Michael Ryan, a member of the Royal Colleges of Physicians and Surgeons and Senior Physician to the Metropolitan Free Hospital, expressed this envy as far as London was concerned in his *Prostitution in London*, published three years after Dr Parent-Duchâtelet's work and drawing heavily upon it:

> As prostitution has ever existed, and will ever exist, in all countries, the French police regulations are intended in every way to diminish the nuisance caused by it, and to regulate the houses devoted to it. The regulations in France, are well calculated to repress crime, while those in this country, are most defective, and hence the frequent murders and robberies, in brothels, so often recorded in the public papers.[1]

The French system was based on the belief of the inevitability, even the necessity, of prostitution combined with the desire to discipline the prostitute, to keep the whole phenomenon contained and subject to authority. As Dr Parent-Duchâtelet put it, 'Prostitutes are as inevitable in a great urban centre as are sewers, roads and rubbish dumps. The attitude of the authorities should be the same in regard to the former as to the latter.'[2] The ideal was considered to be the creation of an enclosed world of prostitutes, a sort of distorted mirror image of the enclosed world of the nun, in which the women concerned would be good 'workers', doing as they were told, and contributing to the stability of society by absorbing the excess sexual energy of men, while remaining invisible to the bulk of the population. It was believed that registration with the police and tight control over the activities of prostitutes would result in the containment of syphilis, a great scourge of the nineteenth century, as well as in the maintenance of stable married life. This was essentially a European attitude, carried to its logical conclusion in the French system of regulation; an entirely different attitude prevailed in New York, for instance, where the emphasis was on the desire to stamp out prostitution altogether. Dr Ryan quotes from an address delivered by the Reverend Mr M'Dowall, Chaplain to the New York Magdalen Asylum, in May 1832 in which he had declared that 'the grand effort of those who would promote reformation, should be directed to arresting, and, if possible, reclaiming, those wretched females, who are the pest and nuisance of society, though equally the objects of our compassion and abhorrence'.[3]

Parent-Duchâtelet's research was conducted and published during the reign of Louis Philippe, a period also known as the July monarchy. The ethos of this monarchy centred on the maintenance of political and social stability and, in the early years of his reign, Louis Philippe's naturally conservative outlook was strengthened by a number of workers' demonstrations – such as the revolts of the Lyonnais weavers in 1831 and 1834, which were brutally suppressed – and by several attempts on his life. Little was done to address the growing social problems arising out of the Industrial Revolution, the workers in the slums having to fend for themselves while the middle and upper classes made money out of them and went dancing and dining on the proceeds. Disease, especially cholera, was rife among the urban population; the cholera epidemic of 1832, which lasted from mid-February to nearly the end of September, claimed the lives of 18,402 Parisians. The glittering façade of Paris masked an under-world of poverty and disease, a dislocation which was a marked feature of Second Empire life but whose seeds were sown during the July monarchy, where the contrasts between rich and poor also provided a natural setting for the growth of prostitution and for the rise of the courtesan.

The backbone of the French system was the registration of prostitutes, a registration which could be entered into voluntarily or enforced following an arrest. Registered prostitutes or *filles soumises* (literally, submissive or compliant whores) had to submit to various regulations, including mandatory health checks for venereal disease, while unregistered ones (*insoumises*) operated outside the law. A *fille soumise* either worked independently, in which case she was known as a *fille libre* or *isolée*, or as a *fille en carte* (because of the obligatory identity card which detailed the dates of her medical inspections as well as any infringements of the rules), or in a strictly regulated and supervised brothel known as a *maison de tolérance* or *maison tolérée*, where she would also live. This latter type of prostitute was known as a *fille de maison* or a *fille de numéro*, by virtue of the number she was given when she was entered in the brothel-keeper's book, though it may also have referred to the fact that the authorities required brothels to display their street numbers in a large size over the door. At the top of the hierarchy were the first- and second-class *maisons*, intended for an aristocratic or bourgeois clientèle, and generally to be found in the centre of Paris, in the area around the Opera House in the rue Le Peletier. Such establishments were lavishly furnished, with thick carpets, mirrors and statuary, and an abundance of mythological motifs in the decorations on ceilings and walls.

Prostitutes who worked independently in Paris were hemmed in by a network of petty restrictions, designed to prevent the innocent and the virtuous from being offended by the too obvious presence of vice which was tolerated only so long as it could be kept invisible except to those who knew where to look, and which increased the difficulties of carrying out their trade. In particular, prostitutes were forbidden to

solicit or even appear in the street or other public places before seven
o'clock in the evening and after ten or eleven at night. Neither were
they supposed to draw attention to their trade by dressing or behaving
provocatively. One way in which such restrictions were circumvented
was through the use of intermediaries or procuresses who, while
appearing to carry on a legitimate business as, for instance, clothing
merchants or outfitters, would also be making appointments for a
number of prostitutes from whose profits they would take a cut. Such
women were likely to have previously been prostitutes themselves and
could now, by their very presence alongside younger women in the
streets, indicate, to those men who knew the signs, the availability of
the latter; they could also direct the interested passer-by to the nearest
brothel. 'The more severe the regulations of the police are made, the
more important to their class these women become.'[4] The extent to
which a prostitute could get away with soliciting varied from area to
area of Paris. Alphonse Esquiros, a phrenologist and social commentator who took up and developed some of Parent-Duchâtelet's
theories in his *Les Vierges folles* (The Foolish Virgins), first published
in 1840, and who, unusually for such commentators, was endowed
with a sense of humour, presents a vivid picture of these differences in
describing how an old hand might instruct a new recruit:

> In the area of the Bourse, the Chaussée d'Antin and boulevard
> de Gand, the prostitute should walk along the pavement,
> discreetly beckoning with her eyes when appropriate; around
> the Palais Royal and in the streets of Saint-Honoré, Montmar-
> tre, Richelieu and Saint-Denis, she should whisper in a man's
> ear; in the Latin Quarter, she should address him as '*tu*' and call a
> spade a spade; finally, in the Cité, in the rue de l'Hôtel-de-ville
> and elsewhere, she should accost the passers-by boldly, seize
> their protesting arms and drag them to her by force, even at the
> risk of being elbowed sharply in the chest.[5]

The most convenient arrangement for a prostitute would be to have a
roster of regular clients, obviating the need for her to solicit for new

ones. A *fille en carte* might have an arrangement whereby a group of gentlemen bought her services *en bloc*, dividing up among themselves who would visit her on which day. Such an arrangement could also be advantageous for the men concerned by lessening the risk – or at least the fear – of contracting a venereal disease, by confining sexual activity within a closed circle of acquaintances.

A distinction was made between those women who registered voluntarily and those registered by the authorities. Voluntary registration was a simple procedure, involving a woman going to the Prefecture of Police armed with her birth certificate and asking to be registered. She would be questioned by the assistant head of the bureau and asked to declare her matrimonial status, the professions of her parents and whether she had any children. She would then undergo a medical examination at the police dispensary. The minimum age at which a girl might legally apply for registration was sixteen. Compulsory registration might be the result of a police raid, of the sort so feared by Emile Zola's Nana in his novel of that name:

> Moreover, Satin inspired [Nana] with an awful fear of the police. She was full of anecdotes about them . . . In the summer they would swoop upon the boulevard in parties of twelve or fifteen, surrounding a whole long reach of sidewalk and fishing up as many as thirty women in an evening . . . [Nana] saw herself hustled and dragged along, and finally subjected to the official medical inspection. The thought of the official armchair filled her with shame and anguish . . .[6]

The compulsory health check, or *contrôle sanitaire*, was detested by prostitutes who, no less than other women of the period, experienced medical examination of the sexual organs as an assault on their modesty. The 'armchair' Nana dreads so much refers to the adapted table on which the women were examined. The doctors preferred to use an ordinary table, with a raised plank at one end for the woman to rest her feet on, but so many prostitutes were in the habit of wearing big hats which they did not want to be squashed as they lay back, that a kind of reclining armchair was devised so that they could remain partially sitting up. The dispensary where the checks were carried out was originally located in the rue Croix-des-Petits-Champs not far from the Louvre and the Tuileries, moving in 1843 to the courtyard of the Prefecture of Police on the quai de l'Horloge on the Ile de la Cité, and it was open from eleven in the morning until five in the afternoon, every day except Sunday. The checks were carried out at speed; on average during the Second Empire, fifty-two women would be examined in one hour. Independent prostitutes were required to attend for the check twice a month, while doctors visited the *maisons de tolérance* to carry out the checks every week.

If a *fille insoumise* arrested during a police raid, or a *fille soumise* attending for her routine check-up, was found to be suffering from a venereal disease, she would be sent to the prison-hospital of Saint-Lazare where she could be detained until she was cured. Registered prostitutes could also be taken there for infringements of the rules. Saint-Lazare was a source of terror, reputed to be filthy as well as harsh, and women were continually devising ways of disguising any tell-tale symptoms of disease, always trying to keep one step ahead of the examining authorities. Some such device, at which Dr Ryan will do no more than hint, appears to have been a form of cup inserted into the vagina and covering the cervix, as it also had the effect of appearing to stop menstrual bleeding:

> It is necessary to abstain from details; but I may mention that this invention has often served to conceal their maladies, and has thus enabled them to elude the watchfulness of the police; and they have also employed it in the hospital to simulate cures, and recover their liberty; but these tricks are now well known, and no longer deceive the persons who are charged with the sanitary *surveillance*.[7]

If, on her first arrest, a *fille insoumise* turned out to be healthy, she would probably be released, while a second arrest was likely to lead to immediate registration. Unless she was in a position to call on some influential protector prepared to vouch for her and to state that she was not after all a prostitute, it would be in the woman's best interest to comply at this point, as refusal to be registered would only result in further detention and investigation.

A further type of institution devoted to the prostitute, in addition to the brothel, the hospital and the prison, was the refuge where she could go to repent and be, to some extent, rehabilitated. Convents had originally provided such a refuge but they had been abolished at the time of the Revolution, and the only institution available to the repentant prostitute at the time of Parent-Duchâtelet's researches was the refuge of the Good Shepherd, founded in 1821 by an association devoted to the education of prostitutes. A woman had to be aged between eighteen and twenty-five to be admitted here, and there was a disturbingly high mortality rate caused, or so Parent-Duchâtelet considered, by the extreme change the prostitute had suddenly to make from her previously unstructured life into this new one of an ordered austerity, involving getting up at five o'clock every morning followed by long hours in chapel: 'they jumped, so to speak, from one extreme to another, and without the least transition'.[8]

Parent-Duchâtelet estimated the number of prostitutes in Paris in 1836 as approximately eighteen thousand,[9] one half of whom were kept women or *femmes galantes*, over whom the police had no jurisdiction because they carried on their affairs in private.

No one, says [Duchâtelet], can deny that these women are really prostitutes; they propagate fatal diseases and precocious infirmities, more than all the others, and they may be considered to be the most dangerous beings in society. The police cannot, however, treat them as prostitutes, for they all have a residence, pay taxes, and conform, apparently, to the rules of decency; consequently, they cannot be refused the outward tokens of respect which are due to virtuous women.[10]

Somewhere between the prostitute and the kept woman came the *grisette*, an untranslatable word which originally referred to a costume

of inexpensive grey fabric worn by working-class women but which
by 1835 was also being used to denote 'a flirtatious young female
worker of loose morals'. Indeed, as early as the seventeenth century,
La Fontaine was using the word in this sense:

> A *grisette* is a treasure today,
> For without any effort at all,
> Or accompanying her to a ball,
> You'll easily go the whole way.
> Say what you like, she'll ask nothing of you,
> The only hard thing is finding one who'll stay true.[11]

A *grisette* would be in employment, most probably as a dressmaker,
milliner or florist, and, bearing out Parent-Duchâtelet and Ryan's
opinion that the most common cause of prostitution was 'an
insufficiency of wages',[12] she would supplement her income by
taking a paying lover. (A working man's wage at the time averaged
three to four francs a day – approximately the equivalent of six to
eight pounds sterling at today's values – but women earned only half
that amount.) There might well be three men in her life: the mature
lover whom she would see on weekdays and who topped up her
meagre wages; her young and not so rich lover with whom she
would enjoy recreation on Sundays; and the working man of her
own class whom she would eventually marry.[13] The money earned
by this sort of light-hearted prostitution would go towards luxuries
the *grisette* could not otherwise afford, and provide some spice in her
life before she settled down to the grind of being a working-class wife
and mother. Henri d'Alméras writes of the *grisette* that her job
provided her daily bread, while love represented the dessert.[14]

On a higher level than both the *grisette* and the common prostitute
were those women known colloquially as *lorettes*, the name initially
awarded by Nestor Roqueplan[15] to the superior class of prostitute
who tended to live in the new houses built near the church of Notre
Dame de Lorette (consecrated in 1836), midway between the
boulevard des Italiens and Montmartre. (The congregating of such

women in this area was a result not only of its proximity to the fashionable cafés and restaurants of the *grands boulevards* where they would go to meet their clients, but also of the low rents of the rapidly constructed, already rather damp housing.) Some of these women would be unable to avoid police registration, while others were able to use both their lifestyles as outwardly independent women and the influence of well-connected clients to keep them off the official lists. Once having been registered, it was not easy to get one's name removed from the list of prostitutes, but it could be done, with persistence and the right connections. Some *lorettes* were separated women, who had perhaps married above their class but subsequently 'fallen'; they nevertheless remained at a higher level and able to command a higher price than the ordinary prostitutes of the street or brothel. The author of *Scènes de la vie de Bohème*, Henry Murger, described the *lorette* as 'an impertinent hybrid, a mediocre beauty, half-flesh, half-unguent, whose boudoir is a counter where she slices pieces of her heart, as though they were roast beef'.[16] Their lives could be complicated, necessitating careful organisation in order not to confuse the appointments of various lovers and to avoid clashes. As Julien Teppe puts it:

> all this required precautions and careful book-keeping. The hairdresser, the pedicurist and the inevitable 'piano mistress' – in reality, her *éminence grise* – completed the universe of the *lorette*, who was also bombarded by her supplier of all kinds of outfit and jewellery. And so, dressed up to sail the high seas of intrigue, all she had to do was inspire tender – and profitable – feelings.[17]

Some *lorettes* aspired to be actresses, while some dreamt – and some, like Thérèse Lachmann who became La Païva, attained their dream – of becoming great courtesans. Parent-Duchâtelet also identifies a class of women he calls '*femmes à parties*', who gave dinners and soirées at which they hired themselves out as attractions amidst the gaming-tables.

The measure by which the level reached by a woman paid for sex could be judged was not only the amount of money she could command but the degree of choice she could exercise in the selection of her clients. The lowest prostitute had to take whatever was on offer; the élite of the *demi-monde*, the renowned courtesan, had an almost infinite number of aspirants to pick from. She might make her choice mainly on the grounds of which man had the most disposable income, rather than because of any personal characteristics, but the choice was hers to make. That, at least, is the rosy side of the picture. The other side was that the more money the courtesan had lavished upon her, the more she spent and the more her expenses grew. It was often part of her side of the bargain to spend, rather than save, the money given her by a wealthy protector, for the conventions of the age demanded that the mistress of a man of the world be an ostentatious status symbol, not someone to be hidden away in a secluded apartment. And so the courtesan would come to depend on a high income and then, with the inevitable ending of a particular relationship, her debts would quickly accumulate and she would need to find an equally wealthy replacement as soon as possible. It was a lifestyle which, once embarked upon, was no easier to abandon than that of the common prostitute, and few *demi-mondaines* succeeded in making adequate provision for old, or even middle, age.

The words used to denote the various classes of prostitute and courtesan tell us something about the attitudes of those who employed them towards the women thus labelled. Most noticeable is the number of words taking their provenance from the farmyard or the zoo, words which inevitably belittle the women to whom they are applied, lending them the characteristics of birds or animals, dehumanising and depersonalising them. At best the men using these terms are regarding these women as pets, and at worst as ravening beasts. One of the dictionary definitions of *grisette*, for instance, is 'a species of warbler, lark, duck, weevil and butterfly'; applying this epithet to the young female worker who takes a paying lover emphasises her triviality and lack of value – she is the little bird or butterfly a middle-class man can amuse himself with for a while. Slightly more substantial than the *grisette* was the *cocotte*, a child's word for 'hen' or for a piece of paper folded to resemble a hen, and applied to a professional courtesan. A frequently used animal word for a courtesan was *biche*, literally 'doe' though also used of a small bitch. *Chameau*, literally 'camel', colloquially 'cow' or 'bitch', was used of a heartless woman out to exploit men, in contrast with *camélia* which denoted the loving prostitute of whom Marie Duplessis – or, rather, the fictionalising of her in *La Dame aux camélias* – became the prototype. A word which sounds like one of these animal or bird words, but is not, is *cocodette*, the feminine version of *cocodè*, a name given in the first instance by the young and dissipated Duke de Gramont-Caderousse to a few of his intimates among the fast set, addicted to gambling, horses and duels.[18] *Cocodettes*, who often had to be booked far in advance and were valued as an adornment, were sometimes married women who nevertheless had all the luxury and allure of a professional courtesan.[19] Such women who maintained their connections with high society while acquiring some of the habits of the *demi-monde* might also be termed *demi-castors*, a word which originally referred to hats made half of beaver and half of wool.

From the mid-1850s courtesans were sometimes disparagingly referred to as *Filles de marbre*, the name of a play by Théodore Barrière and Lambert Thiboust, first performed in the Vaudeville Theatre on 17 May 1853. The protagonist of the first act is a sculptor, Phidias, who creates marble statues of the famed courtesans of Ancient Greece, Laïs, Aspasia and Phryne. He subsequently falls in love with his marble creations, who remain cold and inert. The moral of the story is demonstrated by the arrival of the rich man who commissioned the statues; he offers them money and luxury, at which the marble women turn their heads towards him. The rest of the play is set in contemporary Madrid and Paris, and tells the story of an artist seduced by a heartless courtesan. For a while he returns to his senses, his mother and his virtuous fiancée. But at the end of the play he has a vision of the marble statues – and drops dead. Such a play would have depended for its success on the audience being able to recognise characteristics, or thinking it could recognise characteristics, of certain contemporary courtesans in the portrayal of the marble statues.

The women of the uppermost ranks, the most desirable *demi-mondaines*, were also often referred to by the epithets *grandes* or *hautes* – *grandes cocottes*, for instance, rather than simple *cocottes*. The pseudonymous writer 'Zed' refers in his *Le Demi-monde sous le Second Empire* of 1892 to *grandes abandonnées* (the great abandoned ones), while Frédéric Loliée in his *Les Femmes du Second Empire* of 1907 uses the term *grandes horizontales* (literally, great horizontals, or women flat on their backs). Collective expressions for the great *demi-mondaines* included *la haute galanterie* (literally high gallantry, chivalry or intrigue, and colloquially the top rank of kept women) and *la Haute Bicherie*. The greatest of the great were also known collectively as *La garde* (properly used to refer to the Imperial Guard); these were the top twelve or so courtesans, the aristocracy of the *demi-monde*. At various stages in their careers, Cora Pearl and La Païva would both have been considered as members of *La garde*. Others included Marie Colombier, Hortense Schneider, Blanche d'Antigny, Léonide Leblanc, Anna Deslion and Marguerite Bellanger (who became one of Napoleon III's mistresses). Yet even at this exalted level, the pejorative animal vocabulary could not be escaped, for such women were also known as *lionnes* – queens of beasts, certainly, but still beasts.

Respectable mothers feared that these beasts would devour their sons, breaking their hearts while eating up their fortunes. The men themselves, along with the medical and police authorities, were more afraid of the danger of contracting syphilis, which could lead to madness and early death. By the end of the nineteenth century as many as 20 per cent of the entire population of Paris was affected by the disease. Dr Michael Ryan, for one, did all he could to increase this fear, in the hope of influencing behaviour, by his description of the symptoms:

> In many cases there is partial or total destruction by ulceration or sloughing off of the virile member, and of the female genitals, of the soft palate, of the cartilages of the nose, there are warts on the glans penis, or labia pudendi, various abscesses, pustules, and fissures, in different parts of the body; there are nervous,

neuralgic, and rheumatic pains, falling off of the hair, phthisis or general breaking up of the constitution, and very frequently death closes the scene.[20]

Courtesans and experienced prostitutes could go some way to allay the fear of syphilis by the use of condoms, which carried the added benefit of helping to avoid pregnancy (though Drs Ryan and Parent-Duchâtelet both seem to have believed that a pregnant prostitute was a particularly enticing proposition to many men). In the early part of the nineteenth century condoms – known to the French as *redingotes anglaises* ('English overcoats') and to the English as 'French letters' – were made of sheep gut with a ribbon used to close the open end and, though they also began to be made of vulcanised rubber in the late nineteenth century, they were still being made of animal skins and silk in Europe right into the twentieth. From the 1820s condoms could be purchased from certain shops in the gallery of the Palais Royal, and later in the century they were available in tobacconists or brothels for fifty centimes.

For those courtesans and prostitutes who did not want their way of life interrupted by the advent of a child – and these were most of them – other methods of contraception were also available, although coitus interruptus remained the most common. Vaginal sponges represented one option, some acting merely as barriers while others delivered chemical agents to the vagina. The insertion of a small, damp sponge tied to a ribbon was recommended by English birth controllers and was declared by the French, if accompanied by a douche or the use of a bidet, to be a woman's best protection. Douching itself was increasingly popular, particularly in France (where foreigners were always struck by the ubiquity of the bidet, an invention which had emerged some time in the late seventeenth century). Women douched with various mineral and vegetable solutions, including one which consisted simply of cold water though more often a little vinegar or alum would be added. By the middle of the nineteenth century commercial douches were readily available in pharmacies and were also sold via respectable mail order catalogues, purportedly for purposes of hygiene.

If all the precautions of condoms and douching failed, there remained the emmenagogues – drugs used for the purpose of bringing on late or missing periods. Many newspapers carried small advertisements for women's medicines and, though no one could openly advertise drugs that would induce abortions, they could freely mention remedies for 'irregular' periods. The dividing line between contraception and abortion (or the inducement of miscarriage) was hazy, and herbal teas, purgatives and suppositories were all employed to keep women 'regular'. Patent remedies guaranteed to cure irregular periods began to edge out the traditional remedies, but even the new concoctions were based on traditional emmenagogues, such as aloes, iron, savin, ergot (from rye), rue, tansy, quinine and pennyroyal. And for most women abortion remained a back-up method of birth control.

Abortion had been made illegal in France in 1791. The Napoleonic law codified in 1810 did not, however, punish pregnant women if the drugs they used were self-administered. On the other hand, anyone who assisted or advised them on which drugs to take – whatever their medical status, from physician to midwife – would be guilty of a criminal act. Seven years later the law was amended to apply also to women who brought about their own abortions. But despite the prohibitions in France and other countries, it was possible throughout Europe to obtain information about which drugs were effective for inducing abortions. In 1805, two years after the Ellenborough Act made abortion illegal in Great Britain, the *London Dispensatory* was published. This guide to drugs was based on the official *London Pharmacopœia*, and the items it names suggest that most drugs used for abortion and contraception were sold in chemists' shops. The 1818 edition of the *London Dispensatory* included some references to birth control, however vague. Using language in such a way as not to appear to be proffering advice, an American guide to drugs published in 1836 contained the information that ergot was popularly used by midwives in parts of Germany, France and Italy to induce contractions of the uterus. The guide warned that this could be dangerous. In short, the guides published in the early nineteenth century all indicate that during the period when abortion was criminalised the means of bringing about abortions were commonly known and available. A survey of newspapers in Great Britain during one week in the mid-nineteenth century showed that a hundred of them contained thinly disguised advertisements for abortion; and in France, by the end of the century, claims were being made that between one hundred thousand and five hundred thousand abortions were carried out every year.

When children were born to prostitutes their chances of survival beyond infancy were not high, both because they may have already been infected in the womb with venereal disease and because the mother's precarious way of life and uncertain income did not provide the optimum background for health and stability. It was also a part of the conventional wisdom of the time that prostitutes would make hopeless mothers anyway, by virtue of their innate fecklessness and childishness. In addition to documenting the regulations governing prostitution in Paris and describing the outward circumstances of the women concerned, Dr Parent-Duchâtelet had devoted some space in his *De la Prostitution dans la ville de Paris* to the moral and physical characteristics of prostitutes, assembling a number of stereotypes which had already obtained wide currency in society and thereby ensuring that they continued to be influential for some time to come. Dr Ryan drew upon Parent-Duchâtelet's descriptions to determine whether the same stereotypes applied to prostitutes in London and concluded that, by and large, they did. Neither doctor, however, agreed with everything that was popularly said about prostitutes and listed some of the common beliefs in order to contradict them.

One of the generally accepted stereotypes concerned the mental and emotional immaturity of the prostitute. She was seen as something of a child, who had not yet learnt how to assimilate the values of society as a whole. She was supposed to have rejected work in favour of pleasure, and thus everything about her was perceived as demonstrating this rejection: her laziness, her love of idleness, the shape of her day. The fact that she might be exhausted after hours of plying her trade did not seem to be taken into account to explain her 'laziness', which was considered to be a prime cause for women taking to prostitution in the first place. Quoting Parent-Duchâtelet, Ryan declares: 'it is the desire of procuring enjoyments without working, that causes many young women to leave their places, or to refrain from seeking others when out of service. The laziness, carelessness, and cowardice of prostitutes have become almost proverbial.'[21] It was also believed that women were propelled into prostitution by vanity, 'and the desire of being finely dressed . . . particularly in Paris, where simplicity in dress is actually a subject of reproach, and shabbiness is still more despised'.[22] Both doctors are clear that these are not the primary causes of women turning to prostitution, however, according that honour to poverty and, in many instances, to a first incident of 'seduction' (or what one might sometimes more accurately call rape). One of the reasons for the poverty of women, Parent-Duchâtelet believed, was that men had been usurping jobs more suitable for that sex, such as waiting in restaurants and serving in shops.[23] Further characteristics attributed to the prostitute were instability, turbulence and agitation, qualities demonstrated by her frequent changes of address, as well as by her love of dancing, her sudden shifts of mood and her inability to concentrate. 'Their volatile and changeable turn of mind is so great, that nothing can fix their attention, which is distracted by the most trifling occurrence.'[24] The prostitute symbolised disorder, excess and improvidence, a rejection of the established order. The types of 'excess' identified included a willingness to be carried away by various enthusiasms, an over-fondness for alcohol and food, a tendency to talk all the time and frequent outbursts of anger. Very few prostitutes, it was thought, knew how to save money; they indulged in useless expenditure, particularly on perishable items such as flowers, and they easily acquired a passion for gambling. 'There are three things in the world that prostitutes love most,' wrote Alphonse Esquiros, 'the sun, flowers, and their hair.'[25]

A particular fear, one clearly discernible in Zola's depiction of Nana and her friend Satin, is that prostitutes had a predilection to love one another instead of loving men. This fear seems to have exercised the Parisian authorities more than those in London, as Dr Ryan sounds rather surprised by his French colleague's findings on this score:

> [Parent-Duchâtelet] next alludes to those who from a depraved and unnatural taste, select their lovers from persons of their own sex. These are called *tribades*, and are numerous when long confined in prisons. They are despised and hated by all other prostitutes, but their vice prevails to such an extent, that, notwithstanding the regulation of the police, which obliges every woman to sleep in a separate bed, M. Duchâtelet estimates them at less [*sic*] than one-fourth of the entire number of prostitutes.
>
> These disgusting and monstrous unions, are much more frequent than is generally imagined.[26]

Lesbianism was perceived as a huge threat to the social order of which properly regulated heterosexual prostitution was otherwise seen as representing a safeguard. (It is, I hope, a measure of the gulf between attitudes of the 1830s and those of the early twenty-first century that I must confess to having no idea what Dr Ryan is talking about when he concludes his comments on *tribades* thus: 'It has been remarked that these women are more frequently pregnant than ordinary prostitutes; and this circumstance has become the subject of jokes in the prisons. The explanation must be apparent to every one conversant with human nature.'[27])

On what was perceived to be the positive side, other qualities attributed to fallen women included an attraction to religious piety (despite the tendency not to go to church) – 'Many of them refrain from all religious duties, on account of their unworthiness; though most of them are anxious for religious consolation when dangerous or fatal illness assails them';[28] an attachment to young children (despite, or maybe because of, being incapable of rearing their own); and a nostalgia for their native countryside (many of them having made their way to the big cities from the villages where they had been born). They were also perceived as having a great sense of solidarity with and charity towards other marginalised elements in society, as well as towards those of their own kind who had fallen on hard times. 'In times of scarcity, a great number of these women, have given a loaf of bread a week, or even a day, to old people, to those in bad health, and also to poor families in their neighbourhood.'[29]

Parent-Duchâtelet mentioned only two physical stereotypes, which were to be repeated endlessly: plumpness of figure, ascribed to greed, laziness and the taking of many warm baths, as well as to the clients' preferences, and a raucous voice, which he believed to be caused by social origin, abuse of alcohol and exposure to cold rather than by, as popular prejudice would have it, the practice of oral sex. Dr Ryan went to some lengths to convince his readership that the genital organs of prostitutes were not, as was commonly supposed, any different from those of the general population of married women. Alphonse Esquiros drew up a more detailed physical stereotype of the prostitute:

> Natural prostitutes, if one may express oneself thus, are in general of a powerful and Herculean race. Everything about them speaks of eager appetites: their chest is wide and generous, their pelvis ample, their flesh abundant and firm to the touch; their face radiates highly developed sensual energies; the large and devouring mouth, the flaring nostrils, the deep and rather raucous breathing – there is no element of their physical characteristics which does not indicate an inexhaustible need for material pleasures.[30]

Esquiros did not share Parent-Duchâtelet's views on the inevitability of prostitutes; rather he regarded them as a section of the human race at a lower stage of development than other women, and believed that the continuing progress of humankind would eventually lead to the end of this phenomenon. He agreed, however, that among the main causes of prostitution were poverty and ignorance, though he also thought that heredity played a not inconsiderable part: 'conceived in the midst of an orgy, most of them have prostitution in the blood'.[31]

He also believed that some of them were governed by an over-whelming need to keep eating, such that no ordinary worker's wage could ever buy enough food to satisfy their appetite; this, he thought, was caused by a particular cerebral organ called 'alimentivity'.[32]

Though in many respects the life of the successful *grande horizontale* was a far cry from that of her less fortunate sister, the common prostitute or *fille publique*, the characteristics attributed to the latter were also in large measure attributed to the former and, no matter what dizzy heights women such as Marie Duplessis and La Païva eventually attained, they were never free from these stereotypes which have coloured nearly every subsequent description and judgment of them. They were also in a double bind, for they could be condemned both for conforming and for not conforming to type, either for reinforcing the popular prejudice of the archetypal prostitute (as Marie did perfectly), or for having the temerity to behave differently and attempt to live outside the accepted classifications (as did La Païva). In both cases the reality became overlaid by the stereotype, so that it became very difficult, maybe even impossible, for both their contemporaries and subsequent generations, to see these women clearly.

The assumption underlying much of what has been summarised in this chapter – of both the regulations governing prostitutes' lives and the stereotypes attributed to them – was the weakness of women, of all women. Not only were prostitutes themselves viewed as having been drawn to their way of life through laziness, greed, vanity and inability to cope with poverty in any other way, but even so-called virtuous women were in danger, through their own inherent weakness, of being contaminated by the example of their fallen sisters if prostitution were allowed to be practised openly, without the protecting walls of the brothel or the rules against open solicitation and display. 'The wide road is too tempting for feminine fragility, women have thrown themselves down it; ask the bosses why they search in vain for workers, ask the artists why it is so difficult to find models; unregistered prostitution has seized them and will not let them go.'[33] The virtuous woman needed protection, not only because she might be shocked at witnessing depravity but, even worse, because she was likely to be tempted into abandoning virtue herself. The splendidly attired, ostentatiously wealthy courtesan was viewed as a particular source of temptation to the virtuous, protected but less dazzling wife, and this is one reason for the disquiet evinced by some contemporary writers such as Maxime Du Camp when describing the *demi-monde* and the difficulty of telling it apart from the *haut monde*.

---

1 M. Ryan, *Prostitution in London, with a comparative view of that of Paris and New York*, H. Baillière, London, 1839, p.72

2 A.J.B. Parent-Duchâtelet, *De la Prostitution dans la ville de Paris*, J.B. Baillière, Paris, 1836, p.513

3 M. Ryan, *Prostitution in London*, p.221

4 Ibid., p.59

5 Alphonse Esquiros, *Les Vierges folles*, P. Delavigne, Paris, 1842, pp.97–8

6 Emile Zola, *Nana*, The Modern Library, New York, 1928, pp.309–11

7 M. Ryan, *Prostitution in London*, pp.64–5

8 A.J.B. Parent-Duchâtelet, *De la Prostitution dans la ville de Paris*, p.549

9 Mr Talbot, Secretary of the London Society for the Prevention of Juvenile Prostitution, reckoned that there were as many as eighty thousand prostitutes operating in London at this time, while the Rev Mr M'Dowall of the New York Magdalen Asylum expressed horror at his estimate of ten thousand existing in New York.

10 M. Ryan, *Prostitution in London*, p.58

11 Quoted in Julien Teppe, *Vocabulaire de la vie amoureuse*, La Pavillon, Paris, 1973, p.115

12 M. Ryan, *Prostitution in London*, p.47

13 See Henry Knepler (ed.), *Man about Paris. The confessions of Arsène Houssaye*, Victor Gollancz, London, 1972, p.74

14 Henri d'Alméras, *La Vie parisienne sous le Second Empire*, Albin Michel, Paris, 1933, p.217

15 See S. Kracauer, *Jacques Offenbach ou le secret du Second Empire*, Editions Bernard Grasset, Paris, 1937, p.92

16 Quoted in Julien Teppe, *Vocabulaire de la vie amoureuse*, p.117

17 Julien Teppe, *Vocabulaire de la vie amoureuse*, p.117

18 See S. Kracauer, *Jacques Offenbach ou le secret du Second Empire*, pp.242–3

19 See Julien Teppe, *Vocabulaire de la vie amoureuse*, p.119

20 M. Ryan, *Prostitution in London*, p.402

21 Ibid., p.43

22 Ibid.

23 A.J.B. Parent-Duchâtelet, *De la Prostitution dans la ville de Paris*, p.97

24 M. Ryan, *Prostitution in London*, p.50

25 Alphonse Esquiros, *Les Vierges folles*, p.135

26 M. Ryan, *Prostitution in London*, p.56

27 Ibid., p.57

28 Ibid., p.50

29 Ibid., p.53

30 Alphonse Esquiros, *Les Vierges folles*, p.46

31 Ibid., p.35

32 Ibid., p.46

33 Maxime Du Camp, *Paris: ses organes, ses fonctions et sa vie jusqu'en 1870*, p.351

CHAPTER TWO

The Life of Marie Duplessis

MARIE DUPLESSIS WAS born Alphonsine Plessis on 15 January 1824 in the village of Saint-Germain-de-Clarfeuille near Nonant in Lower Normandy, the younger daughter of a travelling pedlar called Marin Plessis and his wife Marie, née Deshayes, who had married below herself and disastrously. In the year of Alphonsine's birth Charles X, a Bourbon, was enthroned as king of France, succeeding his elder brother Louis XVIII. The eldest brother of the three had been Louis XVI, executed in 1793. Louis XVIII had been restored to the throne by the allies after the defeat of Napoleon I in 1814. He had to flee when Napoleon returned to France from his exile on Elba and was restored a second time in 1815 after Napoleon's final defeat at Waterloo. Charles X, an ultraroyalist, would have liked France to return to the ways of the *ancien régime*, as it was before the Revolution of 1789.

Marin Plessis was the illegitimate son of a priest and a prostitute. He abused his wife – particularly after the birth of Alphonsine, whom he had wanted to be a boy – until she could stand it no longer. She left to work as a maid to an English woman in Paris, hoping to be able to send for her two daughters once she was able to afford to do so. This never happened, as she died when Alphonsine was six, and the daughters, especially Alphonsine (her sister Delphine was two years older), were left at the mercy of their father. Delphine was sent to live with an uncle, where she remained until she was sixteen and was then apprenticed to a laundress. Initially Alphonsine lived with her mother's cousin, Madame Agathe Boisard, who was a farmer's wife and already had three children of her own. She stayed with the Boisards for several years, despite their poverty and the refusal of Marin Plessis to contribute anything to her upkeep. Eventually, however, Alphonsine, who as a young girl was already pretty and a source of temptation to men (Romain Vienne, who, though an unreliable and inventive biographer, demonstrates a degree of insight into Alphonsine's character, claims that she was abused by male workers from the age of eleven and a half[1]), became too much for Agathe Boisard to handle. There was a scandalous incident involving a farmhand – according to Vienne, Alphonsine seduced the seventeen-year-old boy against his will[2] – and she was sent back to her father.

Marin placed her, like her sister, as an apprentice to a *blanchisseuse*, which can be loosely translated as 'laundress'. Such an apprenticeship involved long hours of hard and repetitive physical labour. Emile Zola gave a detailed description of a laundress's establishment in his novel *L'Assommoir*, from which it is possible to reconstruct an idea of Alphonsine's working life at this time.[3] First, piles of dirty linen would be sorted and washed, the actual washing sometimes being done at a communal washroom by a washerwoman, a lower level of worker than the *blanchisseuse*. Much of the work of a *blanchisseuse* consisted of ironing, which would be done at a large table covered with a heavy blanket, itself covered with calico. Several irons were heated on the large cast-iron stove, and it would be the job of the apprentice to keep this stove filled – always being careful not to over-fill it – with coke. The room where the *blanchisseuses* worked would also be full of clothes hung up on wires to dry. On the floor there would be an earthenware pan, containing starch into which the linen would be dipped before being ironed. The *blanchisseuse* herself and her older employees would be busy ironing intricate objects such as caps, shirt-fronts, petticoats and embroidered drawers, while the apprentice could be put to work on the plain items, the stockings and handkerchiefs. The ironing would be done standing up around the table, a flat brick alongside each worker on which to place the hot iron. Work could go on until late at night, particularly on Saturdays, so that the customers could have their clean clothes to wear on Sunday.

Such was Alphonsine's life when she was aged about thirteen to fourteen. Then one Sunday, her father, who had remained in touch with her, took her to visit an elderly acquaintance of his, a bachelor in his sixties or seventies by the name of Plantier. But more than taking her to visit, Marin Plessis left Alphonsine with Plantier; possibly he even sold her to him. For a while she attempted to continue her work with the *blanchisseuse* while spending Sundays and Mondays with Plantier. She was dismissed, however, when her employer realised the situation and Alphonsine returned full-time to Plantier. She was resourceful enough to escape from him after a few weeks and to find herself a job in an inn at Exmes in Normandy, where she lived as a maid-of-all-work for several months. This period of relative tranquillity was again disrupted by the arrival of her father, who this time placed her with an umbrella merchant. After two months of selling umbrellas, Alphonsine was once again removed by her father. There followed a fortnight about which little is known but much has been suspected. Alphonsine refused to talk about it to her biographer Romain Vienne, and the only thing which is known for certain is that Marin took his daughter to live with him for two weeks in a hovel where there was room for only one bed and not many ways of keeping warm. And afterwards the neighbours talked. At least so it has been surmised from the sudden departure, in 1839, of Marin and Alphonsine Plessis for Paris.

On arrival in the capital, Alphonsine was left by her father with some more cousins of her mother, the Vitals. Madame Vital found work for her, initially again as an apprentice laundress, but then as something more to her taste in the shop of a dressmaker, Mademoiselle Urbain, in the rue du Coq-Héron, not far from the Palais Royal. At the time Alphonsine was placed as an apprentice there, early in 1839, she was fifteen years old. The apprentices worked from seven o'clock in the morning until eight at night, for six days a week, and learnt such skills as decorating dresses with lace and embroidery. Mademoiselle Urbain supervised her young apprentices as closely as she could, knowing, as did the forewoman in the shop where Nana was apprenticed in Zola's *L'Assommoir*, 'the dangers that a girl ran in the streets of Paris'.[4] It would be an unusual establishment where at least one or two of the girls were not following the customary practices of the *grisette*. And after Alphonsine's life in the countryside, the city of Paris, where gaslight had been introduced in the late 1820s and the first omnibuses had appeared in 1828, must have seemed a place full of life, movement and adventure. The reign of Charles X had been ended in 1830 by the July Revolution, the ultraroyalists having provoked the opposition of the middle classes, who desired more participation in the government of the country. The insurrection had begun on 26 July and led to the installation of a provisional government three days later and the abdication of Charles X on 2 August. Louis Philippe, previously the Duke d'Orléans, was proclaimed king on 31 July and officially acceded to the throne on 9 August. He had formerly been a part of the liberal opposition to Louis XVIII and Charles X and found his support in the discontented upper middle classes. His reign, known as the July monarchy, marked the triumph of the wealthy bourgeoisie; Louis Philippe was himself known as the 'citizen king' because of his bourgeois manners and dress. Many former officials of Napoleon I's Empire were also returned to positions of influence. The increase in the political power of the bourgeoisie coincided with a growth in their spending power, and money began to take over from birth in determining one's place in society.

According to Nestor Roqueplan, Alphonsine's chief interest on her arrival in Paris was food, in particular the fried potatoes sold from stalls in the street. Roqueplan recalled the first time he saw the girl he later recognised as the courtesan Marie Duplessis: it was near the Pont Neuf, and she was nibbling at an apple while eyeing hungrily the potatoes sizzling in a skillet. He bought her a large portion of the fried potatoes, which she ate greedily, having thrown away the despised apple.[5]

For about six months all went well. Alphonsine lived as well as worked at Mademoiselle Urbain's premises, and spent most Sunday afternoons with her relatives the Vitals. Then one Sunday in summer her life took on a new aspect. Alphonsine and two other apprentices, Hortense and Ernestine, had planned a trip by omnibus into the country, to the royal château of Saint Cloud which was a few miles from Paris, on the left bank of the Seine. But it began to rain and, instead of setting off for Saint Cloud, the three girls sheltered in the galerie Montpensier beneath the arcades of the Palais Royal while discussing how to spend their free time. As usual they were hungry, and they decided that they had just enough money between them to eat in a modest restaurant frequented by the local shopkeepers. There they were approached by the owner of the restaurant, a Monsieur Nollet, who offered them a bottle of wine on the house. Furthermore, after hearing what their plans had been, he invited them to accompany him to Saint Cloud on the following Sunday. And so the next week the three girls set off with him in a hired carriage for the country. For two of the girls this represented a pleasant, but isolated event, just an unexpected treat; for the third, it marked the beginning of a new phase of existence.

Quite who seduced whom, who exploited whom, is debatable: Alphonsine, with her precocious sexual experience, was an easy prey for a man with a certain amount of sophistication on the look-out for a young and pretty mistress, while she was quick to realise that, if she played her cards right, Nollet was in a position to offer her a way out of a life of drudgery and relative poverty. Events progressed rapidly. Within a month Monsieur Nollet had installed Alphonsine in a small apartment in the rue de l'Arcade and given her three thousand francs (about six thousand pounds in today's terms) for her initial needs.

Alphonsine demonstrated no intention of merely supplementing her income in the manner of a *grisette* or of ever returning to her occupation as a dressmaker. Dressed in her new finery, she went to say farewell to Mademoiselle Urbain and her former fellow apprentices, but did not, at least according to Romain Vienne, make any further appearance at the Vitals': 'She didn't dare present herself at her cousin Vital's, but she wrote to ask her forgiveness, and to let her know that she intended to visit her on Sunday morning. She didn't have to wait long for a reply: "If you ever set foot in my house again, I'll chase you out like the vermin you are."[6] Her tastes very soon outstripped the abilities of any potential working-class husband to pay for them or even the resources of a bourgeois lover such as Monsieur Nollet to satisfy them. The few dresses and jewels and relatively modest sum of money with which he provided her awoke the desire for more and more luxury. Nollet retired from the scene, having realised he could not keep up with Alphonsine's expenditure, upon which she had a brief liaison with a young man called Valéry and several others besides. But the pivotal point of her transformation from a young kept woman with a very dubious background into the highly prized (and priced) courtesan was her liaison with Agénor de Guiche, *le beau Agénor*, who makes an appearance in the lives of most of the nineteenth-century Parisian *demi-mondaines*. He has also caused a degree of confusion among historians because of his multiple names: as eldest son of the Duke de Gramont, he bore the title of Duke de Guiche until succeeding his father, when he himself became the Duke de Gramont; the family were also known as the princes of Bidache, and were one of the most ancient and illustrious houses of the French nobility. The only thing Agénor lacked was wealth (or at least enough of it to maintain a long-term relationship with a high-spending courtesan), as the Gramonts had lost much of their fortune at the time of the Revolution.

When Agénor took up with Alphonsine he was twenty-one years old and she was sixteen. He had just left the Polytechnic after two years of studies in which he had not particularly excelled, and he had also just embarked on an army career which would be brief and not particularly glorious. Seriously smitten by Alphonsine, and interested in more than just going to bed with her, he decided he wanted to bring her up to his own level of education and refinement. So he arranged for her to have good teachers, paying for piano and dancing lessons for her. Alphonsine improved her writing and reading skills, amassed a library (by the time of her death she owned some two hundred books, ranging from the novels of Walter Scott, through Rabelais and Rousseau, to Michaud's voluminous *Biographie univer-*

selle and Burette's *Histoire de France*), took lessons in deportment and decorum and became skilled in the art of conversation. During this time of Pygmalion-like transformation, Nestor Roqueplan encountered her again, this time in the Ranelagh pleasure gardens:

> One evening, I felt myself being tapped on the shoulder by a tall young man, fresh as a lily and with the blond curls of a Cupid, the Duke de . . ., the bearer of a great name, a name often illustrious and never insignificant; hanging on to his arm was a charming person, elegantly dressed, who was none other than my greedy girl from the Pont Neuf, and whom he was exhibiting with an inventor's satisfaction.[7]

Agénor spent something in the region of ten thousand francs on Alphonsine in three months. There was a break in their relationship before the end of 1840, when he left for England. On his return the liaison was struck up again, though by this time he was not enjoying exclusive rights (if indeed he ever had). But his effect was lasting, Alphonsine having taken readily to the process of education which he had initiated. And to mark her transformation, she changed her name from Alphonsine Plessis to Marie Duplessis.

She was not unusual, among the *grisettes* and courtesans of Louis Philippe's reign, in deciding to change her name; it was also a very common practice among the ranks of ordinary prostitutes. The choice of a new name (ones chosen frequently included Ninette, Niniche and Nana) could serve both to add a touch of glamour and to depersonalise the prostitute, so that she could feel she was merely performing a role, disconnected from her real self. There was also often a desire to disconnect herself from her previous life and from her family, either out of shame or from a desire to escape and not be easily traced. Parent-Duchâtelet emphasises the need in many cases for prostitutes to conceal their identities in order to avoid pursuit by the courts or the police, as well as their desire not to be recognised by family and erstwhile friends.[8] In Alphonsine Plessis's decision to change her name to Marie Duplessis there was undoubtedly an element of this urge to escape her past, and to reflect the remaking of herself in her name. It has also been asserted[9] that she chose the name 'Marie' in honour either of her mother (Marie, née Deshayes) or of the Virgin Mary. A more likely candidate would be Mary Magdalene, patron saint of the repentant prostitute and whose church of La Madeleine Marie was supposed to have visited on many occasions. One also cannot help being struck by the fact that the name 'Marie Duplessis' is not so very far removed from 'Marin Plessis'; perhaps it was the shadowy figure of her depraved father whom Alphonsine was honouring, or at least unconsciously connecting herself with, in the choice of this particular name. He had been the first to teach her, in leaving her with the old man Plantier, that her sexuality could be used as a source of income. It was a lesson she learnt well and to full effect, proving, in this respect at least, that she was indeed her father's daughter.

In June 1840 Marie had taken up with the young Viscount de Méril, who was the first to introduce her to the delights of Spa, the internationally fashionable watering place near Liège in Belgium. It was here that she discovered her predilection for gambling, a fascination which greatly increased her expenditure. The affair with de Méril, who was attached to the Ministry of the Interior, lasted for more than a year and resulted in Marie giving birth to a son, in Versailles, in May 1841. The child was placed by Méril with a nurse in the provinces, but later died of pneumonia. (That, at least, is one version of the story. Another is hinted at in the assertion that in 1869, many years after Marie's death, a young man by the name of Judelet visited her sister Delphine and asked to see a picture of Marie. She showed him the portrait by Vidal, which remained in her family until 1960, and Judelet, it was said, bore a marked resemblance to the woman depicted in it.)[10] A month after the birth of Marie's son her father, Marin Plessis, died of syphilis, aged fifty-one, in the hamlet of Ginai in the canton of Exmes. There had been no further contact between father and daughter since her arrival in Paris.

Marie made it her trademark to be pale, mysterious and rather distant in public, though she could be quite different with a few acquaintances in her own drawing room. At times she could seem excessively exuberant. She enjoyed singing risqué songs, accompanying herself on the piano, dancing madly and drinking too much champagne. Romain Vienne gives a detailed description of her appearance:

> She was tall and slim, fresh as a spring flower; her bodily beauty perhaps lacked that fullness so appreciated by the Turks, those rich curves without which there is no perfection. A painter would have chosen her as a model, a sculptor never. But she was deliciously pretty. Her long, thick, black hair was magnificent, and she arranged it with inimitable skill. Her oval face with its regular features, slightly pale and melancholy when calm and in repose, would suddenly come to life at the sound of a friendly voice or a warm and sincere word. Her head was child-like. Her sweet and sensuous mouth boasted a display of dazzlingly white teeth. Her hands and feet were so slender that her fingers could almost seem too long. The expression of her large black eyes, with their long lashes, was penetrating, and the softness of her glances gave rise to dream.[11]

Marie's propensity for lying represented the only obvious scar from her dreadful upbringing. The following anecdote is repeated endlessly: 'She had an obsession with lying – I say obsession rather than flaw, because her lies were nearly always harmless. One day when someone asked her why she lied, she replied: "Lying whitens the teeth."'[12]

Marie had many lovers, some of them concurrently, others in rapid succession. Early in 1842 she was living at 28 rue de Mont-Thabor, near the rue de Rivoli, and her expenditure demanded that she keep a constant supply of men able to pay the bills. Hippolyte de Villemessant tells how seven members of fashionable Paris decided to club together to purchase her favours, since she was so expensive to maintain (as mentioned in Chapter 1, this was a not uncommon practice). To inaugurate this arrangement they bought Marie a present: a dressing table with seven drawers so that they could each have one in which to keep their things. In the early days Marie's management of her multiple lovers sometimes went adrift. Shortly after Agénor de Guiche's return from England she made the mistake of taking him for a drive in the blue carriage which had been given to her by another lover, Fernand de Montguyon. The latter saw them, and Marie had much explaining to do. Montguyon was a dissipated young man who gave Marie money to spend on lace and satin and took her to dine in fashionable restaurants such as Tortoni's in the boulevard des Italiens. In addition to the blue carriage, he gave her a dog which she called Tom and used to take for walks in the Bois de Boulogne. Subsequently she managed her affairs better and took care not to offend those who were paying the bills. Agénor was at this stage what was known as an *amant de cœur* – that is, his and Marie's relationship was not a monetary transaction (he could no longer afford for it to be) but a matter of genuine affection and mutual enjoyment. A letter she wrote to Agénor when he was in London in July 1842 demonstrates how fond she was of this particular lover. It also attests to the presence in the background of a man of more substantial means – 'the General' – who has become an obstacle to Marie and Agénor's affair:

> my angel I am very sad I'm very fed up at not seeing you . . .
> I've been pestered since you left by the General who is
> absolutely determined that I should receive him and that I
> should be with him as in the past he should not have changed his
> conduct towards me we would have been so happy if he hadn't
> come to surprise us our life was so well organised . . . tell me
> everything you are thinking what you are doing tell me also that
> you love me. . . . I love you more tenderly than ever I kiss you a
> thousand times on your mouth and all over.[13]

A tactful *amant de cœur* always had to know when to withdraw and had to guard against inappropriate jealousy. Zola portrays one such liaison in *Nana*: '[Clarisse] had seen Madame Bron giving the letter to

Simonne's young man, and he had gone out to read it under the gas-light in the lobby. 'Impossible tonight, darling – I'm booked.' And with that he peaceably departed, as one who was doubtless used to the formula. He at any rate knew how to conduct himself.'[14]

Marie subsequently moved to a more comfortable apartment in the rue d'Antin, acquired for her by a new lover, Count Edouard de Perrégaux. Edouard's grandfather was Jean Frédéric de Perrégaux, a financier who was made a senator by Napoleon Bonaparte and who became the first regent of the Bank of France. His son, Charles Bernardin, was made a count during the Empire. Edouard had fought in Africa against Abd-el-Kader, the great opponent of France's conquest of Algeria, and had acquitted himself very well. Afterwards, however, his conduct deteriorated. He contracted debts, which increased on his return to France. On the death of his father, he found himself with a very large fortune at his disposal. He proceeded to dispose of it as fast as he could, becoming involved in all the high life of Paris. On 3 April 1842 he was admitted to the Jockey Club, the exclusive haunt of the sporting aristocracy, located on the corner of the boulevard des Capucines and the rue Scribe; the annual sub-scription was a thousand francs. He first encountered Marie at a masked ball at the Opera House in the rue Le Peletier, the tradition of masked balls having been revived there in 1839, such events being held every Saturday evening during the carnival time before Lent. Edouard and Marie were intrigued by one another, and Edouard rapidly dropped another courtesan, Alice Ozy, in order to take up with her.

The apartment in which he installed her at 22 rue d'Antin comprised a drawing room, boudoir, dining room and two bed-rooms. The windows, and Marie's bed, were curtained with muslin and silk. Marie ordered her goods and services from a wide range of providers: wines from Madame Tisserant, just opposite in the rue d'Antin; cakes delivered by Rollet from the passage de l'Opéra; glacé fruits from Boissier; mint pastilles from Gouache in the boulevard de la Madeleine. Edouard would join in the consumption of all these luxuries, not stopping to make the calculation that by spending at the rate of three thousand francs a month, which was the absolute minimum Marie required to live on, he would rapidly use up his already depleted fortune.

Marie's daily routine involved getting up at about eleven o'clock in the morning or even later, and having a light breakfast, followed by about twenty minutes' piano practice. She would then read for half an hour or so, before starting on the lengthy process of deciding what to wear, changing her outfit several times until she was satisfied. She might also be visited by outfitters, menders, suppliers and a hairdresser. When all these matters of dress were completed, she would order her carriage and go for a drive, probably to the Bois de Boulogne (which was not yet the landscaped attraction it would become under Napoleon III but which still provided plenty of *allées* for walking along). She would return home towards the end of the afternoon and would then be 'at home' to visitors – not necessarily only lovers or clients, for sometimes these visitors would include poor women or prostitutes hoping for a hand-out from their more fortunate sister and, at least according to Romain Vienne,[15] if she could help them she would. Then it would be time to dress for the evening, to go to the theatre or to go dancing at somewhere like the newly opened Bal Mabille, an enormous garden in the allée des Veuves (now part of the avenue Montaigne), near the Champs Elysées, transformed in 1840 into an enchanted grove by Mabille the dancing teacher. Here, under oil lamps hung from the trees, men watched famous female dancers perform, or couples danced together while an orchestra played. The first Mabille's sons subsequently introduced gaslight, installing five thousand standard lamps, an illuminated sign over the entrance and even little gas jets in the groves for lighting cigarettes. Then would come dinner, and sooner or later Marie would return to her apartment, usually accompanied by a lover. And once she had serviced this paying client and seen him safely off the premises, her *amant de cœur* might arrive and keep her amorously occupied until the early hours of the morning.

Unsatisfied with these few hours at night, wanting Marie to himself and to be with her all the time, Edouard rented a house for her in the countryside at Bougival with the intention of freeing her from this daily round of Paris – and from the exigencies of other men. Here for a few weeks the couple enjoyed a pastoral idyll, though they also made regular excursions into Paris to attend the Opéra and to eat at the Café Anglais or the Maison Dorée. The Café Anglais had opened at 13 boulevard des Italiens in 1822 and consisted of two floors, divided into twenty-two private rooms, while the Maison Dorée or Maison D'Or, with its gilt balconies, opened in 1840 and contained a large room overlooking the street, as well as a number of private rooms. These were just two of the best known of the numerous cafés and restaurants situated on and around the boulevard des Italiens and which enjoyed a flourishing trade. Marie was flattered by Edouard's exclusive passion for her and willing to reciprocate his love as far as she was able and for as long as he was able to continue supporting her. All he wanted to do was keep her happy, and he fell out with his family and friends as Marie continued to dissipate his fortune. It was around this time that Marie began to show signs of illness, coughing blood for the first time.

Then, on their return from a two-month stay in Baden, Edouard realised that he could no longer afford to keep on the house in Bougival. Marie felt she had been deceived as to the extent of Edouard's fortune, and realised that she again needed to find other protectors to support her way of life. Or, as Vienne puts it, 'It was then that she noticed, by the sudden cooling of her sentiments, that she had loved him only superficially, in the intoxication of deceitful hopes; that she had been the dupe of lying appearances, and that she had built her projects on shifting sand.'[16]

Edouard did not make a complete break with Marie, but she returned to dispensing her charms elsewhere. Lovers of all ages were continually arriving at the rue d'Antin. They included Edouard Delessert (a son of the Prefect of Police who would later become a man of letters and a great traveller, his mother Valentine was for many years the mistress of Prosper Mérimée), the Baron de Plancy, Roger de Beauvoir the well-known *boulevardier* and dandy, and Montjoyeux, as well as men who had already enjoyed her favours, such as Montguyon. One of her most notable lovers was Henri de Contades, who was descended from an eighteenth-century marshal of France, Erasme de Contades. Henri had married his cousin Sophie de Castellane when she was eighteen years old, and embarked on his affair with Marie a few years after the wedding. By this time Sophie had already had several affairs herself. Marie also managed to seduce Sophie's brother, Pierre de Castellane. When Henri de Contades died in 1858, Sophie married again and became the virtuous Madame de Baulaincourt.

Another of Marie's lovers, and the most significant for her future reputation, was Alexandre Dumas *fils*; their liaison began in September 1844 and lasted for nearly a year. Alexandre, the illegitimate son of Alexandre Dumas *père* and a serving girl, first saw her in the company of Eugène Déjazet at the Théâtre des Variétés. Eugène was the son of a famous actress, Virginie Déjazet, who provided her adored and spendthrift son with whatever he wanted. The two young men were both twenty years old, the same age as Marie. They were introduced into Marie's apartment through the agency of Clémence Prat, a dressmaker who also acted as a procuress and who lived next door to Marie.

Alexandre, who as a young man did not have the resources even to begin to support Marie, became an *amant de cœur*. It was not a role he found easy. To begin with he was received only between the hours of midnight and six o'clock in the morning. Later he was allowed to join her in her box in the theatre, or at a restaurant. Sometimes she would send him an affectionate little note in the morning, telling him where to meet her, or that he might accompany her during her afternoon drive or walk. But he did not like being only one lover among many and, as one of the more impecunious ones, having no right to do anything about it. He became jealous, dissatisfied with the few hours allotted to him; he did not like to see another man escorting his mistress to the Opéra. After two months they were quarrelling and Alexandre began to distance himself, though the affair struggled on for a further nine months. A short note which Marie sent to him around this time demonstrates her desire to maintain a relationship and is couched in the reasonable tone of a courtesan attempting to keep a young *amant de cœur* in a sensible frame of mind (she addresses him by his initials of 'AD'):

> Dear Adet, why haven't you told me how you are and why don't you write frankly to me? I think you should treat me like a friend. So I hope for a word from you and I kiss you fondly, like a mistress or like a friend, whichever you prefer. In any case I will always be devoted to you.
>
> Marie[17]

Eventually Alexandre felt he could go on no longer. He sent her a note, appearing to end the affair, dated 'midnight' on 30 August 1845. This is a letter redolent of the pain of a young man in love, but also of the hurt pride of the unhappy *amant de cœur* (and containing a certain amount of self-dramatisation):

> My dear Marie. I am neither rich enough to love you as I would like nor poor enough to be loved as you would like. So let us both forget – you a name which must mean hardly anything to you – me a happiness which has become impossible to bear. There is no point in telling you how sad I am – for you already know how much I love you. So farewell – you have too great a heart not to understand the reason for my letter and too good a nature not to forgive me for it. A thousand memories. AD[18]

Meanwhile, during her affair with Alexandre, in the late autumn of 1844 or early in 1845, Marie encountered an elderly gentleman in the spa town of Bagnères. This octogenarian was Count Gustav Ernst von Stackelberg, a former Russian ambassador to Vienna. He claimed to be a widower, and to have been struck by Marie's likeness to his deceased daughter. He offered to become Marie's protector, hoping to save her from the life she was leading. In fact, Count von Stackelberg was not a widower; his wife the Countess was alive and well, living in the rue de la Chaussée-d' Antin, just the other side of the boulevard des Capucines from where Marie lived, and where she held receptions every Friday for diplomats and other foreigners. She died in 1868, having survived her husband by eighteen years. He did indeed have a daughter who had died − Elena, who died in Karlsruhe in 1843 − though she was not his only daughter as he seems to have implied. He was in fact the father of eleven children. Earlier in his life Stackelberg had been known as an 'executioner of virgins', and he was said to keep with him a list of all his conquests. It seems unlikely that his intentions towards Marie were quite as pure as he made out.

Count von Stackelberg set Marie up in style at 11 boulevard de la Madeleine (the present number 15). Her apartment was on the mezzanine floor and comprised a drawing room, a smaller room leading off to the left, and a boudoir, these three rooms sharing five windows which looked out on to the boulevard. The dining room and a large bedroom overlooked the inner courtyard. Stackelberg also provided her with furs, diamonds, horses and carriages. As household staff, Marie enjoyed the services of a coachman, a cook and a chambermaid. There were also providers of various services from outside such as mending and laundry, a hairdresser from Dezoutter in the rue Saint-Honoré who attended her every day, a chiropodist who also cared for the feet of Louis Philippe's court and of famous dancers, a saddler and coachbuilder who looked after the upkeep of the carriages, and a vet. At one time she also had a groom and a footman. She usually had food brought in for lunch, and sometimes for dinner or supper, from the nearby café Voisin. Alternatively she would eat out, often with guests, at the Maison Dorée. She had changed from the days when she voraciously ate a portion of fried potatoes on the street, generally choosing for herself sweet things like biscuits, macaroons and iced meringues; when she was accompanied the order might be for chicken and salad, invariably with wine. She also kept herself well supplied with chocolates and sweets. She used only one toilet water, called 'L'Eau du harem', supplied by Geslin. She also used copious quantities of cold cream.

According to the account given by Romain Vienne, Marie

claimed to spend an average of five hundred francs a day, making a total of about a hundred and eighty thousand francs a year.[19] Such a figure was surely an exaggeration; even to approach it, Marie must have been spending constantly. (As a comparison, schoolteachers were paid three hundred francs a year, priests a thousand, copying clerks one thousand three hundred, and government ministers ten or twenty thousand.) The rent for the apartment in the boulevard de la Madeleine amounted to approximately three thousand two hundred francs a year, payable in quarterly instalments. Another major expense was the upkeep of a carriage and horses; there were also the servants' wages to be paid. Otherwise money was dispensed in a constant trickle on clothes, food, drink and all kinds of luxuries – though Marie was also the recipient of many gifts for which she did not have to pay. The prices for individual items of food which she ordered do not in themselves sound exorbitant – asparagus for three francs, a bottle of champagne for six, a duck for a hundred centimes, an omelette for twenty-five, two dozen oysters or a cutlet for one franc fifty – but to order in fresh every day meant that the bills mounted up and up. Likewise the cost of individual items of dress does not seem high in itself, the material costing more than the labour – Marie paid over one hundred and seventy-four francs for forty-one metres of muslin in November 1842, while having a silk dress made for only twelve francs, and buying a ready-made one at Hirtz *fils* in the rue Française for eighty francs – but her purchase of new things was so constant that the expenditure became vast. And then all these items would require upkeep – cleaning, repairs or dyeing; the cleaning of a long shawl, for instance, cost fifteen francs while three dresses were taken away and cleaned for thirty-six. Pockets and collars were ordered in from tailors, and sewn on by women hired for the purpose; Marie also bought large numbers of hats (which could cost up to eighteen hundred francs each) and pairs of shoes or boots, and ordered chemises and gloves by the dozen. Though many men bought jewels for her, she also bought some for herself, or paid to have them repaired or mounted. Likewise she bought certain items of furniture herself – though the most valuable pieces tended to be bought for her – and she paid the repair bills. Then there were the housekeeping staples, such as candles, matches, cognac and cakes, in addition to heating costs; in December 1842, for instance, Marie paid forty francs for a delivery of firewood and seventy-five centimes an hour to the man who chopped it for her in the cellar.

In addition to the items acquired in the traditional manner, the suppliers arriving at the apartment with their wares or the purchaser dealing directly with the tailor or other craftsman, there was the temptation provided by the new style of shop which had begun to emerge in the 1840s, the *magasins de nouveautés* or fancy goods stores. These were precursors of the modern department store, and towards the end of the decade such shops began to appear everywhere in Paris. They dealt in such things as silks, woollens and other fabrics, shawls, lingerie, hosiery and gloves, and they gradually brought about an end to practices which had done nothing to increase sales, such as the obligation for anyone entering a shop to buy something and the custom of lengthy bargaining over a sale as there were no fixed or marked prices. The most famous of these new stores included the Petit Saint-Thomas in the rue du Bac, the Grand Condé in the rue de Seine and, most conveniently for Marie, the Trois Quartiers on the corner of the boulevard de la Madeleine and the rue Duphot, just a few doors up from her apartment. Here she bought all kinds of items of interior decoration, such as bedspreads, pillow cases and curtains, and paid an extra charge to have them delivered.

Marie was dependent on Count von Stackelberg's willingness to continue to provide her with enough money to cover her rent and all her other expenses, a willingness which lessened as the months went by and it became clear that she had by no means abandoned all her other men in favour of him. As her expenses were consistently and inevitably higher than any budget a protector might try to impose, it seemed absolutely necessary from Marie's point of view to maintain a number of wealthy clients; a single one would never be enough, or not for long. Neither could her need for entertainment be provided solely by the regular visits of an octogenarian, no matter how generous he might be.

Marie loved the theatre and was nearly always to be seen in her box at a first night, the tickets automatically being sent to her by the theatre management, who knew her habits. She would also attend every notable exhibition or concert, and it was at a concert that she first saw the composer and pianist Franz Liszt, who was performing at the Théâtre des Italiens on 16 April 1845. He had split up with his mistress and the mother of his children, Marie d'Agoult, the previous year, and had just returned from a phenomenally successful concert tour of the major cities of France. Liszt was introduced to Marie later that year by Dr David Ferdinand Koreff, a society doctor who prescribed dubious cures for his wealthy female clientèle who included, besides Marie herself, both Liszt's mother Anna and his ex-mistress. Liszt was subsequently a guest at a number of soirées held by Marie in the boulevard de la Madeleine, where he entertained the other guests on the piano. Marie became very attached to him.

Liszt stayed in Paris for several months, but then had to return to Weimar where he had been *Kapellmeister* since November 1842. Marie wanted to go with him. He dissuaded her, but did suggest she might meet him in Pest (modern Budapest) in the spring after he had given some concerts in Vienna and Prague and said he would then take her to the coasts of the Bosphorus. In a letter to Marie d'Agoult dated 1st May 1847 Liszt gave his own, brief account of what Marie Duplessis had said to him and how he had responded:

> she told me . . . fifteen months ago: 'I shall not live; I am an odd girl and I shan't be able to hold on to this life which I don't know how not to lead and that I can equally no longer endure. Take me, take me anywhere you like; I shan't bother you. I sleep all day; in the evening you can let me go to the theatre; and at night you can do with me what you will!'
>
> I have never told you how strangely attracted to this delightful creature I became during my last visit to Paris. I had told her that I would take her to Constantinople, for that was the only reasonably possible journey I could get her to undertake . . .[20]

The plan never materialised.

And then, on 21 February 1846, Marie Duplessis married Count Edouard de Perrégaux at the Kensington Register Office in London. She had obtained a passport from the Prefecture of Police on 25 January which had described her as 'Mlle Alphonsine Plessis, person of private means, living in Paris at 11, boulevard de la Madeleine' and provided the following additional details: '22 years old, height one metre 65 centimetres, light brown hair, low forehead, light brown eyebrows, brown eyes, well-made nose, medium-sized mouth, round chin, oval face, ordinary complexion'. On 3 February she obtained a visa from the Ministry for Foreign Affairs, and she and Edouard set off for London. The entry in the marriage register upgrades Marie's father Marin Plessis to the status of 'gentleman' and awards him the Christian name of 'Jean'. The address for both Edouard and Marie is given as 37 Brompton Row, Kensington.

Husband and wife never lived together after this mysterious marriage. It was perfectly regular according to English law, and Edouard could have made it valid for France by having it properly announced according to article 170 of the Civil Code. Instead he abandoned his wife immediately after the wedding and let her return alone to Paris. Marie kept the surname Duplessis but began to use the title of Countess for certain business matters. (Some of the invoices found after her death were made out to Madame la Comtesse du Plessis, de Plaissy or other orthographic variations.) With the help of a specialist she designed her own coat of arms, using part of the arms of her husband, and had them emblazoned on her carriage, her linen and her silverware.

Marie was already gravely ill by the time of her marriage. She had been consumptive for years, a condition which cannot have been helped by her life of excess and by her peculiar diet, with its emphasis on snacks and sweets. Towards the end of her life she lived ever more feverishly. On 16 June 1846 she was present at a grand official ball in Spa. Her gambling had become extremely reckless, and she had left a mountain of debts behind her in Paris. She also travelled to Baden, Wiesbaden and Ems that summer, accompanied only by her maid, desperately seeking health but growing ever weaker. She returned to

Paris in mid-September. Stackelberg, tired of her deceptions, had lessened the frequency both of his visits and of his financial offerings. Between March 1846 and January 1847 there were nineteen instances of Marie having recourse to a pawnshop. She also took the precaution of having various valuables removed from her apartment to prevent her creditors seizing them, her friend Julie being entrusted with the task of renting other apartments in the passage Tivoli, the rue de la Chaussée d'Antin and the rue des Dames in which to store items of furniture, ornaments and jewellery. Meanwhile the seven gentlemen who had shared Marie's favours removed their belongings from the communal dressing table. The only men who did not desert her during her final illness were Pierre de Castellane, Olympe Aguado and Edouard Delessert.

The invoices from her last months detail a litany of doctors' visits. Dr Manec of the Salpetrière paid her thirty-nine visits between 18 September and 19 November. Drs Chomel and Louis, the latter a professor at the Hôtel-Dieu, were called in for special consultations. The services of Dr Koreff, to whom Marie owed fourteen hundred francs, were dispensed with (she claimed that he was poisoning her). It later transpired that he was indeed hastening her end by the daily administration of a centigramme of strychnine. Her habitual consultant was a Dr Davaine, one of the most reputable medical specialists in Paris, to whom she showed her gratitude by giving him, some time before she died, a miniature of herself. He paid her three visits in September, thirty-seven in October, forty-four in November, thirty-five in December, thirty-nine in January and eight in February (by the end he was visiting her two or three times a day). Prescriptions she was given by Drs Davaine and Chomel in November 1846 included refreshing drinks, goats' milk, calming potions, grilled meat, fish, eggs and vegetables. She was advised only to go out in mild weather, to talk little and to sleep on a horsehair mattress. None of this did any good. Meanwhile, one by one her old friends fell away and her debts accumulated. She was cared for by her maid, Clotilde, who also tried to protect her from her creditors – despite being one of them herself. In the final weeks deliveries from suppliers were made not to the apartment but to the *concierge*, Pierre Privé, who paid for them out of a sum advanced to him by Clotilde. They included the delivery of a half-bottle of champagne, urgently requested by Marie, costing two francs. Another time she ordered a 'camphor cigar', believed to be of benefit to the respiratory system.

Marie's last appearance in public, in either December 1846 or January 1847, was to attend the theatre. She died at three o'clock on the morning of Wednesday, 3 February 1847, aged just twenty-three. Her funeral took place two days later at the church of the Madeleine, a few hundred yards from her apartment. The mourners included Montjoyeux; Tony, the famous supplier of horses to elegant Paris; Romain Vienne, who signed the register at the Madeleine as a witness; and several prostitutes who had been helped by Marie in the past. The funeral expenses came to one thousand three hundred and fifty-four francs, and it is possible that some of Marie's erstwhile lovers clubbed together to cover them. Her obsequies may also have benefited from the flowers and decorations provided for a grander ceremony, the other funerals taking place that day at the Madeleine being for the Countess d'Augier, the Count d'Escherny and an old man called Monsieur Ducamp de Bussy, who lived in the same building as Marie. The coffin was followed from the Madeleine to the cemetery of Montmartre by Edouard de Perrégaux, who appeared overcome with remorse; behind him came Olympe Aguado, whose twentieth birthday it had been on the day Marie died, and Edouard Delessert. Marie was initially buried in an unmarked temporary grave, and then exhumed and reburied in a permanent plot where a stone bearing the words 'Here lies Alphonsine Plessis' and the dates of her birth and death was erected, under the orders of Edouard de Perrégaux, on 16 February. That day happened to be Mardi Gras and, while the exhumation and reburial were taking place, a carnival procession was winding its way down the butte Montmartre, the revellers in masks and fancy dress undeterred by the falling rain.

1 Romain Vienne, *La Vérité sur la dame aux camélias*, Paul Ollendorff, Paris, 1888, p.13

2 Ibid., p.14

3 See Emile Zola, *Drunkard*, tr. Arthur Symons, Elek Books, London, 1958, pp.128–46

4 Ibid., p.332

5 Nestor Roqueplan, *Parisine*, J. Hetzel, Paris, 1869, pp.64–5

6 Romain Vienne, *La Vérité sur la dame aux camélias*, p.44

7 Nestor Roqueplan, *Parisine*, pp.65–6

8 A.J.B. Parent-Duchâtelet, *De la Prostitution dans la ville de Paris*, p.127

9 See Joanna Richardson, *The Courtesans: The demi-monde in 19th-century France*, Phoenix Press, London, 2000, p.99

10 See ibid.

11 Romain Vienne, *La Vérité sur la dame aux camélias*, pp.105–6

12 Gustave Claudin, *Mes Souvenirs. Les boulevards de 1840–1870*, Calmann Lévy, Paris, 1884, p.40

13 Quoted in catalogue of the sale of a book collector, Jacques Launay, at Drouot's on 6 December 1984

14 Emile Zola, *Nana*, p.175

15 Romain Vienne, *La Vérité sur la dame aux camélias*, p.221

16 Ibid., p.131

17 Quoted in Micheline Boudet, *La Fleur du mal: La véritable histoire de la dame aux camélias*, Albin Michel, Paris, 1993, p.187

18 Quoted in catalogue of the sale of a book collector, Jacques Launay, at Drouot's on 6 December 1984

19 Romain Vienne, *La Vérité sur la dame aux camélias*, p.189

20 Franz Liszt, *Selected Letters*, tr. and ed. Adrian Williams, Clarendon Press, Oxford, 1998, pp.249–50

CHAPTER THREE

La Dame aux camélias

ON 9 FEBRUARY 1847 a notary, Monsieur Ducloux, accompanied by a Monsieur Nicolas Ridel, had made an inventory of
the possessions and personal effects of the late Marie Duplessis, and on
Thursday, 18 February an announcement of the sale of her goods
appeared in *Le Moniteur des Ventes*. Viewing commenced at noon on
the following Tuesday and the auction took place, in her apartment
on the boulevard de la Madeleine, from Wednesday, 24 to Saturday,
27 February. Much of fashionable Paris attended the sale, fascinated
to see the interior of an apartment few would have deigned to enter
during the courtesan's life. Among items up for sale were furniture,
including pieces in rosewood and marquetry, wardrobes, beds, tables,
dressing tables, armchairs, other chairs, mirrors and a piano by Ignace
Pleyel, curios, including clocks and candelabras, clothes, silverware,
diamonds, other jewels, curtains, carpets, books, pictures, horses and a
carriage and its accoutrements. Despite the pecuniary difficulties she
had been in before her death, which had led to her selling or pawning
many of her more expensive clothes, Marie left a wardrobe of about a
hundred and fifty articles, including dozens of pieces of lingerie,
twenty-seven peignoirs, more than thirty gowns, masses of lace, boas
and shawls. She also left a stash of invoices stuffed in a drawer,
detailing the myriad purchases she had made over several years from
dressmakers, milliners, restaurants, pastrycooks, florists, booksellers
and other suppliers.

The sale realised just over eighty-nine thousand francs, of which
nearly fifty thousand went to her creditors, who had been waiting for

her to die in order to claim at least some of what was owing to them. One of her dissatisfied creditors was Dr Koreff, who had sued her executors for unpaid medical bills.[1] He even requested Franz Liszt's support in the case against them, but Liszt replied (in a letter of 12 February 1847, Dr Koreff having wasted no time after Marie's death in pressing his claim) that he was unable to help, and that he had not even known Marie at the time of the medical treatment in question (May to June 1845). The remainder of the proceeds of the sale went to her sister Delphine, who now lived in Saint-Evroult-de-Montfort and was married to a man named Paquet. Delphine had been present at neither the death nor the burial of her sister.

The brief, turbulent, extravagant and finally tragic life of Marie Duplessis seems to match almost too perfectly the stereotype of the prostitute drawn up by Dr Parent-Duchâtelet and repeated by Dr Ryan and others. She is a textbook case, the ideal illustration of what could happen to a vulnerable young girl on the streets of Paris. She even managed to die of the right disease to please the moralists and social reformers, for Dr Ryan wrote of consumption or 'phthisis' that 'this direful, and I believe incurable disease . . . is often accelerated by venereal excesses'.[2] This belief came about because of the change in breathing patterns observed during the sexual act; it was thought that this must be harmful to the respiratory organs, so that a surfeit of 'erotic spasms'[3] was likely to be among the causes of consumption.

'Insufficiency of wages', Drs Parent-Duchâtelet and Ryan had declared, was the chief cause of prostitution, and Marie fits neatly into this diagnosis. Her work as an apprentice had provided her with a roof over her head and enough food to prevent her from starving, but she was constantly hungry and pleased to accept a portion of fried potatoes from the first man to offer them to her. Then the doctors remind us that a first case of 'seduction' is nearly always a contributory factor, and again Marie is the perfect exhibit. Left to fend for herself from an early age, she was probably abused by farmhands, was given to an elderly man to service his sexual needs and may have been abused by her own father as well. She had no moral upbringing of any kind. Seeing in Monsieur Nollet an opportunity to acquire expensive dresses for herself, instead of having to repair those belonging to other women, there was no need for an inner struggle. Vanity won the day because there was no opposition, no reason to refuse Nollet's proposition.

All that cannot be argued with. Marie's case merely proves that Parent-Duchâtelet and Ryan got at least part of their diagnosis right. What is more suspect, what leads one to question whether descriptions of Marie's behaviour and character are a reflection of preconceived ideas about the nature of the prostitute or courtesan rather than the depiction of a real person, is the way she appears to fit the prescribed mould temperamentally, the way even her smallest character trait seems to match the stereotype. The prostitute was supposed to be immature and rather child-like; Marie's head, according to Vienne, resembled that of a child. In particular, descriptions of Marie accord with the characteristic traits ascribed to the prostitute of instability and agitation, the sudden shifts of mood and inability to concentrate. Gustave Claudin wrote of her in his memoirs: 'her times of nervous gaiety were always quashed by sudden fits of sadness. She was whimsical, capricious and foolish, adoring today what she had hated yesterday, and vice versa.'[4] Marie's constant enemy was *l'ennui*. She seemed always to be searching for new experiences and for an elusive happiness, a characteristic interpreted, according to Parent-Duchâtelet's diagnosis, as 'a sign of an interior discomfort and proof that [prostitutes] are searching everywhere for a happiness which eludes them'.[5] Romain Vienne wrote: 'When she was bored with a protector, or tormented by the fever of her temperament, she would obey the sudden impulses of her heart and nerves, and seek consolation in a passing love which, more often than not, lasted as long as roses last, but which allowed her to expend her energy and sensibility.'[6] In Marie's case the stereotypical instability and 'agitation' seemed to be intensified by premonitions of an early death, as reported again by Claudin and Vienne, both writing some time after that death and claiming that they are writing of their memories. Claudin declares: 'Marie Duplessis was slim and pale and had magnificent hair which reached right down to the floor. Her delicate beauty and fine skin, with its tracery of small blue veins, indicated that she was consumptive and would die young. She had a presentiment about this.'[7] Vienne elaborates on Marie's need for instant gratification:

> Refusing to be shackled, she tolerated no obstacles to her desires, and obeyed only her whims of the moment, like a spoilt child. If she had a sudden urge to leave for some seaside resort, she would immediately put the plan into execution; so much the better if her protector or, failing him, a lover agreed to accompany her; if not, she would set off with her chambermaid. The good which the thermal waters should do her was one reason which she was justified in invoking; but that motive was only a pretext for the opportunity to satisfy her ruling passion – for gambling. At Hombourg, Baden or Spa, her boldness in risking considerable sums, and her calm expression, whether she was winning or losing, would disconcert the most intrepid gamblers and the most daring risk-takers.[8]

Gambling was, of course, considered to be another typical vice of the prostitute.

Equally striking are the number of positive stereotypical traits of the prostitute attributed to Marie. She was known to be pious, frequently visiting the Madeleine to pray, and among the personal effects found after her death was an order for a prie-dieu covered in velvet fixed with gilt nails. She also had a reputation for good works and was believed to give away as much as twenty thousand francs a year to charity.

If prevailing conventional views about the nature of the prostitute contributed to the myth of Marie Duplessis and went some way to veil the reality from sight, then the contribution made by Alexandre Dumas *fils* to this process was even greater. He had received the news of Marie's death several days after the event, on 10 February, having been abroad for some time with his father and unaware that Marie was suffering the final stages of her illness. He was back in Paris in time to attend the sale in the apartment where he had previously been received as a lover, and immediately afterwards he wrote the eighty-eight lines of verse which became the last poem in his collection *Péchés de jeunesse* (Sins of Youth). The poem was preceded by a blank page bearing only the initials 'M.D.'. It begins with a recollection of the ending of his affair with Marie – 'We quarrelled; I can't remember why' – and goes on to lament the fact that he can now never make up the quarrel. He alludes to having revisited the apartment where he had previously spent such happy hours with Marie, and he remembers their love-making, in which the feverish heat generated by illness mingles with sexual ardour:

> Do you remember those nights when, a burning lover,
> Your desperate body contorted beneath kisses,
> Consumed by that ardent fever, you found
> The longed-for sleep in your exhausted senses?

He ends his poem by paying tribute to those few mourners who accompanied Marie on her final journey:

> You who loved her and who followed her
> Were not like the dukes, marquesses or lords
> Who prided themselves on maintaining her life
> But saw no pride in accompanying her death.[9]

Alexandre subsequently lost no time in transmuting what he had known of Marie Duplessis into his novel *La Dame aux camélias*, in which Marie is transformed into the 'prostitute with a heart of gold', Marguerite Gautier. Published in 1848, it is the work which made his name. He also adapted it for the stage, as a play which opened at the Vaudeville Theatre on 2 February 1852. The final transmutation of Marie's story is in the form of Verdi's opera *La Traviata*, based on *La Dame aux camélias* and premièred in Venice on 6 March 1853.

   La Dame aux camélias tells the story of Armand Duval, a young man who, at the opening of the novel, is racked with remorse over his treatment of a young woman, Marguerite Gautier, who has recently died. Armand, like Alexandre, was away from Paris at the time of the death and learning of it has come as a horrible shock. The narrator, also a young man who had known Marguerite, at least by sight (for what young man about Paris would not have known this beautiful young courtesan?), attends the sale of her effects (Dumas *fils* places this in the apartment in the rue d'Antin, where Marie lived when he first knew her, rather than in the boulevard de la Madeleine) and there he buys a copy of Prévost's novel *Manon Lescaut*, belonging to Marguerite and inscribed by Armand Duval with the words 'Manon to Marguerite, Humility'. Armand discovers on his return to Paris that the young man has bought this book and he comes to ask if he may have it back.

Thus the stage is set for the telling of Armand's story, which he begins by giving the narrator a letter to read. In this letter, which is from the dying Marguerite, she regrets that she will never see Armand again and directs him to go on his return to her friend Julie. There he will receive a journal which Marguerite has been writing and which will explain certain past events to him. There follows a gruesome scene in which the narrator accompanies Armand to the exhumation of Marguerite's body, which is in the first stages of putrefaction.

Armand subsequently falls ill, but during his convalescence he starts to tell the narrator his story, beginning with his first encounter with Marguerite Gautier, which replicates Alexandre's own first encounter with Marie Duplessis, at the Théâtre des Variétés with a friend. Armand is fascinated by the vivacious and restless young woman with her multiplicity of lovers who is already exhibiting symptoms of the disease which will kill her, and he becomes her *amant de cœur*, a role he finds no easier than did Alexandre himself. This relationship, however, soon develops into a more overwhelming love than Alexandre ever seems to have enjoyed with Marie, and Marguerite begins to abandon her other, paying, lovers for him. She even gives up the elderly duke who has been paying most of her bills, and she and Armand retreat to a country house at Bougival, as had Marie and Edouard de Perrégaux. For a time they live there without concerning themselves for the future, but then Armand discovers that Marguerite has been selling off her jewellery and other luxury items in order to maintain their way of life, now that he has become her exclusive lover. She tells Armand that she never wants to return to her former life as a courtesan and that her plan is to sell off all the material goods she has accumulated over the last few years, settle all her debts and use the surplus to buy an apartment in which she and Armand can live. He agrees to her plan and then, unknown to her, visits his lawyer to request that arrangements be made to transfer his income to her.

Meanwhile Armand has been avoiding communicating with his father and his sister, aware that they would be disturbed by the course his life has taken. The lawyer having warned Monsieur Duval senior of the way events seem to be progressing, the father, who cannot believe that Marguerite's motives in the affair are other than venal, arrives to remonstrate with his son. Armand refuses to give up Marguerite. His father's next line of attack is to appeal directly to Marguerite herself, and he arrives in Bougival one day when he has ensured that Armand will be away in Paris. He persuades Marguerite that if she really loves Armand she will give him up, both for the sake of his own future and for that of his sister, who is engaged to be married but whose fiancé will call the wedding off unless his future brother-in-law stops being a cause of scandal for living with a courtesan, even if she wants to be an ex-courtesan.

Marguerite, who longs to be able to perform a redeeming act which will bring her the respect of people like Monsieur Duval and his virtuous daughter, agrees. She realises that Armand loves her too much ever to leave her voluntarily and so, for love of him, she resolves to make him hate her – and she does this by returning to her life as a courtesan and her former lovers. Her ploy works so well that Armand does indeed come to hate her and, whenever he happens to meet her in Paris, he is spiteful and contemptuous towards her. The pain this gives her contributes to the downward path of her health, and she becomes more and more ill.

The couple do have one final night of passion, on the occasion of Marguerite visiting Armand to ask him to stop tormenting her (she never explains to him why she left, knowing that this would make him abandon his father and sister and return to her) and in that night they make love with a fever and a depth they have never before attained. On the next day, overcome by jealousy at the thought of Marguerite with other men, Armand commits his cruellest act towards her by leaving some money at her house to pay her for the night before. He never sees her again. He departs on his travels, and while he is away she dies. The journal which she writes during her last days has explained everything to him, and he is overcome with remorse at having so misunderstood, mistrusted and hurt this girl who had loved him so much that she had sacrificed all her chances of happiness, and even life itself, for what she believed to be his own good.

Because Dumas *fils* had used certain well-known aspects of the life and character of Marie Duplessis in his portrayal of Marguerite Gautier, while changing or inventing other aspects, and because his novel, and then his play, became so popular so quickly, it very soon became impossible to disentangle the myth from the reality, to know whether various descriptions of her are based on genuine memories of Marie or whether they have become entirely overlaid with the image of Marguerite. The hair is one case in point; did Marie really have thick, almost black hair as so many memoirists claim to remember and with which Dumas *fils* endows Marguerite Gautier, or was the description on her passport of 'light-brown hair' closer to the mark? The trademark camellias are another point at issue: Dumas *fils* claimed to have invented this touch himself – that Marguerite Gautier wore or carried white camellias every day, except for four or five days in the month, when they were exchanged for red ones – and that Marie Duplessis had never been known in her lifetime as '*la dame aux camélias*'.[10] Romain Vienne, however, claims that she was indeed given this sobriquet, by a female employee of the Opéra.[11] Marie certainly bought camellias on several occasions, this being confirmed by invoices from a florist called Ragonat in the rue de la Paix. In any event, these flowers became such a powerful symbol, prostitutes capable of falling in love being henceforth known as *camélias*, that they were taken up by commentators and 'remembered' as a salient feature of Marie's life. Nestor Roqueplan, writing towards the end of the 1860s, introduces camellias into this romanticised description of the dead Marie:

The beauty of this young girl now she was dead was another marvel. She had been so well adorned by the touching taste of her friend, with a coquette's tenderness! Her head was encircled by Alençon lace; her joined hands held a bouquet of camellias, her favourite flower, from the centre of which rose a crucifix, indulgently uniting with this frivolous emblem of a life of dissipation.[12]

If it has been assumed that the fictional Marguerite Gautier was to all intents and purposes a portrait of the real-life Marie Duplessis, much speculation has surrounded the identity of the 'real' Armand Duval, whom she loved so much. In a letter he wrote to the actress Sarah Bernhardt on 28 January 1884, Dumas *fils* claimed this identity for himself; this letter accompanied his gift to the actress, for her portrayal on stage of Marguerite Gautier, of a special copy of *La Dame aux camélias* into which he had pasted his letter to Marie of 30 August 1845, breaking off the relationship. Alexandre certainly used some aspects of his own affair with Marie, including this same letter, in writing his novel and he also gives his hero Armand Duval his own initials, so that he is able to use the affectionate nickname 'Adet'. Yet he also made use of what he knew about Marie's relationships with other men such as Agénor de Guiche and particularly Edouard de Perrégaux; he would have learnt some of the details directly from Marie herself (the most intense phase of her affair with Edouard was over before Alexandre entered her life, and an *amant de cœur* made the perfect confidant), and possibly from Edouard, who could well have needed someone to talk to after Marie's death. Thus Armand Duval became to some extent a composite of Alexandre Dumas *fils* and Edouard de Perrégaux.

But this is a novel, not a biography, and all the characters have necessarily undergone the transformations of fiction. Where *La Dame aux camélias* departs from reality entirely is in the motives ascribed to the heroine. Whereas Marguerite is persuaded to give up Armand by his father, for his own good and to ensure the happy and respectable future of his sister, Marie's relationships with both Edouard and Alexandre broke down over issues of money – neither young man could afford to maintain the exclusive relationship with her that they both desired, because she was too expensive. Marguerite goes on loving Armand to the end, despite all his mistreatment of her, and the clear implication is that it is the circumstances of life, rather than any defects in her own character, that have forced her to lead a life of immorality and excess. This is Marie as Alexandre might have wished her to be, not as she really was. Nevertheless there are glimpses of a real person, of the restless, dissolute and difficult girl who may have been Marie, particularly in the early parts of the narrative. Hervé Maneglier has suggested[13] that Alexandre wrote the book as a form of expiation, in remorse at the way he had abandoned Marie, who had died too soon to be able to forgive him or to tell him of her forgiveness – and maybe there is an element of this in his idealised portrait. On the other hand, he also recognised a good plot when he saw one, and knew how to use the young woman's short life and romantically early death to good effect. For this novel, despite all its idealisation and over-romanticism (the exhumation scene is particularly grisly, for instance, and ignores the fact that this was a perfectly standard procedure) is still tremendously affecting and this fact, combined with Marie's conformity to the more appealing aspects of the stereotypical prostitute – her reputed religiosity, her charitable donations and her love of small animals – contributed to the mythologising of her into the type of the saintly courtesan, the acceptable face of the fallen woman.

Among the characteristics ascribed to Marguerite Gautier by her creator, and deemed to have been those of Marie Duplessis by those who wrote about her, was a relative simplicity of dress (despite the number of items in her wardrobe), her preference for light, pastel shades and the grace with which she knew how to drape a cashmere shawl around her slim body. In the poet and dramatist Théodore de Banville's account, this simplicity of dress becomes symptomatic of Marie's innate 'chastity' and distinction: '. . . this young girl whose gracious and pure face beneath her simply arranged hair, whose long swan-like neck and large, gentle and dreamy eyes gave us, despite everything, a sense of chastity, and whose slim, lithe body seemed so comfortable in her close-fitting and unadorned dress, with a plain cape whose shape was suitable only for a nun or a duchess!'[14] Dumas *fils* himself stated explicitly in the preface to his play of *La Dame aux camélias* that he had based Marguerite Gautier on Marie Duplessis, and he also refers to her 'distinction': 'She was one of the last and only courtesans with a heart . . . She possessed a natural distinction, she dressed with taste and moved gracefully, almost with nobility.'[15] Romain Vienne offers more of the same: 'The way she walked was so imposing, with a style of such decorum and reserve, that everyone would watch her go by with a surprise mingled with admiration and respect.'[16] The myth grew up that Marie was particularly discreet about her profession, that she never flaunted herself, that during her drives down the Champs Elysées or to the Bois she would sit, alone and as near invisible as possible, in the recesses of her carriage (certainly this is how Dumas *fils* described Marguerite Gautier).

This supposed aspect of Marie's character was reinforced by the account given by Madame Judith of the Comédie Française, who records in her memoirs[17] that Marie came to visit her during the actress's illness, having first sent bouquets anonymously, out of modesty. Madame Judith writes that she was greatly impressed by Marie's charm, by her melancholy black eyes and beautiful silken hair, but above all by this modesty, so unexpected in a renowned courtesan. After her recovery, Judith visited Marie in her apartment in the boulevard de la Madeleine, which she describes as 'embalmed' with flowers and rather like being in a museum, with Marie demonstrating the knowledge and passion of a connoisseur about each piece of furniture and ornament. She asserts that Marie told her she was not really happy, that she had entered on this life because of her irresistible need for luxury and that she had desired to experience the 'refined pleasures of artistic taste'. Marie went on to declare, according to Judith, that she had been in love, but that her love had never been reciprocated, and that courtesans were wrong to have a heart. She then began to cough, accusing sadness of killing her, whereas happiness would have made her well. Madame Judith further recounts that one day she encountered Marie in the Bois and invited her to get out of her carriage and walk with her, which she duly did. This was a great mark of friendliness – not to say condescension – on Madame Judith's part, and it was duly noticed and remarked upon, with disdain or approbation, depending on the attitude of the onlooker. Marie later repaid Madame Judith for her gracious gesture by warning her off about a man scheming to marry her for her money. The memoirist goes on to get the year of Marie's death wrong, which hardly inspires confidence in the accuracy of her highly romanticised account.

The way such sentimentalising can lead to the widening of the rift between reality and myth is demonstrated in the description of Marie's last days given by John Forster, the close friend and biographer of Charles Dickens, writing in the mid-1870s. Much of this account, presumably gleaned from the 'talk' in Paris to which he alludes, is pure invention:

Not many days after I left, all Paris was crowding to the sale of a lady of the demi-monde, Marie Duplessis, who had led the most brilliant and abandoned of lives, and left behind her the most exquisite furniture and the most voluptuous and sumptuous bijouterie. Dickens wished at one time to have pointed the moral of this life and death of which there was great talk in Paris while we were together. The disease of satiety, which only less often than hunger passes for a broken heart, had killed her. 'What do you want?' asked the most famous of the Paris physicians, at a loss for her exact complaint. At last she answered: 'To see my mother.' She was sent for; and there came a simple Breton peasant-woman clad in the quaint garb of her province, who prayed by her bed until she died. Wonderful was the admiration and sympathy; and it culminated when Eugène Sue bought her prayer-book at the sale.[18]

Yet despite all this exaggeration, sentimentality and confusion of Marie Duplessis with Marguerite Gautier, there remains a kernel of truth, a part of the real Marie, which genuinely impressed onlookers – an innate quality unusual, to say the least, in a woman with her way of life and her background. For only a few days after her death, well before Dumas *fils* had been able to present his version of her, an obituarist wrote of her in *L'Epoque* in terms which draw attention to that 'distinction' so frequently commented upon by others:

> A woman has just died who was once one of the most irascible and most charming of those foolish virgins who fill a whole capital with the noise of their commotion and their loves . . . At the very least you know this woman by name, even if you have never met her: she was called Marie Duplessis. She had received from God the kind of elegance and distinction which would make a great lady envious. Gracefulness came as naturally to her as scent does to a flower. Like Diana Vernon in *Rob Roy*, slender and beautiful, Marie was burning to live yet seemed to run towards death.[19]

The adulation aroused by Dumas *fils'* novel and play was by no means universal. The anonymous 'Chroniqueuse' who provided monthly accounts of Paris life for readers in England wrote in November 1860, when *La Dame aux camélias* was produced at the Gymnase Theatre, of 'that detestably vulgar piece'.[20] Neither did the cantankerous diarist Count Horace de Viel Castel, who saw the play when it first opened, have anything good to say about it or its author:

> This play is a disgrace to the era which supports it, to the government which tolerates it and to the public which applauds it . . .
> Alex. Dumas the younger is a young good-for-nothing, for

whom, it must be said in his defence, everything has been lacking: family example, moral instruction, honest companions. All he has ever seen at his father's house are prostitutes. He and his father frequently share the same mistresses and wallow in the same orgies . . .[21]

It was no doubt with such critics in mind that A.D. Vandam defended Dumas *fils* and his subject. He also underlines the fact that options were limited for a young woman of Marie's class who desired to earn more than subsistence wages:

The world at large, and especially the English, have always made very serious mistakes, both with regard to the heroine of the younger Dumas' novel and play, and the author himself. They have taxed him with having chosen an unworthy subject, and by idealizing it, taught a lesson of vice instead of virtue; they have taken it for granted that Alphonsine Plessis was no better than her kind. She was much better than that, though probably not sufficiently good to take a housemaid's place and be obedient to her pastors and masters, to slave from morn till night for a mere pittance, in addition to her virtue, which was ultimately to prove its own reward – the latter to consist of a home of her own, with a lot of squalling brats about her, where she would have had to slave as she had slaved before, without the monthly pittance hitherto doled out to her.

She was not sufficiently good to see her marvellously beauti-ful face, her matchless graceful figure set off by a cambric cap and a calico gown, instead of having the first enhanced by the gleam of priceless jewels in her hair and the second wrapped in soft laces and velvets and satins; but, for all that, she was not the common courtesan the goody-goody people have thought fit to proclaim her.[22]

Marie's early death, of what mistakenly came to be viewed as a fashionable, romantic disease (the very word 'consumption' conjuring

up the image of someone languorously wasting away, while occasionally coughing a little blood), was another factor which contributed
to her idealised portrayal. Combined with the misconception which
equated her with Marguerite Gautier, it enabled her to be seen as a
tragic heroine. As early as 1867, according to Dumas *fils*, Marie's grave
was becoming a place of pilgrimage, particularly for women. Later in
the century, the Countess Néra de la Jonchère put fresh camellias on
her tomb every day for many years. In 1950 Edith Saunders, a
biographer of Dumas *fils*, found out that her rather daunting *concierge*
was in the habit of taking flowers to Marie's tomb every Sunday. Even
today, the tomb is seldom without some floral tribute.

The story of Marie's life and death also provided ideal subject
matter for moralists, who could draw the inference that she brought
her early, painful death, abandoned by former lovers and plagued by
creditors, on herself as a direct result of the sinful excesses of her life.
John Forster indicated that Dickens had toyed with the idea of using
Marie's story in this way, and he was not alone. The legend of Marie
Duplessis fitted as neatly into stereotypes about the most appropriate
death for a courtesan as into those pertaining to a prostitute's life:
'Though she may have been no more than a *fille de joie*, according to
the moralists, or a *fille de tristesse*, as Michelet says when speaking of
her sort, death made of her a martyr. She endured a long and painful
agony during which she repented and begged forgiveness from
heaven for having loved pleasure.'[23]

It is striking that, in this case of a young woman whose biography is
so overlaid with stereotypes, fiction and moralising, and of whom it is
very difficult to catch more than glimpses of the actual person, several
of the books which have been dedicated to her life claim to be the
'true' or 'real' story. First off the mark was Romain Vienne with his
La Vérité sur la dame aux camélias (The Truth about the Lady of the
Camellias), published in 1888. Vienne claims to have been a childhood friend of Marie's, and much of what he relates is supposed to
have come direct from her own account in conversations with him.
He was, however, writing many years after her death, and his
narrative (in which he further confuses the issue by disguising the

names of the men involved with Marie) is undeniably coloured by
the idealisation which had gone on since then. He is dazzled by the
image which he himself has helped to create:

> If I have decided to write the story of Marie Duplessis, whom I
> have known since her earliest infancy, and who was worthy of a
> better fate, it is because she was not at all like the common run of
> courtesans, and because she was the heroine neither of extra-
> romantic affairs, nor of sensational scandals, nor of crazy duels;
> because she shone with a dazzling lustre, in a world apart where,
> by a combination of superior qualities, by her beauty, her mind,
> her distinction and her beneficence, she had managed to make
> an exceptional place for herself.[24]

Charles A. Dolph in 1927 also claims to be writing about the 'real' lady
of the camellias[25] and Micheline Boudet, writing in 1993, maintains
the tradition with her title *La Fleur du mal: La véritable histoire de la dame
aux camélias* (Flower of Evil: The True Story of the Lady of the
Camellias). Boudet's work is more scholarly and factual than anything
that has gone before, but she makes her own contribution to the myth
of Marie by building up the short-lived liaison (if that is even what it
was) with Franz Liszt into an affair of far more significance than the
only real evidence – Liszt's affectionate, but brief, mention of her in his
letter to Marie d'Agoult – would appear to justify. Boudet's reason for
doing this is the attempt to find some plausible explanation for Marie's
sudden, apparently unpremeditated, marriage to Count Edouard de
Perrégaux; Boudet suggests Marie married Edouard in order to
achieve respectability so that she could join Liszt in Weimar as a
legitimate countess rather than as a courtesan with a scandalous
reputation, no fit companion to the worthy *Kapellmeister*.[26] This seems
to me quite as far-fetched as any other aspect of Marie's legend.

After divesting her of legend and stereotyping, is there anything
left of the 'real' Marie Duplessis, or is she too closely bound up with
her own legend for such divesting even to be possible? A particularly
interesting aspect of Marie which can be discerned, and which makes

the disentangling of reality and legend doubly difficult, is the use she herself made of the myth of the ideal courtesan, the way she contributed to the building up of her own legend. This is noticeable in the account Madame Judith gives of their meeting, for instance; if the actress's memory serves her correctly, then Marie fed the kind of information to her that chimed with her own sentimental preconceptions of the life of a courtesan – luxurious but melancholy, loving and never loved, forever seeking an elusive happiness while dying romantically of misery. Such an account suggests that Marie was adept at playing to her audience, living up (or down) to their expectations and reaping the rewards of their sympathy and, in the case of wealthy men, their money. An ability to dramatise and sentimentalise her own life is also apparent throughout the narrative provided by Romain Vienne, if it is indeed based on what Marie told him. And if Count von Stackelberg fabricated aspects of his own life story the better to persuade Marie to accept him as a protector, it is more than likely that she was playing the same game herself, exaggerating her desire to be a reformed character, if only he would provide the money for her to do so. Vienne relates the story of Marie being approached by a 'Baron de Ponval', who pressed his suit by presenting her with a box of twelve oranges, each wrapped in a thousand-franc note. If such a character existed, this was not his real name, but Vienne takes this opportunity to have Marie deliver a speech, a kind of apologia for her way of life and her attitude towards the men who made it their business to fund it – and this is a speech which does have the ring of psychological truth:

Baron, I follow an unpleasant profession; but I must not leave you ignorant of the fact that my favours are very expensive. I spend, on average, five hundred francs a day, and sometimes I indulge in extravagant expenditure which doubles this figure. Therefore my protector needs to be very rich to cover my household expenses and to satisfy my many, varied and strange caprices. At present I am approximately thirty thousand francs in debt, which is very reasonable for me. I find nothing alarming about this figure, and don't mind admitting that it is sometimes higher. There it is, it's an obsession I have, along with plenty more; it is not my fault, after all; it is not I who dance too fast, it is the violins who can't keep up. When my current debts have been paid, I will lose no time in contracting new ones to justify the old and so as not to get out of the habit; it is stronger than I . . .

In addition, I must point out to you that, in my lover's company, I wear only those outfits which his generosity has provided. As for the old ones, I either make them into relics or give them as presents to those less fortunate than myself . . .

I think these confidences are sufficient to explain to you why I always have new outfits; they do honour to those who love me. I am always frank: I intend to remain, at all times, absolutely free in my movements and mistress of my fancies; I give the orders, I do not receive them; I have no desire at all to be compelled to receive a lover whenever he expresses the wish to see me. I have also the misfortune to believe neither in promises nor in fidelity; it is enough to tell you that I acknowledge sincerity only when it has been proved to me.[27]

Thus one aspect of Marie's character which comes over very clearly from her way of handling to her own advantage the expectations of the people she encountered, despite all the myth-making and embellishment – and even because of them – is her manipulativeness. Marie had a gift for telling her hearers what they wanted to hear, as well as what could prove useful for herself; neither should one forget her prescription for white teeth. She also had an innate cleverness, further attested by the speed with which she assimilated the education in culture and decorum provided for her by Agénor de Guiche among others. Moreover, the very fact that this young man wanted to offer her some education, desired to raise her to his own level, suggests that he found in her far more than a girl he paid for sex, that he saw qualities in her which made him desire her companionship. Likewise what we know of her relationships with Alexandre Dumas *fils*, Franz Liszt and Agénor himself, through the few letters which survive, suggests that this girl was not only capable of inspiring love but of loving – even if that love was inconsistent and needed the buttress of financial comfort (she was, after all, still very young) – and that for all her undoubted vanity and extravagance, and despite the exaggerations of her idealised portrait, she was indeed 'not the common courtesan the goody-goody people have thought fit to proclaim her'.[28] Marie also comes across as very sexy, knowing how to ensnare a succession of men of all ages, her seductiveness all the more effective for being understated, her lifelong promiscuity veiled beneath a beguilingly virginal appearance. The young men who featured prominently in her life all longed to make her their own, but she eluded them, flitting like a butterfly from one man to the next, from one experience to a new one. Edouard de Perrégaux went to the lengths of marrying her, but even that could not hold her still. The most obvious explanation for her marriage, it seems to me, was that this was yet another new experience for her, involving the thrill of a clandestine trip to another country and further evidence of her power over this young man, as well as the material benefits of the right to a title (and surely being able to call herself 'countess' was another amusing game for Marie, who cannot have helped but be amazed at the distance she had travelled from her childhood of being dragged from pillar to post by her feckless father). Stable married life can have held little attraction for this restless girl, and whatever she said to Edouard immediately after their marriage was sufficient to drive him away.

In the end it was Alexandre Dumas *fils* who thought he had finally pinned Marie down by capturing her in fiction. But the very nature of fiction and the questions it raises about its relation to reality have ensured that the real Marie remains as elusive and as beguiling as ever, endlessly fascinating and enigmatic, a young woman whose very short, dissolute and extraordinarily full life became a symbol of a paradoxical purity and against whom the lives of other courtesans would be judged.

---

1 See Alan Walker, *Franz Liszt, Vol. 1: The Virtuoso Years, 1811–1847*, Alfred A. Knopf, New York, 1990, p.391

2 M. Ryan, *Prostitution in London*, p.312

3 Ibid.

4   Gustave Claudin, *Mes Souvenirs*, p.40

5   A.J.B. Parent-Duchâtelet, *De la Prostitution dans la ville de Paris*, p.118

6   Romain Vienne, *La Vérité sur la dame aux camélias*, p.144

7   Gustave Claudin, *Mes Souvenirs*, p.40

8   Romain Vienne, *La Vérité sur la dame aux camélias*, pp.223–4

9   The poem is reproduced in Christiane Issartel's *Les Dames aux camélias de l'histoire à la légende*, Chêne Hachette, Paris, 1981, p.62ff

10 Alexandre Dumas *fils, Théâtre complet*, Vol.1, p.8

11 Romain Vienne, *La Vérité sur la dame aux camelias*, p.222

12 Nestor Roqueplan, *Parisine*, p.68

13 Hervé Maneglier, *Les Artistes au bordel*, Flammarion, Paris, 1997, p.100

14 Théodore de Banville, *La Lanterne magique. Camées parisiens. La Comédie Française*, G. Charpentier, Paris, 1883, p.254

15 Alexandre Dumas *fils, Théâtre complet*, Vol.1, p.8.

16 Romain Vienne, *La Vérité sur la dame aux camélias*, pp.216–17

17 Paul Gsell (ed.), *Mémoires de Madame Judith de la Comédie Française et Souvenirs sur ses contemporains*, Jules Tallandier, Paris, 1911, pp.221–9

18 John Forster, *The Life of Charles Dickens*, Cecil Palmer, London, 1972–4

19 Quoted in L. Graux, *Les Factures de la dame aux camélias*, Paul Dupont, Paris, 1934, p.75

20 La Chroniqueuse, *Photographs of Paris Life*, William Tinsley, London, 1861, p.335

21 Comte Horace de Viel Castel, *Mémoires sur le règne de Napoléon III (1851–1864)*, Vol.2, Chez Tous Les Libraires, Paris, 1884, pp.34–6

22 A.D. Vandam, *An Englishman in Paris (Notes and Recollections)*, Chapman & Hall, London, 1893, pp.110–11

23 Gustave Claudin, *Mes Souvenirs*, p.41

24 Romain Vienne, *La Vérité sur la dame aux camélias*, p.58

25 Charles A. Dolph, *The Real 'Lady of the Camellias' and Other Women of Quality*, London, 1927

26 Micheline Boudet, *La Fleur du mal*, pp.203–5

27 Romain Vienne, *La Vérité sur la dame aux camélias*, pp.189–91

28 A.D. Vandam, *An Englishman in Paris*, p.111

CHAPTER FOUR

The Creation of La Païva

I N 1819 A DAUGHTER was born to a Jewish couple living in
Russia. The parents' names were Martin and Anna-Marie Lachmann, Martin being of Polish origin and Anna-Marie, whose maiden
name was Klein, possibly being of German extraction. Life was not
easy for Jews in Imperial Russia in the first part of the nineteenth
century. The partitions of Poland in 1792, 1793 and 1795 had
brought some four hundred thousand Jews into the Russian Empire
and, in spite of their remarkable culture and talents, most of these
Jews were poor, partly owing to the discrimination long practised
against them and partly because of the economic decline of eighteenth-century Poland.[1] From the outset the Russian government was
concerned not only to integrate them, but also to protect other
nationalities against them. When the Moscow merchants petitioned
in 1791 to be shielded from their competitors, the government
responded with a decree forbidding Jews to settle in the capital cities
of Moscow and St Petersburg. This decree became the basis for the
creation of the Pale of Settlement, which extended from the Baltic to
the Black Sea and included Belarus, the Ukraine and Moldova.
Various regions of Russia, including those of the Volga, the Urals,
Siberia, Moscow and St Petersburg, were not within the Pale and
only certain categories of Jews (such as lawyers, doctors and craftsmen
who belonged to guilds) were officially allowed to live there. Up to
the middle of the nineteenth century, the Jews in the Russian Empire
suffered both from popular prejudice and from the government's
inability to match its aspirations to integrate them into society with

practical measures. The Jewish Statute of 1804, for instance, admitted Jews without restriction to education at all levels; or, if they wished, they could set up their own schools provided the pupils were taught Russian, Polish or German. In reality, however, Russian schools of any kind were so few and far between that very few Jews were able to take advantage of them. Furthermore, conversion to the Orthodox Church became a pre-condition for Jews to enjoy the normal rights of Russian subjects, and the vast majority chose not to convert.

The daughter born to the Lachmanns was given the names Esther Pauline; she later chose to change her first name to Thérèse, signifying from an early age her fascination with France and the French. Nothing is known for sure about her childhood and youth. It has been generally asserted that she was born in the 'Moscow ghetto'[2] without much close enquiry as to whether there was such a place in the early nineteenth century. If the Lachmann family did indeed live in Moscow and live there legally, Martin Lachmann must have been a craftsman belonging to a guild, and thus one of the better off among the Jewish community. Alternatively, the family may have been living illegally in an area of Moscow near the present-day Rossiya Hotel which was the centre of Jewish settlement there, and where there were always Jews living, either legally or illegally. A third possibility is that they did not live in Moscow at all, as the evidence that Thérèse (or Blanche, as she later called herself) was born there comes from the certificate of her third marriage, which contains other misleading information. It may have been that, to the average Frenchman, a Russian in Paris inevitably came from either Moscow or St Petersburg, anywhere else being too remote to be countenanced.

Her father was probably a clothing merchant or a craftsman, the family may have lived in Moscow, and it has been asserted that Thérèse was baptised at the age of seven.[3] No firm evidence has been found to support this assertion but, if there is any truth in the rumour, it would suggest that her parents were unusual among their community in being prepared to renounce their ancestral faith, at least on behalf of their daughter, and that they may have wanted to provide her with some opportunity to lead a broader life than they themselves had been able to, and to try to ensure that some form of education was available to her. The theory that the Lachmanns did not adhere closely to Jewish tradition in the upbringing of their daughter is supported by the fact that she was not already married by April 1835, when new legislation for Jews came into force which, among other things, forbade marriages under the age of eighteen for the groom and sixteen for the bride. By this time Thérèse was already going on sixteen, and in most Jewish families in eastern Europe it was traditional for children to be married between the ages of thirteen and sixteen and for them to reside in the paternal home. The age restrictions in the new code were a reflection of Austrian and Prussian practices designed to restrict population growth among the Jews.

If Martin Lachmann had a broader outlook on life than many of his fellow Jews in Russia – an outlook which he passed on to his daughter – it may have been gained through his activity in the export trade. Jewish merchants travelled annually in large numbers to fairs abroad, particularly to the one held in Leipzig, to buy merchandise and export products such as furs and skins. The legislation of April 1835 also allowed certain classes of merchant to visit the two capitals and the sea ports, as well as the big fairs of Nizhny Novgorod, Kharkov and other Russian cities, for wholesale buying and selling. If the family was not already living in Moscow, it is possible that Thérèse accompanied her father on one of these business trips to the capital, for it was in Moscow that she married on 11 August 1836. She was seventeen; her husband was a twenty-six-year-old tailor called François Hyacinthe Antoine Villoing. Antoine, as he was known, was of French extraction and had been born in Paris. Though it is not known how he came to be in Moscow, there was nothing unusual about his presence there; there were many Frenchmen in Moscow at that time, and French was the language most commonly used in society. If Thérèse had not previously been baptised, she would now have had to convert, as the wedding was celebrated in an Orthodox church.

The main attraction that Antoine Villoing held for Thérèse

Lachmann was his French nationality. He had connections in Paris and at some point would return there – sooner rather than later, if Thérèse had her way. Paris was known throughout Europe not only as a fashionable and sophisticated city, but as a place where Jews as well as Gentiles could have an opportunity to succeed and enjoy the good life. Thérèse believed that Paris could offer her a far brighter future than any prospects she had in Russia, and that marrying Antoine Villoing would be the first step in attaining her goal.

But Antoine was in considerably less of a hurry to leave Moscow than was Thérèse, who in 1837 gave birth to a son, also called Antoine. Her family may have expected that she would now settle into the role of wife and mother, but less than a year later Thérèse left for Paris – without husband or child. It is more than likely that she found another man to take her there; there were plenty of Frenchmen of various sorts living in Russia, working as actors, tutors, or musicians, and Thérèse had great powers of persuasion, not to mention a seductive presence. Antoine had served to inflame her imagination with the desire for another life; perhaps through him she had obtained some glimpse of that inviting city portrayed by Maxime Du Camp in the opening words of his comprehensive study *Paris: ses organes, ses fonctions et sa vie jusqu'en 1870*:

> Throughout my life as a traveller, I have seen many capital cities, some being born, some growing, some flourishing, others dying or dead, but I have seen no other city produce as great an impression as Paris or so clearly convey the sense of a tireless, nervous people, equally active during sunshine or by gaslight, breathless for its pleasures and its business affairs, and with the gift of perpetual motion.[4]

But Antoine had fallen short of providing this new life for her. And so Thérèse took matters into her own hands.

It is not known by what route she travelled to France, nor whereabouts she settled on arrival in Paris. But it is not hard to work out how she earned her living. It may be that she had imagined, as she later hinted, that with the knowledge she had already acquired of French, German, Russian and Polish, she could become a teacher. But at this stage she had no veneer of culture or any idea of how to live in Paris. While she was learning, her only marketable asset was her body, and it was very marketable: 'With her large rather prominent eyes which shone with a conquering flame, her full red lips, her firmly delineated bosom and her generous curves, she was armed with all she needed to stimulate the sensuality of men.'[5] Alphonse Esquiros paints a picture of the kind of fate most likely to befall a girl such as Thérèse:

> A young peasant girl arrives in Paris, bringing with her her figure, her innocence and her seventeen years. Ambition has brought her from the countryside; Paris has been described to her as a magic city where lovely clothes and a comfortable life await young girls. She books into a hotel which has been recommended to her. The expenses of the journey have emptied her small purse; but she easily obtains credit. She spends the first few days looking for work.[6]

No work is forthcoming, her debts mount, and she begins to despair. Meanwhile, she notices that men are continually arriving to visit other young women in the 'hotel'.

> And then one day the landlady, seeing that the girl is desperate and doesn't know where to turn, makes it clear to her that all she has to do is fulfil certain duties towards the house. At last – but too late – the unfortunate girl realises the nature of the trap she has fallen into. Weary and exhausted from searching, in a strangle-hold from the obligations she has contracted, she yields . . .[7]

If something like this did indeed happen to Thérèse, and she began her life in Paris in a *maison de tolérance*, she had the energy and determination not to stay there for long. Instead she exercised all her powers of attraction, as well as her prodigious willpower, to persuade one or several of her clients to help her buy her way out of the brothel and establish herself in a matter of months as an independent, higher class of prostitute.

This early period of her life in Paris was not one on which Thérèse ever chose to dwell, and little is known of her until in 1841, at the age of twenty-two, she set off for the spa town of Ems in Prussia. Ems, or Bad Ems, had been one of Europe's most famous spas since the late seventeenth century and was an ideal venue for making conquests. For her to be in a position to enter the social world of Ems, Thérèse's first two or three years in Paris must have been sufficiently lucrative to have enabled her to acquire respectable clothes and at least fake jewellery. In Ems her fortunes rose to a new level, for it was here that she encountered the pianist Henri Herz.

Henri (or Heinrich) Herz was born in Vienna on 6 January 1808. He was a child prodigy, performing in public and composing from the age of eight. In April 1816 he was admitted to the Paris Conservatoire, and in the 1830s and 1840s he became one of the most famous virtuosos and popular composers in Paris. A. Marmontel, a professor at the Conservatoire (and something of an amateur phrenologist) describes his physical appearance thus:

> Henri Herz's physiognomy is of the Israelite type; the forehead is prominent, the nose aquiline, the bright, wide open eyes suggest clarity of thought and benevolence. The mouth is accentuated, framed by firm lips, and the chin is rounded. There is nothing that is not straightforward and candid in this face with its decisive lines; there are no distinguishing characteristics, apart from the habit of holding the head slightly to one side with a questioning look. His height is a little above average; his rhythmic gait betrays a slight tendency to limp.[8]

At the age of thirty-eight, when Thérèse met him, Herz was at the height of his virtuosity and charm. He had been delighting young women in particular with his performances in Paris, London, Berlin and Vienna; nor did he refrain from seducing them when he had the chance. He spoke several languages fluently and was very wealthy.

It is clear from the style in which he couched his memoir about his tour of America that Herz was a man of 'sensibility', given to high-flown expressions of emotion and displays of enthusiasm. Thérèse, recognising this quality in him, deployed her powers of seduction by swooning at one of his concerts, thus ensuring that he noticed her and was attracted to her. Her genuine love of music played its part in the development of their relationship, and what began as piano lessons ended with Thérèse moving in with Henri in Paris where, in 1842, he became professor of piano at the Conservatoire. He was also involved in the running of his family's piano factory and owned a concert hall in Paris, the Salle Herz.

Thérèse Villoing and Henri Herz lived together for several years in what was then the eleventh (and is now the ninth) arrondissement in the rue de Provence, near the Salle Herz which was situated at 48 rue de la Victoire. More than just living together, they passed themselves off as married, Thérèse having cards printed for Monsieur and Madame Herz. At the same time she chose to change her first name to Blanche, partly, as in the case of Marie Duplessis, to mark a break with her past, to dissociate herself from the woman who had been Thérèse Villoing, and to remove herself symbolically from the life of prostitution which she had been following until then. For what could be purer, or whiter, than 'Blanche'? According to the reminiscences of a former pupil of Henri's brother Jacques, however, her underskirts were not always as white as they might have been at this period, her hems having been trailing in the mud.[9] Her skills at remaking herself became more refined as time went on.

The mysterious origins of this woman – she seemed to the onlooker to have come out of nowhere, after having perhaps been glimpsed in the streets of Paris as a twenty-year-old *lorette* – provided fertile ground for speculation, as did her prodigious powers of attraction, which were almost as mysterious as her origins. She herself fed the speculation, both to cover up what could be considered a not very interesting or a sordid background and to add to her aura of exoticism. And so she spread around the rumour that she was not a Lachmann at all, but the illegitimate daughter of Prince Konstantin Pavlovich, a grandson of Catherine the Great. Neither did she discourage the romanticising of the journey she had made from Moscow to Paris, a tale which included the rumour that she travelled via Constantinople where she had become the head of a harem.

The *raison d'être* for such a rumour was partly an attempt to explain her undeniable, but indefinable, sexual allure – she must have learnt the arts of seduction somewhere exotic, went the reasoning. She was not conventionally beautiful, yet she exerted some kind of power which many men seem to have resented at the same time as being in thrall to it. Physical descriptions of her are noticeable for their similarity to that of the stereotypical prostitute given by Alphonse Esquiros, with his suggestion of large, well-shaped breasts, a sensual face and, in particular, flared nostrils.[10] Marcel Boulanger writes, for instance (not that there is any evidence that he ever saw her), that Thérèse's 'nose was strange, broken at the end like a Kalmuk's, and her large nostrils quivered indecently'.[11] He also describes her as resembling the sort of female devil Cossacks might gallop away with, or a gipsy reading the tarot, and asserts that she had enormous shining eyes, like those of a dragonfly, and that her body was light, arched and wild, poised to spring like a female faun.[12] Frédéric Loliée writes of her in her youth (this again can only have come from conjecture and hearsay) as possessing 'an extraordinarily slim figure, a Grecian, not to say English-style bosom . . . luxuriant hair of bronze hue, a face more expressive than fine and superb slightly prominent eyes'.[13]

Thérèse (or rather Blanche as she now was) travelled with Henri on various of his concert tours, including to London, where he was always very warmly received. The couple enjoyed mixing with artistic society there, and Blanche added a knowledge of English to her accomplishments. Through Henri, Blanche also met various musicians, journalists and literary men in Paris, including Richard Wagner, Hans von Bülow, the pianist and son-in-law of Liszt, the novelist, poet and journalist Théophile Gautier and the editor and newspaper proprietor Emile de Girardin. Such connections sowed the seeds of her career as a hostess. Blanche used Henri to educate herself musically and culturally; she learnt much about how to conduct herself in society – and she learnt how not to handle money. Blanche also had a daughter by Henri, named Henriette, who was entrusted to the care of Henri's brother Jacques and his wife. She was a delicate child, and Jacques Herz decided to send her to Switzerland where he owned property near Berne.

Stories were circulated about Blanche at every stage of her life, usually in an attempt to denigrate her out of resentment at her arrogance and success (her demeanour could not have been further removed from that of the 'modest' courtesan, Marie Duplessis), and her period as Madame Herz was no exception. The stories often arose from some factual incident and were then embellished. The most famous story of the Herz period concerns a reception at the Tuileries, to which Henri Herz had been invited by Louis Philippe and the Queen. Herz attempted to take his 'wife' with him but, unfortunately for Blanche, enquiries had been made into her background and marital status and, as she stood in the queue at the foot of the stairs, a member of the palace staff approached her and, on establishing her identity, asked her to leave. According to Frédéric Loliée, she was so enraged that she broke her fan and threw the pieces in Herz's face for having been unable to prevent her from sustaining such an insult.[14]

By 1846 living with Blanche was beginning seriously to deplete Henri's resources. Business was also going badly and, in consultation with Jacques, he decided to liquidate the piano manufacturing business and to embark on an extensive concert tour of America, on which he would charge very high fees in order to recoup his losses and rebuild some capital. This time he decided that Blanche would not be coming with him but that she should be entrusted, along with Jacques, with the business of the liquidation and management of Henri's other affairs in Paris. He promised to send large amounts of money to her from America, both for her to live on and to pay the staff. It was envisaged that the concert tour would last for six months.

On 2 November 1846 Henri embarked at Liverpool on the

steamer *Caledonia* which was to take him to Boston. Years later, this is what he wrote about his departure:

> Armed with a good piano – my tool, – with an overnight bag and one small suitcase, I left for the new world as others might leave Paris to watch the fountains play at Versailles.
>
> I bade farewell to old Europe with a heart full of the feverish yearning, mingled with vague fears and melancholy, which is the traveller's first and perhaps most delightful emotion.
>
> For I was leaving relatives, friends and land! – but going to see America, to live a life replete with enticing dangers, over this liquid world called the Ocean; I was going to enjoy a new sky, breathe in the scents of unfamiliar vegetation, tread the mysterious ground discovered by the genius of Columbus – and these were noble and poetic compensations for the tranquil pleasures of the sedentary life.[15]

In the event, Henri stayed in America for five years. He was accompanied everywhere by his piano, which continually posed immense logistical difficulties, and he crossed both North and South America several times, giving more than four hundred concerts.

Meanwhile Blanche and Jacques got on with the work of liquidating the piano factory. Blanche quickly proved to Jacques that she was a skilled businesswoman when it came to raising money and calling in debts. He was less impressed by the fact that she spent the money at least as fast as she raised it, and he was disturbed by the constant arrival of new gowns and jewellery. Moreover, creditors kept arriving, demanding settlement of unpaid bills in the name of Madame Herz. Jacques decided to inform Henri about her overspending; the latter wrote a few mildly remonstrative letters to Blanche, about which she groaned but which had no effect whatsoever on her behaviour.

Jacques had not yet informed his brother of Blanche's other misdemeanours – of what a good time she seemed to be having in his absence. Eventually, however, the truth broke. A servant who had been sacked by Blanche decided to tell Jacques that she and Henri

Official portrait of the Emperor Napoleon III by Franz Xavier Winterhalter.
Napoleon III ruled France from 1852 to 1870; his rise and fall was mirrored
in the lives of the ostentatious courtesans who flourished during his reign.

Miniature of Marie Duplessis. Romain Vienne described how 'Her oval face with its regular features, slightly pale and melancholy when calm and in repose, would suddenly come to life at the sound of a friendly voice or a warm and sincere word.'

Watercolour of Marie Duplessis at the theatre, by Camille Roqueplan. Marie loved the theatre, and was regularly to be seen in her box at a first night.

Photograph of Alexandre Dumas *fils* by Gaspard Félix Tournachon, known as Nadar. Alexandre, who was one of Marie's *amants de cœur*, immortalised her in his novel and play *La Dame aux camélias*.

Portrait of the pianist and composer Franz Liszt by Henri Lehmann. Marie
Duplessis developed a grand passion for Liszt, and dreamt of running away with
him but nothing came of the relationship.

Watercolour of Apollonie Sabatier by Vincent Vidal. Before becoming the mistress of Alfred Mosselman, Apollonie spent some of her time working as an artists' model, and always enjoyed the company of artists and writers.

L'Atelier du peintre (The Artist's Studio) by Gustave Courbet.
Apollonie is shown looking on (wearing a shawl).

The Recital by Ernest Meissonier. Apollonie appeared repeatedly in the paintings
of Meissonier, a life-long friend. Here she is shown standing on the right.

Above: Photograph of the poet Charles Baudelaire
by Nadar. The poet's tortured relationship with
Apollonie Sabatier inspired several of the poems
in his major work *Les Fleurs du mal*.

Right: *Polichinelle* (Mr Punch) by Ernest
Meissonier. Originally painted on a door panel
in Apollonie's apartment in the rue Frochot,
this little figure seems to encapsulate the
lascivious way in which so many men gazed on
'La Présidente'.

Photograph of the Duke de Morny by Eugène Disdéri. Auguste de Morny, one
of the many conquests of Cora Pearl, was the Emperor's illegitimate half-brother
and a central figure in the political, business and cultural life of the Second Empire.

Portrait of Napoleon Joseph Charles Paul Bonaparte, known as Prince Napoleon, by Hippolyte Flandrin. Prince Napoleon, cousin of the Emperor, was another of Cora Pearl's significant conquests. Cora described him as 'an angel to those who pleased him ... demon, roué, madman, unhesitating insulter towards others.'

were not legally married. This was the last straw for Jacques, who informed his brother of everything Blanche had been getting up to, both financially and in other areas. The fact that Henri made no attempt to patch things up with Blanche, but immediately stopped sending her further money and decided to extend his American tour, suggests that some of 'Madame Herz's' exploits involved other men. Perhaps he had also found other women in America who were as prepared as Blanche had been to swoon over his performances. There were terrible scenes between Blanche and Jacques. The latter demanded that she vacate the apartment in the rue de Provence and refused to let her have any further contact with any member of the Herz family, including her own daughter.

Blanche and Henri Herz never met one another again. Their daughter Henriette died at the age of twelve, having never really known either parent. Henri continued to be a pianist adored by his public. On his return from America in 1851 he re-established the piano factory and also co-founded with Jacques and their elder brother Charles a school for pianists, the Ecole Spéciale de Piano de Paris. He clearly continued to attract young women: 'The number of women pianists trained at Henri Herz's school is considerable and forms a brilliant cohort. Unfortunately for music, most of the girls who dedicate themselves to virtuosity soon renounce it in favour of the austere duties of the family.'[16] The instruments made in the Herz factory were regarded by his contemporaries as equal to those of Erard and Pleyel, and one of his pianos won first prize at the Paris Exposition of 1855. His compositions consist largely of variations and fantasies on themes by other composers, but they also include eight piano concertos, as well as various dances, salon pieces and exercises.

So in late 1846 or early 1847 Blanche (who for the time being retained her expropriated surname of Herz) found herself almost back where she had started, in the position of having to find herself a protector, or several, of being well off for a few months or even weeks at a time and then, in between lovers, having to pawn her jewellery and find some cheap accommodation. The identities of her protectors at this period are unclear. She may at some point have been involved with Agénor de Guiche, and she certainly became a well-known figure in the *demi-monde*. A story related in the Journal of the Goncourt brothers in 1863, some sixteen years after it was supposed to have happened, involves an encounter between Blanche and Théophile Gautier, who was already a friend of hers.

The story goes that Blanche was ill and in financial difficulties. She had only been able to find a very cheap hotel to stay in, the Hôtel Varlin on the rue des Champs Elysées, where she had a modest room on the fourth floor. She asked Gautier to visit her there and, in a feverish state, adumbrated her plans for the future to him. She declared that she would one day build the most beautiful house in Paris – 'just there' – pointing out of the window toward the avenue des Champs Elysées. Théophile was unconvinced, though he did not tell Blanche so. This rather hand-to-mouth existence came to an end, probably in 1848, partly through the agency of another courtesan, Esther Guimont, who spoke on Blanche's behalf to Camille, a well-known milliner and purveyor of fashionable clothes, whose client Blanche had been during her liaison with Herz. Camille herself occupied a position on the fringes of the *demi-monde* as what was commonly known as an *ogresse* or, more accurately, *entremetteuse* – that is, she acted both as a procuress and as a facilitator, being prepared to extend sufficient credit to a woman of Blanche's calibre and obvious pulling power to enable her to be dressed as befitted a fashionable woman of the world (or the half-world) and thus to enter the circles where the truly wealthy might be found. Such women understood the value of appearances, in this world of display and ostentatious finery, and knew that to appear wealthy was the first step in becoming so. To this end, an *ogresse* would even supply her client with ready cash – not only for spending, but as a final touch to help create the illusion of being an expensive woman, of the sort that a man of the world would be drawn to and desire to possess. This was the service Camille agreed to perform for Blanche, whose potential she had already assessed during her days as the consort of Henri Herz.

Appropriately attired and bejewelled by Camille, with a 'float' to keep herself going for a few weeks, and determined to make enough money to be able to save so as to avoid the humiliating necessity of having to depend in the future on the whims of a succession of men, Blanche decided that her field of operations should be London. This was a shrewd move on her part. As his reign had gone on, Louis Philippe had become increasingly unpopular. Since 1847 there had been a food crisis in France, due to a series of poor harvests, and there was much poverty in the country. Factories were closing and workers being laid off. This economic recession spread discontent among an already miserable working class, a discontent exploited by numerous secret revolutionary societies, while on the right the King had to contend with both the Legitimists, who wanted the restoration of the Bourbon line, and the Bonapartists. Louis Napoleon Bonaparte had already made two unsuccessful attempts at staging an insurrection, one in October 1836 when he had tried to persuade the garrison at Strasbourg to rise up in support of him and another in August 1840 when he had attempted to take Boulogne. After this second effort he had been sentenced to 'permanent imprisonment' at the fortress castle of Ham, but in May 1846 he had escaped and gone to live in London. Meanwhile Louis Philippe had himself contributed to the evocation of glorious memories of the name of Napoleon both by inaugurating the statue of Napoleon I on top of the Vendôme column in July 1833 and by arranging for the return of his remains from Elba; they were translated to the Invalides, amidst great pomp and ceremony, on 15 December 1840.

The ferment of opposition to Louis Philippe increased throughout 1847 and was formalised in a series of banquets held to promote demands for electoral reform. The banning of one of these banquets, planned for 22 February 1848, led to disturbances, barricades in the streets of Paris and, two days later, the abdication of the King. The Second Republic was proclaimed on 26 February and on 2 March Louis Philippe left for exile in England, where he died on 26 August 1850. But the February Revolution, as it became known, did nothing, at least initially, to improve the economic situation. Blanche realised that Paris was not currently the best place to be for a woman in need of men prepared to lavish their riches upon her. Neither were other regions of continental Europe much more likely to yield the appropriate fruit, in this year of revolutions and popular unrest. By contrast, the ruling classes in London were relatively free of anxiety. Moreover, Blanche was already acquainted with London through her visits there with Henri Herz; she had herself been accepted there as Madame Herz. It was thus the obvious place for her to go.

Little is known for sure about Blanche's stay in London, except that it was entirely successful in its objective. It is said that she appeared one evening, luxuriantly attired, in a box at Covent Garden, and that all male eyes were immediately drawn to her. The most widely spread rumour as to her conquests concerns Lord Edward George Geoffrey Smith Stanley, the 14th Earl of Derby. He was very rich, a man about town and a dandy, yet also a most serious gentleman and a connoisseur of all types of pleasure. Married to a daughter of Lord Skelmersdale, he came second in precedence only to the Earl of Shrewsbury. He was a member of the Tory party and for a long time the right-hand man of Sir Robert Peel. He was himself three times prime minister – in 1852, from 1858 to 1859, and finally from 1866 to 1868. English through and through, this lover of pictures and books, of horse-racing, hunting and women knew how to combine business, duty and pleasure, and it is reputed that for a while Blanche came into the latter category. He possessed a large amount of land in Lancashire as well as considerable property in Ireland and he would, by today's standards, have been a multi-millionaire.

Lord Derby was by no means Blanche's only conquest; judging by the wealth with which she returned triumphantly to Paris, she must have had many rich lovers during her brief sojourn in London. Another rumour typical of the kind which surround her life concerns this money-making expedition: she was supposed to have returned by way of Moscow with a consumptive young prince in tow, who conveniently died and left her all his money. There is no evidence to substantiate this rumour and there are no candidates for the identity of the prince. On her return to Paris Blanche took up residence at 30 place Saint-Georges, near the church of Notre Dame de Lorette, in an unusual *hôtel*, or mansion, decorated with gothic sculptures, which had created a sensation when it was built in 1840 by the architect Renaud. There she received men who could afford her, if and when she chose. She also began to invest the money she had amassed, ensuring that she would never again be penniless.

A few months after the February Revolution Prince Louis Napoleon Bonaparte had also returned to Paris from London and was elected to the National Assembly. In December 1848 he defeated General Louis Eugène Cavaignac in the presidential elections by an overwhelming majority, his success being due both to his prestigious name and to his rather vague politics which allowed people of different parties and persuasions to see him as being on their side. As President of the Second Republic he was limited by law to one term of office, but he soon began to strengthen his position, taking special care to conciliate powerful conservative forces such as the Church.

On 16 June 1849 a notary's clerk arrived at the place Saint-Georges to inform Blanche that François Hyacinthe Antoine Villoing had died in Paris, on the previous day, of cholera. (A cholera epidemic had broken out in March of that year. It lasted until the end of the summer and claimed over sixteen thousand lives.) It is not known how long Antoine Villoing had been in Paris, or precisely what his relations had been with his wife. Clearly the notary had been made aware of her existence and knew where to find her. The notary's clerk also informed her that her son was currently at the boarding school run by the Frères des Ecoles chrétiennes at Passy. Blanche subsequently provided Antoine junior with an allowance of two hundred and fifty francs a month, just enough for him to live on as a schoolboy and later as a medical student. Blanche never saw him herself, the allowance being remitted to him via an official intermediary. He died of tuberculosis at the age of twenty-five.

One day soon after the death of her husband one of Blanche's friends from the literary and artistic circle she had been cultivating since the time of her liaison with Herz introduced her to a Portuguese gentleman who was already well known in the fashionable world. His

name was Albino Francesco de Païva-Araujo, and Blanche took note
of him. He had a reputation as something of a Don Juan, passionate
about gambling and women. Dressed by the best tailors, he was tall
and dark and sported a fine moustache, trimmed in a style similar to
that of the President, Louis Napoleon. He had not been in Paris long,
but was already well established in the crowd of fashionable spend-
thrifts. It was believed that he was the heir to a great fortune; he was
forever talking about the money he would one day inherit from his
mother. In fact, by the time he met Blanche he had already spent
most of it.

Albino Francesco de Païva-Araujo had been born in 1827 in
Macao, a Portuguese possession in the Far East, and was the only
son of a rich businessman who had died there in 1842. Francesco was
in Paris when he learnt of his father's death, being at the time a
boarder at the same school in Passy which the young Antoine
Villoing was to attend a few years later. On the death of her husband,
Francesco's mother left Macao and returned to live in Portugal
where, at eighteen, Francesco rejoined her. He had studied as little
as possible at school, having decided that his wealth made it unnecessary for him to follow a profession. As soon as he had attained his
majority he asked his mother for his inheritance and, after a little
prevarication, she agreed.

Francesco's first port of call was Bad Ems, where he sustained
severe losses in the casinos. Then, arriving in Paris, he moved into a
luxurious apartment at 2 rue Rossini, near the main boulevards and
the Opera House. He became a regular at the casinos, restaurants and
theatres, and also took to styling himself 'Marquess'. (The assumption
of a spurious title was not uncommon among foreigners arriving to
live in Paris; they believed it improved their creditworthiness and
helped them become established in society.)

The shrewd Madame Herz soon noticed that the 'Marquess' de
Païva was on the path to ruin, that he was crippled with debts, having
to borrow constantly, giving as his guarantee the property which he
claimed to possess in Porto and Macao. She realised that this was only
bluff, and she also began to lend him money herself. Before long

Païva found himself at her mercy, with no one knowing that she was partially funding him. It was as though he were being drawn into a spider's web. When Blanche felt that Francesco could no longer hold off his creditors or even the forces of the law, she offered him an escape route. She would pay off his debts and provide him with a monthly allowance so that he could have the appearance of independence. In return, he would marry her. He agreed.

The marriage contract was signed on 4 June 1851 in front of a notary, Monsieur Noel. Giving the same address as Francesco – 2 rue Rossini – Blanche was careful to stipulate that all the furniture in that apartment belonged to her. The civil wedding ceremony took place in the town hall of the eleventh arrondissement, while the religious ceremony was celebrated on 5 June at the Pensionnat des Frères in Passy. (One cannot help wondering whether the young Antoine Villoing caught a glimpse of his mother at this point.) The witnesses were Théophile Gautier, a painter called Barclay who lived at Passy, the secretary of the Portuguese Legation and a notary public. The marriage was announced in the Paris newspapers on the following day.

During that same year, after the defeat in the Assembly of a constitutional amendment which would have allowed Louis Napoleon to serve as President for more than one term, he and his closest advisers began to make plans for a *coup d'état*. This took place on 2 December 1851, various Assembly leaders having been arrested during the night of the 1st. Once again there were barricades in Paris and about two hundred people were killed in clashes with the army. A plebiscite conducted on 20 and 21 December overwhelmingly endorsed the Prince President's action, and a new constitution was promulgated on 14 January 1852 which gave him dictatorial powers and created a Council of State, a Senate and a Legislative Assembly all subservient to him. In November another plebiscite was held, this time to seek the people's approval for the re-establishment of the Empire. That approval was forthcoming, and on 1 December 1852 Louis Napoleon was proclaimed the Emperor Napoleon III.

A distant cousin of Blanche's new husband was the Portuguese chargé d'affaires; he remained in this post during the Second Empire until he committed suicide in Berlin in 1868. Francesco held no office but this did not worry Blanche any more than the fact that his title was fictitious; she adopted for herself the name of Marchioness de Païva with no less aplomb than Louis Napoleon had adopted that of Napoleon III. This had been her aim in marrying the 'Marquess', and for ever afterwards she was known as 'La Païva'. Having attained her object, Blanche became less inclined to keep bailing her husband out. After two years at the most, she advised him to return to Porto and plead his cause with his mother. She made it clear that she herself wanted nothing more to do with him. And so, with no resources or credit remaining to him in Paris, the *soi-disant* Marquess de Païva returned to Portugal. He carried beautiful English suitcases with him, but they were virtually empty. He left behind a few debts which Blanche refused to settle.

The story of this marriage and of Païva's subsequent dismissal was strange enough in itself to give rise to embellished accounts and fanciful descriptions of what may have gone on between the couple. Viel Castel most famously exercised his imagination on this score:

The day after the wedding, when the newly weds woke up, Madame de Païva spoke more or less as follows to her satisfied lover:

'You wanted to sleep with me, and you have managed it by making me your wife. You have given me your name, and last night I performed my duty. I have acted as an honest woman, I wanted a position, and now I have it, but you, Monsieur de Païva, all you have for a wife is a whore, you cannot present her anywhere, you cannot receive anyone; we must therefore separate, you to return to Portugal, and I to remain here, a whore, with your name.'

Païva, ashamed and confused, followed his wife's advice, and hid the memory of his regrettable adventure in the solitude of a Portuguese castle.[17]

His mother did agree to pay off his debts, but she could not forgive him for his marriage. She refused to fund him to the extent he considered necessary, and in future they barely saw one another. He lived in a small house on the edge of his mother's estate. He only left it by night, and spent his days sleeping and eating. A valet would bring him meals from his mother's kitchen.

Blanche de Païva continued to live alone in the place Saint-Georges, the most sought-after of courtesans, at a time when the city of Paris was beginning to enjoy some of its most scintillating years. There were those, such as Victor Hugo, who predicted doom for the Second Empire from the start, as well as those who were conscious of the less benign aspects of Napoleon III's dictatorship – principally, the muzzling of all opposition – but these concerns were not shared by the majority. As Gustave Claudin recalled in his *Souvenirs*: 'If the Empire did not grant much liberty, it offered on the other hand a great deal of security. It dissatisfied the liberals who concerned themselves with politics, but the dissatisfaction was not general, and was not felt at all by those, of whom there are so many in this world, who dream above all of a quiet and happy life and who worry little about politics.'[18]

The ruthlessness with which Blanche had cast off her spendthrift husband once he had served her purposes contributed to her image as a heartless and mercenary woman. She never, it was believed, allowed herself the luxury of sentiment, and in much of what has been written about her one can detect the fear and bewilderment of men in the face of a powerful woman who somehow knew how to get the better of them and who could not be manipulated.

She took care to armour-plate her heart, in order to make herself inaccessible to all emotion. In the course on which she was embarked, nothing could make her hesitate, no force in the world was capable of bending her inflexible will. Entirely devoted to her aim, she remained the self-interested and cold woman, who knows only one thing: money – because for her, money was everything and she knew that through it she could triumph and obtain all the rest. Her constant preoccupation was to be rich in order to be in control.[19]

A marked element of anti-semitism, as well as a general mistrust of foreigners and of foreign women in particular, cannot be denied in some of the judgments made on Blanche de Païva by her contemporaries and by later commentators. There is no escaping the anti-semitism of mid-nineteenth-century Paris, despite the official acceptance of Jews. Count Horace de Viel Castel noted in his diary on 19 August 1853, for instance: 'Since I've been in a position to see the Jews close up, I can understand the edicts of our kings who used to banish them. Today we are more than ever their prey, France's money passes through their hands.'[20] The tendency to ascribe certain characteristics (or supposed characteristics) of La Païva to her 'race' continued long after her death. One commentator who does so is Georges Montorgueil, writing in 1911:

> This Païva's physiognomy is of a singular complexity. A parvenue courtesan, she is not however representative of her class. She presents a unique phenomenon, which is not connected to time or place, but to race. It is the wandering and victorious Jew. No similarity between her and the pretty free spirits of the Second Empire, alluring and fidgety, obsessed with those bodies for which men went mad, queens of the fête, prodigal with the gifts of their beauty and projecting, across the splendours of the régime, the brazen laugh of la Belle Hélène. Madame de Païva did not know how to laugh. She moved towards her goal, proud and mysterious, coldly calculating. She had a powerful instinct of domination, the hidden spring of her life.[21]

Blanche did demonstrate a singular determination to achieve the goals she set herself, chief among then being to attain financial independence, and this single-mindedness as well as her most unstereotypical ability to manage money (after the early débâcle and learning experience of the Herz finances) made a deep impression on her contemporaries and on subsequent male commentators in particular, who have generally viewed this woman as unusually ambitious and unnaturally strong in willpower. Emile Le Senne presents the standard picture when he writes:

> Her understanding of the social order was simple, to her way of thinking there were only two categories of people: the haves and the have-nots. And what was the point of living in wretchedness and poverty while others lived in opulence?
>
> She possessed an unbounded ambition in whose service she placed a will of iron.
>
> She was convinced that for something to happen, it was enough to want it, firmly and fiercely. Power is will.[22]

Or, as Georges Montorgueil has it in his preface to Le Senne's book: 'There was no place for a sudden impulse in this foreign woman's soul; she left nothing to chance or to the imagination; for her everything was deliberate and willed. She slept with a compass under her pillow and, naturally prudent, she never lost the north.'[23]

1 See Geoffrey Hosking, *Russia: People and empire 1552–1917*, HarperCollins, London, 1997

2 See, for instance, Marcel Boulanger, *La Païva*, Editions M-P. Trémois, Paris, 1930, p.13 and Joanna Richardson, *The Courtesans*, p.50

3 Marcel Boulanger, *La Païva*, p.13

4 Maxime Du Camp, *Paris: ses organes, ses fonctions et sa vie jusqu'en 1870*, p.7

5 Comte Fleury and Louis Sonolet, *La Société du Second Empire*, Vol.4, 1867–1870, Albin Michel, Paris, 1913, p.358

6 Alphonse Esquiros, *Les Vierges folles*, p.87

7 Ibid., p.89

8 A. Marmontel, *Les Pianistes célèbres: silhouettes et médaillons*, A. Chaix & Cie, Paris, 1878, p.36

9 See Frédéric Loliée, *La Païva*, p.31

10 Alphonse Esquiros, *Les Vierges folles*, p.46

11 Marcel Boulanger, *La Païva*, p.16

12 Ibid.

13 Frédéric Loliée, 'La Païva'. La Légende et l'histoire de la Marquise de Païva, Editions Jules Tallandier, Paris, 1920, p.13

14 Ibid., p.34

15 Henri Herz, Mes Voyages en Amérique, Achille Faure, Paris, 1866, pp.3–4

16 A. Marmontel, Les Pianistes célèbres, p.39

17 Comte Horace de Viel Castel, Mémoires sur le règne de Napoléon III (1851–1864), Vol.4, 1885, p.39

18 Gustave Claudin, Mes Souvenirs, p.222

19 Emile Le Senne, Madame de Païva: Etude de psychologie et d'histoire, H. Daragon, Paris, 1911, p.10

20 Comte Horace de Viel Castel, Mémoires sur le règne de Napoléon III (1851–1864), Vol.2, 1884, p.231

21 Georges Montorgueil, Preface to Emile Le Senne, Madame de Païva, p.ix

22 Emile Le Senne, Madame de Païva, pp.7–8

23 Georges Montorgueil, Preface to Emile Le Senne, Madame de Païva, p.xiii

CHAPTER FIVE

La Femme piquée par un serpent

IN FEBRUARY 1822, in the town of Mézières in the southern Ardennes, Sergeant André Savatier, of the 47th Infantry Regiment garrisoned in this town, made a declaration, part of which read as follows:

> [he] has before these persons here present freely and voluntarily declared that he is responsible for the pregnancy of Miss Marguerite Martin aged twenty-four years, a washerwoman living at Pont-de-Pierre, in the district of Mézières, the daughter of Charles Théodore Martin, deceased, a distiller at Mézières, and of Marie Jeanne Plumat, his wife, the said Miss Marguerite Martin being about seven and a half months pregnant by him, that he is not and never has, any more than has the said Miss Martin, been engaged in the bonds of matrimony . . .[1]

This was not the first time the beautiful young washerwoman Marguerite Martin had been pregnant. Her first child, Joséphine, had been born of an unknown father on 26 April 1819 but had died in early infancy. The outcome of the pregnancy referred to in Sergeant Savatier's declaration was another daughter, born on 7 April 1822 and christened Aglaé-Joséphine – though the bearer of this name would later assert that her mother had wanted to name her Apollonie, but that the officiating priest would not agree to such an unchristian name. She would also assert that her father was not after all Sergeant Savatier, but rather the Viscount Louis Harmand d'Abancourt,

Prefect of the Ardennes from 1819 to 1823. The story goes that Marguerite worked as a laundress in the house of the rich and married d'Abancourt, who seduced her and subsequently persuaded Savatier to become the expected child's official father. D'Abancourt, who represented Ardennes in the Chamber of Deputies from 1824 to 1831, was forty-eight at the time of Aglaé's birth. He died in 1850, when she was twenty-eight, but there is no record of his having anything further to do with his daughter once he had resolved the paternity issue and ensured that Marguerite was provided for through the arrangement with Sergeant Savatier.

Savatier, who could neither read nor write but who had been made a chevalier of the Legion of Honour for his exploits in the Napoleonic Wars, seems not to have objected to this further award of a young and attractive woman, along with her offspring. His military status precluded an immediate marriage, but did not stop the couple living together. Savatier's wartime experiences had taken their toll physically; he suffered from various infirmities, including fits of uncontrollable trembling. Nevertheless he still represented a more secure future than the (at least) twice-seduced and fatherless Marguerite Martin may have dared hope for.

In 1825 the family, already increased by a boy, Alexandre, moved with Savatier's regiment from Mézières to Paris. Sergeant Savatier finally obtained permission to marry Marguerite, and the marriage ceremony took place in the town hall of the sixth arrondissement when Aglaé-Joséphine was three and a half years old. In 1827 Savatier was awarded a retirement pension of four hundred francs a year, and the family returned to Mézières where it was easier to make ends meet than in Paris and where another boy, Louis, was born in 1828. The final addition to the family was Irma Adelina, known as Bébé and later as Adèle, who was born on 6 September 1832. Shortly afterwards Sergeant Savatier died, and Marguerite moved with her children back to Paris. Some years later she married again, her second husband, Mathieu Cizelet, also being a former soldier. The family settled in the outskirts of the city, in what was then the village of Les Batignolles (and is now an area of Paris near the Porte de Clichy), where Marguerite supplemented the household's income by taking in sewing.

By the time she was fifteen, in 1837, Aglaé-Joséphine was helping her mother to keep house, doing some of her paid work and looking after her five-year-old sister, Bébé. She had inherited her mother's beauty, and was the kind of girl people were drawn to. The head-mistress of a local *pensionnat* offered to take her as a pupil at a reduced rate. This headmistress also realised that Aglaé was very musical, and arranged for her to have free piano and singing lessons. She was a sociable girl and also used to attend dances organised by local societies. At one of them, during carnival time, she dressed in the traditional costume of a peasant woman from La Bresse, in which costume she was painted by two young students of Delaroche, Auguste Blanchard and Charles Jalabert. She was tall and well-proportioned, with exquisite hands and luxuriant copper-coloured hair which glinted when it caught the light. She began to frequent artists' studios as a model, and became involved in bohemian life. When she was sixteen she had an affair with a wealthy young man called James de Pourtalès. Had she been a prudent character she might have married him and had an easy life thereafter, but Aglaé demonstrated early on her tendency to follow her heart rather than her head, and the relationship with Pourtalès foundered when she fell in love with Prosper Derivis, a young opera singer at the start of his career and therefore impecunious. Aglaé seems to have enjoyed this bohemian existence for the next few years, still living for the most part with her mother but involved in a series of liaisons, while studying music – though how seriously is open to debate – and obtaining some work as an artist's model. She seems to have lived on the fringes of the *demi-monde* – half in and half out of this half-world – enjoying its freedoms while not being dependent on it for her daily bread. Her mother clearly had a very *laisser faire* attitude to the bringing up of her daughters and, unlike many other parents of her time, never disowned them whatever they did.

Aglaé's rather unsettled, if carefree, way of life changed in 1846, at the age of twenty-four, when she accepted as her protector the wealthy industrialist and patron of the arts Alfred Mosselman. Alfred, who was twelve years older than Aglaé, came from an old bourgeois Belgian family; his sister Fanny had married the Belgian ambassador Charles Le Hon and was also the mistress of Auguste de Morny, the illegitimate half-brother of Louis Napoleon Bonaparte. From 1832 to 1837 Alfred was himself an attaché at the Belgian Legation, and in 1835 he married Eugénie Gazzani, a daughter of the receiver-general of the finances of the Eure in Upper Normandy, by whom he was to have four children between 1836 and 1845. His father was a banker and the owner of some very prosperous mining enterprises in Belgium, and in 1837 Alfred left the diplomatic service to concern himself with the family business which, on 24 May of that year, was constituted as a Belgian company under the name of the Société des Mines et Fonderies de zinc de la Vieille-Montagne. Its first president was Charles Le Hon and the principal administrators were Auguste de Morny (until 1857) and Alfred Mosselman. As a patron of the arts, Alfred was particularly fond of Romantic painting, and he frequented the circle of writers and artists who used to meet in the apartment of Fernand Boissard – musician, painter, art collector and man of letters – at the Hôtel Pimodan on the quai d'Anjou on the Ile Saint-Louis. This was where the *club des haschichins* used to meet at which Charles Baudelaire and Théophile Gautier, among others, experimented with the effect of eating hashish in the form of green jelly. Aglaé was also acquainted with this artistic circle, though there is no record of her having joined in the hashish-eating episodes, and it was at the Pimodan that she first met Alfred Mosselman. He may have caught his first glimpse of her from the Pimodan's balcony as she was returning with two girlfriends from a swimming lesson in the cold-water swimming pool for ladies, newly constructed at the end of the island.[2] Aglaé allowed Alfred to set her up in a sec-ond-floor apartment at 4 rue Frochot in the quartier Bréda, not far from Notre Dame de Lorette and an area renowned for its kept women. Around this time she changed her first name from Aglaé-Joséphine to Apollonie, the name she claimed should have been hers from the beginning and which she valued for its classical resonances and its suitability for a woman playing the role of muse to a circle of men. She also made a slight change to her surname, altering the 'v' to a 'b'; this reflected her desire both to distance herself from her adoptive father, Sergeant Savatier, and to dispense with the connection to *savate*, a word meaning an 'old used slipper', hardly appropriate for a beautiful young woman. From now on she was most often known as Madame Sabatier.

The rue Frochot leads off from what is now the place Pigalle and in Apollonie's day was the barrière Montmartre. It is an area which continues to be associated with sex and prostitution, while the avenue Frochot, with its gated access at forty-five degrees to the *rue* of the same name, provides an oasis of tranquility. Number 4 rue Frochot itself is now a three-star hotel. The building was constructed in 1838, and Apollonie's apartment consisted of seven rooms: an antechamber, drawing room, dining room, two bedrooms, a large bathroom and a kitchen, and then a large balcony looking out on to the gardens of the private and secluded avenue Frochot. Alfred furnished the apartment with care, he and Apollonie choosing many pieces from antique dealers on the Ile Saint-Louis. The table in the dining room was wide and rectangular, large enough to seat a dozen people, and the square-backed chairs were upholstered in olive green velvet. In the evening, light came from Louis XVI candelabra attached to the walls and from a polished brass chandelier, and in the day the apartment was filled with sunlight. The garnet-red fabric on the walls provided a fine background for the array of pictures, Delft plaques and plates acquired for his mistress by Alfred. The drawing room was to the left of the dining room, and its windows opened on to a view of the street. Everywhere there were rich hangings, pouffes, cushions, rugs and drapes. The apartment was reached by a narrow staircase and through a double door. The quartier Bréda was an area not only of kept women, but also of artists and writers. Apollonie's neighbours included Théodore Rousseau the landscape painter, Théodore Chassériau who had recently decorated the chapel of Sainte-Marie-l'Egyptienne in the church of Saint-Merri, the painter Eugène Delacroix, the composer Hector Berlioz, the poet and short story writer Gérard de Nerval, Théophile Gautier, the impersonator Henri Monnier, and the writers Henry Murger and Maxime Du Camp. Her nearest neighbour was the painter Eugène Isabey, the windows of whose second-floor studio at 5 avenue Frochot looked directly into Apollonie's.

In order to keep his relationship with Apollonie relatively discreet, Alfred found it useful to employ his friend Fernand Boissard as a confidant and go-between. Thus Apollonie maintained her links with the habitués of the Hôtel Pimodan, who included the painter Ernest Meissonier, already a firm friend of Apollonie's, along with his wife Emma. There were even those who thought that Apollonie was Boissard's, rather than Mosselman's, mistress, but he was living with Maryx (or Marix), a young and striking Jewish woman who modelled for the artists Ary Scheffer and Paul Delaroche.

The first few months in the rue Frochot marked the beginning of a significant time for Apollonie, released from any need to earn her own living. She further developed her artistic sense and discrimination, absorbing knowledge and ideas from the men around her. Alfred Mosselman made an excellent mentor, cultivating her taste to match his own while according her freedom to pursue her independent interests as well. She settled into what was in many ways a very easy life.

One thing has always been rather bewildering about accounts of the beginning of Apollonie's liaison with Alfred Mosselman, and that is the apparent ease with which she gave up what several writers have portrayed as a promising singing career to become his mistress[3] (even though there is no particular reason why she could not have been a professional singer as well as a wealthy man's mistress; several women of the period, such as Hortense Schneider and Alice Ozy, combined quite happily the dual roles of actress and courtesan). At one moment, according to these writers, Apollonie was studying under a very eminent singing teacher indeed, Madame Damoreau-Cinti, one of the foremost opera singers of her day and a professor at the Paris Conservatoire, and the next she had abandoned all idea of a musical career and was entirely contented to be only a kept woman, a *femme galante*. It has even been frequently asserted that she first met Alfred Mosselman, not at the Hôtel Pimodan or among their mutual friends, but at a charity concert which he was backing and at which Apollonie herself was singing, in order to gain experience of professional performance, alongside another pupil of Madame Damoreau-Cinti, Madame Ugalde, who went on to enjoy a distinguished solo career. Even stranger, then, that Apollonie should abandon her singing just when her career appeared about to blossom. Was meeting Alfred Mosselman really such an overwhelming experience that all other thoughts and aspirations flew out of her head?

What we have here in fact is a case of mistaken identity. There was in Paris another singer by the name of Madame Sabatier who turns up in various concert notices between 1839 and 1849 and whose maiden name was Bénazet. She was two years older than Apollonie and married Louis François Sabatier at the church of Saint-Eustache in 1839. This Madame Sabatier did indeed sing in a charity concert at the Salle Herz with Madame Ugalde on 15 February 1847, and maybe Alfred Mosselman heard her there – but he had already installed his Madame Sabatier in the rue Frochot some months previously. Apollonie herself was an excellent amateur singer, as evidenced by the fact that in subsequent years composers such as Ernest Reyer were happy to accompany her in an informal setting, but it is unlikely that she was ever the pupil of anyone as illustrious as Madame Damoreau-Cinti and she made no great sacrifice of ambition in accepting Alfred Mosselman as her protector.

The exaggeration of Apollonie's singing talents is only one of the pieces of false information concerning her life before the beginning of her liaison with Alfred. An unsubstantiated assertion made, in the first instance, by Louis Mermaz[4] and repeated by both Claude Pichois[5] and Joanna Richardson,[6] is that she had an affair with Ernest Meissonier, travelling with him to Italy in 1840. The fact that Meissonier was already – and happily – married, however, should not be taken as evidence one way or the other, as he had very clear views on what an artist's wife should be expected to put up with:

> The woman who marries an artist ought to realise that she is
> entering on a life of self-sacrifice. An artist's wife must not
> understand fidelity in the ordinary humdrum sense of the term
> . . . Even if the matrimonial horizon should be darkened by
> fleeting storms, it should be her part to restore peace and good
> will. If you have not the courage to include these items in your
> matrimonial budget, do not marry an artist![7]

The images of Apollonie Sabatier created out of mistaken or misleading information, images of her as a professional singer or as a more
promiscuous young woman than she probably was, have something
of a life of their own alongside the real woman and go on existing
despite evidence to the contrary. They had, however, no particular
effect on her in her lifetime, unlike the most powerful image created
of her at this period of her life, an image very much based on reality –
at least on physical reality. The annual exhibition of contemporary
art, the Paris Salon, included among its exhibits in 1847 a sculpture by
Auguste Clésinger entitled *La Femme piquée par un serpent*. It represented a naked, supine woman, ostensibly having been bitten by a
snake, but who really appeared to be in the throes of orgasm. The
model for this sculpture was Apollonie.

It was Alfred Mosselman who had commissioned the statue of his
mistress from Clésinger, whose studio he had visited to be shown his
works in progress. Auguste Clésinger was the son of a sculptor from
Franche-Comté and had himself taken up sculpture at an early age.
The start of his career had been fraught with financial difficulties – he
had either too few commissions or too little marble – but by 1843 he
had a studio in Paris in the rue de l'Ouest near the cemetery of
Montparnasse, and a couple of years later his reputation was steadily
growing. His supporters included Alexandre Dumas *père* and Emile
de Girardin. It was *La Femme piquée*, however, which brought him
celebrity.

Another item of misinformation repeated by various writers, such
as Louis Mermaz, Jean Ziegler and Henri Troyat, was that Apollonie
had also had an affair in her earlier days with Clésinger. In some

accounts there is confusion between Clésinger and Meissonier, and in any event there is no evidence to back up either assertion.

The process of creating *La Femme piquée* began with the making of a cast, and Apollonie was initially resistant to the whole idea. She did not, however, have a great deal of choice in the matter, once Alfred Mosselman had decided that this was what he wanted and Auguste Clésinger had determined on the technique he intended to use. It cannot have been a particularly pleasant experience for her, involving, as it did, having each part of her body in turn encased in plaster. Although the skin would be protected with oil, the sensation as the plaster cooled would have been very oppressive. After the casts had been made the sculptor assembled the pieces into the required position, making various adjustments and corrections where necessary. Some attempt was made to preserve Apollonie's anonymity, in that the head was sculpted separately and was not copied from her own. Then Clésinger created a marble statue based on the cast, and it was this statue which was exhibited in the 1847 Salon, as was a bust Clésinger also made of Apollonie, entitled *Bust of Mme A.S.*

La Femme piquée par un serpent is now on permanent display in the Musée d'Orsay, lying at one end of the central hall of sculptures. This marble statue of a naked woman consumed by sexual ecstasy – both the snake wrapped around her ankle and the title were added as afterthoughts, in an attempt to disguise the overt sexual nature of the piece – continues to draw the crowds. *La Femme piquée* is beautiful, tactile, enticing – and it is as though a living, breathing woman is lying or, rather, writhing there. People reach out to touch her – the marble is deteriorating because so many have done so – and it is as though they are touching an actual young woman. Apollonie herself – the roundness of her buttocks, the fullness of her breasts, the curve of her stomach and the shapeliness of her legs – seems to be stretched out on that plinth, exposed in all her seductiveness and vulnerability. Every detail of her anatomy is revealed for public inspection, and no attempt has been made to distance her by awarding her some mythological name. In 1847 the blatancy of this naked display riveted the attention of both public and critics, who were divided according both to their moral standpoint and to their beliefs as to what constituted art.

Théophile Gautier was supportive, writing about *La Femme piquée* in *La Presse* on 10 April 1847:

> A young sculptor, M. Clésinger, who is now a great sculptor and has at his first attempt irresistibly captured the attention of artists, poets and public, has had the audacity, unheard of in our time, to exhibit without any mythological title a masterpiece which is neither goddess, nymph, dryad, orcade, drowned sprite nor oceanide, but quite simply a woman . . . There has been no such original work of sculpture for a long time . . . The quivering body is not sculpted, but moulded; it has the texture and bloom of skin.[8]

The aspects of the sculpture which Gautier singled out for praise – the lack of mythological title, the lifelikeness of the body – were precisely what more orthodox critics such as Gustave Planche took exception to.

> Clésinger's work does not have the character of a sculpted figure, but of a moulded one. The model has various imperfections, paltry details which serious art disdains and ignores and which M. Clésinger has not known how to efface. He has reproduced the folds of the stomach, because the plaster reproduced them. He has preserved the flexion of the toes of the left foot which signifies nothing other than the habit of wearing ill-fitting shoes, etc. etc.[9]

Clésinger did not allow critics such as Planche to dishearten him, and the overwhelming reaction of the public was enthusiastic.

This was a momentous year for Auguste Clésinger, for not only did he attain notoriety with his Salon exhibit but in May he married Solange Dudevant, the daughter of the writer George Sand. On 8 June Sand's lover, the musician Frédéric Chopin, wrote to his family in Poland, deploring Solange's choice of husband and including the following remarks:

> The statue which Clésinger exhibited recently represents a naked woman in a particularly indecent pose – so much so that *in order to justify it*, he had to add a snake around one of the statue's legs. It's alarming how this statue squirms. The truth of it is that it was commissioned by Mosselman (the brother of Madame Lehon, the former Belgian ambassadress whom I've often mentioned to you) and it represents his mistress – his and plenty of other men's, because *she's a kept woman who's very well known in Paris.*[10]

It is clear from Chopin's remarks that, despite the attempts which had been made at anonymity, those who knew Alfred Mosselman and Apollonie Sabatier knew perfectly well that she was the subject of *La Femme piquée*. And this knowledge, the sense that she was spread out naked for them all to view, while also being displayed as the property of Alfred Mosselman, would have a profound effect on how the men whom she gathered around her in the rue Frochot would relate to her, – men unable to forget, for all Apollonie's apparent unattainability, this sight of her naked body in its sexual pleasure, an image calling forth a response which was a curious mixture of reverence and contempt.

1 Quoted in Jean Ziegler, *Gautier-Baudelaire: un carré de dames*, A.G. Nizet, Paris, 1977, p.78
2 See Léon Séché, *La Jeunesse dorée sous Louis-Philippe*, Mercure de France, Paris, 1910, pp.272–3
3 See, for instance, André Billy, *La Présidente et ses amis*, Flammarion, Paris, 195, pp.19–20 and Joanna Richardson, *The Courtesans*, p.108
4 Louis Mermaz, *Madame Sabatier. Apollonie au pays des libertins*, Editions Rencontre, Lausanne, 1967, p.11
5 Claude Pichois, *Baudelaire*, tr. Graham Robb, Vintage, London, 1991, p. 205
6 Joanna Richardson, *Baudelaire*, John Murray, London, 1994, p. 151

7 V.C.O. Gréard, *Meissonier, Part II: The Artist's Wisdom*, William Heinemann, London, 1897, pp.181–2

8 Théophile Gautier, *Correspondance générale*, Vol.3, ed. Claudine Lacoste-Veysseyre, Librairie Droz, Geneva/Paris, 1988, p.174

9 A. Estignard, *Clésinger: sa vie, ses œuvres*, Librairie H. Floury, Paris, 1900, pp.51–2

10 Quoted in Jean Ziegler, 'Alfred Mosselman et Madame Sabatier', *Bulletin du Bibliophile*, 1975, p.371

CHAPTER SIX

Salons

A LETTER FROM Théophile Gautier to Apollonie Sabatier, dated 19 October 1850 and supposedly posted from Rome, begins as follows:

> President of my heart,
>   This filthy letter, intended to replace Sunday's dirty talk, is long overdue, but that's the fault of the filth and not of the writer. Modesty reigns in these solemn but ancient places, and I'm very sorry I can't send you more than this shit-stained and not very spermatic mess . . .[1]

This long and rather tedious letter borders on the pornographic but is more scatological than anything else – full of bums, arses, cunts and haemorrhoids. The reader is treated to such things as a description of the author getting an enormous erection from the effect of the jolting of a poorly sprung carriage, and it ends in the vein in which it began:

> Present my most erectible indecencies to Mlle Bébé – heh! heh! – and my condolences to Fernand's spinal cord, myelitous to the third degree. If this document were not so frivolous and bum-wiperish [*torcheculatif*], I would ask you to present my affectionate greetings to Alfred, but I dare not pay homage against that wall.[2]

It is generally agreed that this is not the finest work of Gautier the poet, reviewer, belles-lettrist and apostle of 'art for art's sake'.

The reference to 'Sunday's dirty talk' suggests that this letter was intended to be read aloud at one of the regular Sunday evening gatherings which took place at the rue Frochot. Ever since Apollonie had taken up residence there, a group of literary, musical and artistic men – many of whom were already part of Alfred Mosselman's circle or were old acquaintances from the Hôtel Pimodan – had begun to form around her, and she soon developed the habit of inviting them to dinner on Sunday evenings. It was Alfred who proposed, after one particularly enjoyable Sunday, that these dinners should become a weekly event, and his offer was accepted with enthusiasm. The selected guests agreed to attend regularly, with the proviso that if another pressing engagement or reason for non-attendance arose, they could cancel by sending a note.

The list of regular guests at these Sunday evenings reads like a roll call of the intellectual élite of mid-nineteenth-century Paris. Théophile Gautier, famed for his bohemian taste in clothes which could encompass a rose-pink doublet and green slippers, was there from the start, as was Louis de Cormenin, son of the Viscount Louis-Marie de Cormenin who had been one of the most celebrated pamphleteers during the reign of Louis Philippe, writing under the pseudonym of 'Timon'. The twenty-three-year-old Louis had accompanied Gautier on his trip to Italy (during which he was supposed to have written the famous letter) and he had for some time been assisting him in the writing of his theatre criticism for *La Presse*. If Gautier had to leave before the end of a play, or if he missed it altogether, then Cormenin would write a draft review which would need little correction, as he was skilled at copying the style of his master. Cormenin married in 1854, after which his visits to the rue Frochot became less frequent. Other regular guests at the Sunday evenings included the painter Eugène Emmanuel Amaury-Duval, the sculptor Auguste Préault, Henri Monnier, the lithographer, writer and inventor of the satirical character Monsieur Joseph Prudhomme, Edouard Delessert (last encountered accompanying Marie Duplessis's coffin to Montmartre), Roger de Beauvoir, the critic Paul de Saint-Victor, the novelist, playwright and journalist

Edmond About, Charles de la Rounat, Fernand Boissard and Ernest Meissonier. Charles Jalabert (one of Apollonie's early portraitists) and the sculptor Christophe came because they were neighbours. Several of the regular guests were initially introduced by Gautier, such as the painter Ernest Hébert (who, with his olive skin, yearning eyes, long dark hair and bushy beard, was said to resemble his own paintings) and Julien Turgan, a doctor at the hospital of the Pitié, who would soon give up medicine for journalism. Gautier also introduced a young composer from Marseilles called Ernest Reyer, who had just arrived in Paris after a long stay in Algeria. Reyer was strongly influenced by Hector Berlioz, whom he succeeded as music critic of the *Journal des débats*. He was normally the only pianist present and he would generally sit down at the piano to accompany his hostess in song, or to play some of his own, or others', compositions. Along with Meissonier and Hébert, Reyer provided a link between Apollonie's salon and the world of official and academic art, of honours and worldly recognition.

Maxime Du Camp, a childhood friend of Louis de Cormenin who had introduced him to Gautier in January 1848, returned to Paris on 3 May 1851 from a tour of Egypt, Palestine, Greece and Italy in the company of Gustave Flaubert. Flaubert himself stayed on for a while in Italy, having arranged to meet his mother in Rome. On Du Camp's return, he was taken by Gautier and Cormenin to the rue Frochot where he was immediately adopted as one of the inner circle. From then on a place was always laid for him on Sunday, on Apollonie's left. He had a reputation as a womaniser who had gone through a string of affairs. If he made any advances to Apollonie, she was skilled enough to turn them down without giving offence. Du Camp was one of the best informed of Apollonie's guests, in terms of both literary and worldly matters. He and she were exact contemporaries (his date of birth was 8 February 1822) and they delighted in the fact that he had been born on St Apollonie's day. Shortly after he joined Apollonie's circle he was followed by his close friend Frédéric Fovard, a lawyer, who soon found himself taking on the legal business of various members of the group.

Gustave Flaubert was a more irregular guest than many of the others, because he spent much of his time writing at his family home of Croisset, about seven miles from Rouen. But from 1855 he developed the habit of living in Paris for six months at a time, renting an apartment at 42 boulevard du Temple. He was always warmly received at Apollonie's dinner table and given an open invitation to attend. A very hard and slow worker who refused most distractions, he nevertheless rarely missed a Sunday evening at the rue Frochot when he was in Paris. And whenever he was in attendance he was likely to be accompanied by his acolyte, the poet Louis Bouilhet.

The novelist and dramatist Ernest Feydeau had to angle for an invitation, though subsequently he became a regular guest. As he confesses himself: 'I found my friends were being very slow to introduce me to Madame S . . ., so I decided to introduce myself, and was no less well received for that.'[3] In addition to the regular guests, for whom the table would be laid in advance, there were also occasional guests brought by one of the regulars. Such visitors included Eugène Delacroix and Paul Joseph Chenavard, an artist from Lyons, who was particularly welcome for his outstanding skills as a conversationalist. Another occasional guest was Gérard de Nerval, who was brought by Gautier (the two men had been fellow students at the Lycée Charlemagne) in between two periods in a mental hospital. (De Nerval committed suicide in January 1855, an upsetting event for many of Apollonie's friends.) The distinguished critic and writer Charles Augustin Sainte-Beuve, known to enjoy good food, was also sometimes in attendance. And from time to time Gautier would bring people who happened to be passing through Paris, such as the Cuban singer Maria Martinez.

Women were greatly outnumbered by men. The singer Ernesta Grisi, Gautier's long-term companion and the mother of his two daughters, would sometimes accompany him (she was a good friend of Apollonie's in her own right). The courtesan Alice Ozy was occasionally present, though she and Apollonie tended to keep some

distance between themselves. An undated letter from Alice to
Théophile Gautier reads:

> Have I told you that I'm giving a little soirée on Sunday 10th?
> and that I'm counting *on you*. You'll be coming from Mme
> Sabatier's. I can't invite her again as she's already turned me
> down but if she would like to come with you she'll be very
> welcome. The 10th without fail.[4]

Alice had first made the acquaintance of Gautier during the time of
her liaison with Edouard de Perrégaux (who had abruptly left her for
Marie Duplessis); at one period she had even had a brief liaison with
Gautier as well.

Apollonie's sister Adèle, or Bébé, who had followed her sister's
example in changing her surname to Sabatier, was quite often present
on a Sunday evening. In 1848, at the age of only sixteen, Bébé
became the mistress of Fernand Boissard, a development which
initially came about through his need for consolation after his
previous mistress, Maryx, had left him for a Danish diplomat. In
April 1849 she and Boissard moved into a house together near the rue
Frochot, and in December Bébé gave birth, at her sister's house, to a
daughter, Fernande Ernesta Jeanne Sabatier (known as Jeanne).
Boissard, contrary to the expectations of all their friends, refused
to acknowledge the child as his, though at Ernest Meissonier's
insistence he did agree to make some financial provision for her.
Apollonie and Meissonier acted as godparents at the baptism at Notre
Dame de Lorette on 12 February 1850. Bébé spent the next two years
still hoping to marry Boissard, who kept stringing her along despite
the fact that he was already becoming involved with a young woman
called Edwina Broutta. Edwina was the same age as Bébé but
belonged to a different world. She came from a wealthy family
and was a musician, both qualities which appealed to Fernand
Boissard who proposed to her in February 1852. The future looked
uncertain for Bébé, who for the next few years continued to live in
the shadow of her elder sister.

Another occasional visitor was Elisa de Lucenay, who would be a lifelong friend of Apollonie's, noted for smoking and for wearing a large number of bracelets. Elisa Nieri (sometimes spelt Gnerri or Gnierri), a friend of the Italian revolutionary *Carbonari* and admirer of Orsini (an Italian patriot who attempted to assassinate Napoleon III, whom he saw as an obstacle to revolution, outside the Opéra on 14 January 1858), was sometimes in attendance; a friend also of La Païva's, she and Apollonie used to go to the theatre together on occasion. Apollonie's closest female friend was Emma Meissonier, but she preferred to visit when Apollonie was alone. They corresponded incessantly about clothes and recipes, exchanged confidences and gossiped about their acquaintances. There were plenty of times when Apollonie was the only woman present on a Sunday evening, surrounded by a crowd of admiring men. Alfred Mosselman was nearly always in attendance, his infrequent absences occasioned by business trips.

When Mosselman inaugurated the Sunday evenings as a regular weekly event, the gathering decided to elect a 'President'; they chose Henri Monnier, as the most senior man present. Gautier suggested that they also needed a female President, and so 'La Présidente' became Apollonie's title and it was used frequently by the guests. (Her intimate friends, including Mosselman, also knew her as Lili or Lilette.) Monnier, however, was never known as 'Le Président'. The other regular guests, as well as certain other literary figures about whom they talked but who never made an appearance at the rue Frochot, also received nicknames over the course of time. Thus Victor Hugo was always referred to as '*le père Hugo*', Sainte-Beuve was known as '*l'oncle Beuve*', while Flaubert went by the title of '*le sire de Vaufrilard*'. Bouilhet was known as 'Monseigneur', because of his bishop-like paunch and dignified bearing. And Mosselman was referred to among the group as 'Mac-Ha-Rouilh'. Feydeau, who supplies this list of nicknames in his book about Gautier, states that no one had any idea why Mosselman was given this strange-sounding name, but it is noticeably similar to the word '*maquereau*' which was used to denote a *maquignon* or trader of women and in modern parlance is equivalent to 'pimp'. This word was sometimes abbreviated to '*mac*', '*macque*', '*maca*', or '*macchoux*'. The feminine version, '*maquerelle*', referred to a woman who recruited prostitutes from such places as hospitals and railway stations; it is a term used in this way by Parent-Duchâtelet. Thus in awarding this particular nickname to Alfred Mosselman, the habitués of the rue Frochot were making a rather more than tacit allusion to his status as Apollonie's purchaser.

Apollonie soon proved her ability to provide a congenial atmosphere for her guests where they could relax, say what they thought, and enjoy the company of a woman who did not expect to be treated with deference merely on account of her sex. Looking back on his life, Ernest Meissonier paid eloquent tribute to her gifts as an intelligent and sensitive hostess:

> She had a supreme talent for attracting famous men about her, and for organising a salon, in which it was always a pleasure to find one's self. Refined, subtle and genial, smiling and intelligent, admirably balanced, excelling in all she undertook, she adored light, gaiety, sunshine. They were part of herself, indeed. For a weary, busy man it was an exquisite rest and refreshment to find her always the same, always equable, a true refuge from the cares of life, which she gracefully banished for you.[5]

Every Sunday this almost exclusively male group would come to dinner at six o'clock and stay on into the evening, these evenings becoming a cherished weekly ritual. According to Pierre de Lano, Apollonie shared this gift for putting men at their ease with other women of the period: 'The woman of the Second Empire, while inspiring violent desire, allowed Don Juan to relax in her presence. She accorded him the liberty of his brains – if I can put it that way – and he would forget himself, through her and for her, in all the brilliance of his speech, if he was witty, in all the simple charm of conversation, if he was just a chatterer.'[6] Feydeau recorded that Madame Sabatier showed no particular preference for any of her guests, treating them all the same and so dispelling any sense of rivalry.[7] (François Porché's comment on this apparent lack of preference is that each man could interpret her rather mocking laugh as being directed at one of the others.[8]) Food and drink were always excellent *chez* La Présidente, who herself had a zest for eating and drinking. Sunday had been chosen as this was generally the day for seeing friends in Paris; the Goncourt brothers received on Sunday morning, Flaubert and Du Camp were also 'at home' during the day – in fact, many guests would come on from Du Camp's *hôtel* in the rue du Rocher to the rue Frochot.

Many of the guests were already well acquainted with one another, so that there was little need for introductions and breaking of ice. Gautier and Cormenin worked together, Bouilhet could usually be found anywhere that Flaubert went, Maxime Du Camp knew everybody. The *Revue de Paris*, a journal inaugurated in 1850 by Gautier, Du Camp, Arsène Houssaye and Cormenin, could be seen as having been born in the rue Frochot, as it was here that these four first discussed the idea.

Sometimes the guests would play charades, a pastime very much in vogue. At other times they might read to one another. One evening a fancy dress party was held. Théophile Gautier came dressed as a Turk, Gustave Flaubert as a Red Indian with a kitchen utensil for a tomahawk, Maxime Du Camp as a Hindu, Louis Bouilhet as a Chinese-speaking cleric in a cassock, and Ernest Reyer as a chimpanzee. Another memorable evening was 27 March 1859, when Gautier returned from a long visit to Russia. He arrived back in Paris that evening and rushed straight to the rue Frochot without even going home first to change, startling and delighting the other guests by his sudden and unexpected appearance in a fur hat and voluminous overcoat just as they were sitting down to their soup. (Feydeau provides the added detail that it was a macaroni consommé, sprinkled with parmesan.)[9] More often than not, the Sunday evenings were passed in discussion, smoking, drinking and drawing. The artist Gustave Ricard sketched La Présidente among her guests, and Gautier drew her profile in pastel. She had an album which she would pass around for people to write or draw whatever they liked in it.

Ricard, whom Apollonie had first met at the Hôtel Pimodan, also produced a more serious portrait of her entitled *La Dame au petit chien* (The Lady with the Little Dog). Apollonie was very fond of this portrait, in which she is depicted wearing a black velvet Venetian dress with cherry-coloured satin sleeves. The little dog on her lap was brought back for her from Italy by Alfred Tattet, a friend of two other Alfreds – Mosselman and de Musset. Just as *La Femme piquée* made Clésinger's reputation, so *La Dame au petit chien*, which was exhibited at the Salon of 1850, marked a turning point in Ricard's career. He subsequently became one of the most highly regarded portraitists of his time. Apollonie hung this portrait in the middle of a panel in her drawing room.

Other works of art in Apollonie's apartment included another portrait of herself, this time by Meissonier, a pastel drawing by Rosalba, a landscape with animals by Karel Du Jardin, two small Franck *le jeunes*, a copy of a portrait of Philippe IV by Velasquez, a copy of a portrait of a man by Van Dyck (both copies having been made by Wagrez *père*), a watercolour, an etching and two sketches by Meissonier, a study of a red-haired girl by Ricard, a group of people walking in the Tuileries gardens drawn in two colours of crayon by Célestin Nanteuil, a landscape at Fontainebleau by Boissard, nymphs by Camille Fontallard and dogs by Hayrault. On a white plinth stood the bust that Clésinger had made of her, and beneath the portrait of her by Ricard stood a violetwood piano, chosen at Erard's by Ernest Reyer. But what Apollonie prized above all was a piece of Sèvres porcelain, a biscuit figure by Falconet, of a seated woman entitled *Vénus adolescente et pudique*.

On a door panel in Apollonie's boudoir Meissonier had painted a *Polichinelle* (Mr Punch), a favourite motif of his (he painted a whole series of them on the staircase of his own house at Poissy). The expression on the face of this little figure – cheerfully lascivious, with a wicked glint in his eye as he views the inhabitant of the boudoir disrobing – is in keeping with the way most of the men around Apollonie gazed on her, at least in their imagination and in recollection of the naked orgasmic body of *La Femme piquée*. It also fitted in well with the bawdy talk for which Apollonie's salon was famous. It was nearly all talk, and there is no evidence that talk led to action. The men who gathered in the rue Frochot seemed to experience a *frisson* at being able to 'talk dirty' in the presence of a woman who would neither pretend to be shocked nor make any demands on them, who – unlike their wives or their potential wives, for several of them were married while others would eventually become so – had stepped over the borders of respectability and into the *demi-monde*, and yet retained an aura of unavailability by virtue of belonging to Alfred Mosselman, whose identity as her possessor was acknowledged in his nickname of Mac-Ha-Rouilh. His presence also sanctioned the lewd talk, for if he did not object to it going on in the presence of his mistress, how could she? It could lead nowhere: there is no suggestion that Apollonie had sexual relations with her guests or that she was even tempted to do so – she seemed genuinely fond of Alfred and content to be his mistress. And so the salon at the rue Frochot provided an outlet for a frankly adolescent streak in many of the literary and artistic men who met there each week. Gautier expresses the need for such an outlet in an undated letter to Apollonie in which he laments: 'I have a huge sack of filth to empty; I haven't said anything indecent for three weeks.'[10] This is not to say that some of the men did not fantasise about what might happen if Alfred Mosselman were removed from the scene; Gautier clearly had a soft spot for Apollonie, as did Gustave Flaubert, and Julien Turgan once revealed his feelings in a letter to Ernesta Grisi: 'In the event of my death, be so good as to tell La Présidente that I would have loved her if there had been a way. That won't compromise her much, and it will make me happy. Don't talk about it until I'm well and truly rotting in a nice cemetery.'[11]

It is likely that on at least one occasion the evening's entertainment consisted of a reading of Gautier's scatalogical 'Lettre à la Présidente' alluded to at the beginning of this chapter. Such readings were not confined to the rue Frochot; the Goncourt brothers make mention in their Journal of an evening in December 1857 when Paul de Saint-Victor read the letter to a group of men including Henry Murger, Emile Augier, the journalist Gustave Claudin, the composer Victor Massé and the Goncourts themselves. This was the first time that the brothers had heard the letter, though they had previously known of its existence. Though it was clearly intended to be read aloud in this way and its humour is very male, the fact it was ostensibly addressed to a woman, and a woman who was sometimes present when it was read aloud, provided an extra thrill for the men who listened to it so avidly. In a way it was the literary equivalent of Clésinger's sculpture; though of far less artistic value, it too presented Apollonie as a sexual, though essentially passive, being, delivering up an image of her being sexually pleasured in public.

When Théo, as Gautier was known by his friends, was not flirting or indulging his delight in smut, his dealings with Apollonie generally concerned tickets to concerts and plays. As a prolific critic he was very useful to his friends as a dispenser of free tickets; he also found that good company could relieve the tedium of having yet another event to review. The first known letter from Théo to Apollonie is dated 4 February 1849:

Dear Présidente
   I'm in despair. I'm dining at Ronconi's, having been invited yesterday; Ernesta has a concert at the Winter Gardens and, if it isn't too cold, I'll send her to you and then come and collect her in the evening, which will allow me to contemplate your countless delights. Don't expect anyone after half past six. I don't know what time the music will finish.

                                                    Yours ever
                                                    Théophile Gautier[12]

In a letter of Thursday, 15 March 1849 Théo invited Apollonie to accompany him that evening to a masked fancy dress ball at the

Winter Gardens to celebrate Mi-Carême (mid-Lent, when the rigours of these weeks could be briefly abandoned in a return to a carnival atmosphere). *La Presse* advertised this ball as follows:

> The piquant programme of this carnival night promises a masked ball such as has not been seen for a long time in Paris. There will be polkas of flowers and birds, followed by burlesque quadrilles of animals and fish, by our best dancers. At two o'clock, the quadrille from *Hell*, with devilry and general illumination of the gardens.[13]

Théo rarely gave much notice of his invitations, usually offering a ticket to something on the day on which it was taking place. On Sunday, 15 April 1849 he offered Apollonie a ticket for a concert by Berlioz that evening: 'I'll come to collect you so that your presence will lighten up this musical entertainment for me.'[14] On 8 October he invited her to share a box with him and Ernesta Grisi to see 'la Zélie' dance; 'la Zélie' may possibly have been Ernesta's older sister, Carlotta, to whom Théo was sentimentally attached for the whole of his life.

A kind of low-level bawdiness pervades most of Théo's letters to Apollonie; it became so habitual that it really cannot be taken to mean very much – it was just a style of writing, as in the following short note:

> My dear Lili,
> Don't forget that you're grazing in my dump this Wednesday with Mlle Virginie Huet. The casseroles are steaming and the macaroni is turning horny, like virile members under the grill. If Alfred is with you, bring him too and that's final.[15]

At other times he is more explicit, as in this letter of 2 June 1854 which refers to his failure to secure Apollonie a seat for the first performance of his ballet *Gemma*: 'You know I adore you and I'm ready, like a large King Charles' spaniel, to lick between your fingers and your buttocks, and your gusset. I needn't mention the clitoris,

that goes without saying and is understood.'[16] But even this is not
intended as an actual proposition; the sex is all on paper. Some of the
letters, however, contain a hint that, if Apollonie were not already so
decidedly 'taken', Théo might have ventured on a physical relationship with her:

> My dear Présidente
>   I'm sending you this little pastel daub which would be prettier
> if your image showed through it, but you know it has passed to
> the feather duster, which is better for the mahogany than for the
> picture. Try to find a place for it among your knick-knacks, and
> believe me your most devoted friend (for want of anything
> better).[17]

And often, despite all the bawdy talk, a genuine concern and affection
shines through in even the briefest of notes, as in the following one of
10 December 1854, on the occasion of a performance of Berlioz's
L'Enfance du Christ:

> My dear Présidente,
>   I know you want to hear Berlioz's music: here's a numbered
> seat in the stalls. Ernesta has the other and will make her own
> way to the salle Herz.
>   Much love; rejoice your ears as you rejoice my eyes.[18]

Théo's erotic fantasies became a reality, at least briefly, with Bébé,
who never seems to have shared her sister's inaccessibility. As he put
it, in a note accompanying tickets for a box at the Théâtre Français:
'Let Bébé know; you are my love, she is my vice, and I will be happy
to dream a winter night's Dream between your two charming
realities.'[19] Théo and Bébé had a short-lived affair in the autumn
of 1853, at a time when they both needed cheering up.
   It is noticeable that, though from about 1850 Théo invariably
addresses Apollonie as '*tu*' in his letters to her, she never deviates from
calling him '*vous*' in the surviving letters from her. She did not appear

to object to his use of '*tu*', but neither did she find it appropriate to respond in kind. Gautier was known to address almost everyone as '*tu*'; such familiarity was one of his hallmarks. One might have expected Apollonie to respond as familiarly to such a long-standing and dear friend, but she maintains a respectful distance, at least in her correspondence, with Théo as with others of her male acquaintance. Her great-great-nephew Thierry Savatier stresses how much of an equal Apollonie was among the men of her circle – we might almost say she was 'one of the boys'; but such deference on her part makes one wonder whether she was exercising quite as much choice in her relationships and in the manner in which they were conducted to be consistent with such a viewpoint. She also retained a certain timidity, despite all her social contacts, and had a tendency to blush and stammer on meeting a friend unexpectedly.[20]

In a letter she wrote to Théo some time during the first half of 1852 Apollonie strikes a particularly deferential tone, and is apologetic over some request she had previously made which he had not been able to fulfil. This letter also conveys a flavour of her need for distraction; not every day was Sunday, and for much of the rest of the week Alfred Mosselman had either to be at work or with his family. There is something of the caged bird in Apollonie's situation, as she waits to be visited by Alfred, invited to the theatre by Théo (whose approval she requires before going to visit the singer Maria Martinez, in case this is an inappropriate thing for a *demi-mondaine* to do), or taken out by one of her circle.

My dear Théo, I'm going about it a bit better this time. Forgive me for having troubled you over something which I should have seen was impossible. It won't happen again. So if you can let me have anything at all for the show this evening, I'll be most grateful. I must admit that I get very bored in the evenings, and it would be more than your life's worth to see me turning into a fish, which is bound to happen very soon because I yawn hugely until bed-time. Such is my sad situation, don't put your slave to any bother, make mine run along instead and give her Mme

Martinez's address. I want to pay her a visit, but only if you think that wouldn't be indiscreet.

Clara told me that you came by the other evening. I'm really cross not to have been here, but I was dressed up and wanted to make the most of my outfit. If I don't see you before, I'll see you on Thursday, and do bring la Mariquita. We'll dine together. Remember me to Ernesta when you write to her.

Fondest regards
La Présidente[21]

The following extract from a letter by Théo to Ernesta Grisi, dated 7 May 1852, suggests that the relationship between Apollonie and Alfred Mosselman was not always easy and that Apollonie was as ready to flirt as men were willing to seduce her with words; it also mentions Madame Herz (despite the fact that Blanche was by now the Marchioness de Païva):

Bébé has a *monsieur* who has furnished an apartment for her at 27, rue d'Aumale . . . and who gives her enough money; the morganatic marriage was celebrated about a fortnight ago; the P[résidente] is perhaps a little jealous of her sister's success but she's putting a brave face on it and continues to show a lot of cleavage and to cavort about on sofas. Besides she is always charming to me and the best person in the world . . . Mosselman appears to have had it up to the ears with the Présidente, and it is even rumoured that he has another mistress. Alice [Ozy] is playing the role of the page in *La Vie de Bohème* and Madame Herz is putting on white powder from the love of pastel shades . . .[22]

The correspondence of Blanche de Païva with Gautier, who also knew him as 'dear Théo', could not be more different in tone from that of Apollonie. Though her notes also largely concern arrangements about theatre tickets, they contain no hint of deference (and she is often in a position to offer him a ticket, rather than always being a suppliant like most of his friends). In his letters to her, unusually for him, he invariably addresses her as '*vous*'. The idea of indulging in any 'dirty talk' with her would be unthinkable.

They were friends long before she became 'La Païva', many of her notes to him being signed 'Blanche Herz'. One of the few sympathetic comments made about Blanche by her contemporaries is contained in the reminiscences of Gautier's mistress Maria Mattei, preserved in the Collection Spoelberch de Lovenjoul at the Bibliothèque de l'Institut in Paris:

> On the death of his mother whom he adored, T.G. was deeply upset. He was always grateful to Madame de Païva who used to arrive on horseback to collect him and would seek to distract him by riding with him in the Bois de Boulogne. She wouldn't say a word to him but in this way helped pull him out of his sorrow by forcing him to come out of himself without noticing. This delicate way of handling his grief had greatly touched him.[23]

Théo's mother died on 26 March 1848. Though it is difficult to work out quite how this ties in with Blanche's sojourn in London around this time (for which, however, we have no precise dates), there is certainly the ring of truth about this account; Blanche was known to be an able horsewoman and this practical, non-sentimental way of handling grief and caring for her friend seems in character. Neither would there have been any reason for Maria Mattei to invent such a sympathetic anecdote about another woman's relationship with her former lover. There was in the friendship Blanche enjoyed with Théo a sense of equality entirely absent from his relationship with Apollonie (and this had nothing to do with their relative ages as Blanche was only three years older than Apollonie and pretended in later life to be younger; Théo himself had been born in 1811 and was thus eight years older than Blanche and eleven years older than Apollonie). Blanche trusted Théo, as is clear from a letter she wrote to him on 9 December 1850:

Could you, my dear Théo, do me the service of furnishing yourself with *someone or other* for tomorrow Tuesday at three o'clock. I will come and collect you and take you to the notary Maître Noël to be my witness to the deed that you know about.

You will easily understand why, apart from you my true friend, I prefer to have in my confidence someone who knows me little if at all.[24]

This is a very tantalising note, with its mysterious mention of 'the deed that you know about' and which Blanche clearly did not wish anyone else to know about. Maître Noël was the same notary before whom the marriage contract with Païva had been signed; possibly 'the deed' related to dealings with Païva, or it may have concerned her son by Villoing, whose existence this courtesan with her cachet of exclusivity would indeed have wanted to keep secret.

Some of Blanche's notes to Théo are inviting him to call:

Thursday morning

My dear Théo,

I'm in need of a good gossip for a few hours, in other words you would give me great pleasure by coming to see me

B. Herz

PS. I'll be in all day[25]

and

Monday morning

How are you, my dear Théo, are you able to come out and see me if not I warn you I'm determined to break into your house so choose

Sincerely yours
B. Herz[26]

and, from the period after her second marriage:

My dear Théo,

If you've nothing important to do, I'd be very pleased if you were to come and have dinner with me today of course it wouldn't prevent your doing something else with your evening

Bl. de Païva[27]

Blanche did not trouble herself overmuch about punctuation.

She also established regular soirées, and several of Apollonie's guests (including, of course, Gautier) were hers too. But the characters of these two salons were very different. Blanche held two evenings each week: on Fridays there would be only ten guests, on Sundays twenty. Men such as Paul de Saint-Victor, Arsène Houssaye, Augustin de Sainte-Beuve, Edmond About and Théo himself would have to decide which hostess to grace with their presence on a Sunday evening, or possibly they would manage to dine in one place and join the after-dinner conversation in the other.

In 1848 Paul de Saint-Victor had been secretary to the poet and politician Alphonse de Lamartine and had subsequently become a journalist. Charming and very handsome, he was passionate about art and loved to discuss philosophical questions. A great traveller, when in Paris he lived at 49 rue de Grenelle in a ground-floor apartment full of art objects, paintings and ornaments, all mixed up in wonderful disarray. He and Blanche were very dissimilar but got on very well, becoming great friends and confidants. Arsène Houssaye, who turns up in most social gatherings and at most artistic events of the period, was appointed in 1849 as general administrator of the Comédie Française, a post he held for seven years. In 1875 he became director of the Théâtre Lyrique. He was, in turn and sometimes concurrently, a novelist, poet, non-fiction writer, playwright and historian, excelling at none of these things. The balls and fancy dress parties he gave at his *hôtel* were particularly spectacular. Among La Païva's regular guests were also Léon Gozlan, a brilliant chronicler who had been Balzac's secretary, and Jules Lecomte, who could be relied upon to know everything about what was what and who was who in Paris. Emile de Girardin was also a frequent presence, keeping Blanche up to date in political matters and enlivening the dinners with a steady stream of anecdotes.

La Païva was an exacting hostess who expected stimulating conversation from her guests. Houssaye reports that her friends were given *carte blanche* to bring other guests to her dinners, but that people incapable of talking entertainingly would not be invited a second time.[28] In common with Madame Sabatier's salon, as indeed with every other salon of the period, the vast majority of the guests were male. Only one woman was regularly invited to La Païva's soirées, and that was Roger de Beauvoir's wife, Aimée, formerly Mademoiselle Doze of the Comédie Française.

The food and wine Blanche provided were of the best; never, Houssaye declares, were artists and men of letters more royally fêted.[29] Théo was her chief adviser on whom to invite and her chief arbiter on questions of style. Two other regular guests were a Monsieur de Reims, who was the emissary in France of the Duke d'Aumale and who acted as Blanche's financial adviser, and Dumont de Montcel, a connoisseur of good food and wine who served as her 'taster'. Théo was also gifted with a prodigious appetite and a strong appreciation of wine. He was known for drinking only water during a meal, leaving all the wine until he had finished eating, when he would sample every label on offer, becoming ever more voluble. There are some reports that, despite Théo's best efforts, conversation could become stilted at La Païva's – partly because of the high standards she demanded, though possibly also because the guests were at times more interested in eating and drinking than in talking. Neither were the topics chosen for conversation consistently high-minded; everyone enjoyed discussing their minor ailments, as well as indulging in gloomy prognoses about the future. Eugène Delacroix records that he attended one of La Païva's soirées on 2 May 1855. He claims not to have enjoyed himself very much, finding both the company and the conversation 'useless' and 'insipid' and the atmosphere 'pest-laden'.[30]

Despite all La Païva's efforts at artistic and intellectual sophistication, and despite La Présidente's natural abilities as a hostess and the quality of the guests that both these women invited, in a sense neither was more than a superior *femme à partie*, the sort of kept woman for whom, according to Parent-Duchâtelet, 'beauty alone was not enough; they had to have in addition the graces and charms of a cultivated mind. In general, to be admitted *chez elles*, a man would have to be introduced by one of the regular visitors to their gatherings.'[31] Several of the men who frequented the salons of La Présidente and La Païva were also regularly received by a hostess of a rather different order, at least in worldly terms: her Imperial Highness (as she was styled when her cousin Louis Napoleon became Emperor in 1852) the Princess Mathilde.

In 1840, at the age of twenty, Laetitia Wilhelmina Mathilde Bonaparte had been married off to the rich, but dissolute and sadistic, Russian Count Anatole Nikolayevich Demidov. It was a disastrous marriage which was ended by separation in December 1845. As Demidov's wife, however, Mathilde was able to settle in the France of Louis Philippe despite the law banning all Bonapartes, and to live there comfortably after the separation, on an annual allowance of two hundred thousand roubles secured for her by the Tsar. She never saw her husband again. An ardent Bonapartist, Mathilde worked for Louis Napoleon's political success before his election as President in December 1848, and from 1849 until his marriage to Eugénie de Montijo in January 1853 she served as his hostess at the Elysée and Tuileries palaces. On the restoration of the Empire she received an additional income of two hundred thousand francs per year (later increased to five hundred thousand), with which she purchased her country estate of Saint Gratien, near Lake d'Enghien, an hour's journey from Paris. Her personal life was not so very far removed from that of a *demi-mondaine* – except for the crucial differences that during her long-term liaison with the married Count Emilien de Nieuwerkerke she never had to ask him for money and her imperial status ensured her respectability and her place in high society. Nieuwerkerke was a sculptor who, under Mathilde's aegis, became Director of Museums and eventually Superintendent of Fine Arts.

Princess Mathilde was the most distinguished hostess of Second

Empire Paris, giving not only dinners and receptions but fancy dress balls and theatrical soirées. She also held a special celebration every year to mark the Emperor's birthday. L. de Hegermann-Lindencrone wrote in a letter of 1865: 'The Princesse Mathilde receives every Sunday evening. Her salons are always crowded, and are what one might call cosmopolitan. In fact, it is the only salon in Paris where one can meet all nationalities. There are diplomats, royalties, imperialists, strangers of importance passing through Paris, and especially all the celebrated artists.'[32] Princess Caroline Murat is fulsome in the praise of her relative, and describes how she divided up her guests over various evenings:

> Dignified as Imperial Highness, the niece of two emperors, and the cousin of a third, she had more illustrious family connections than the Emperor himself, and she had the ambition and the faculty to rule. She must have been uncommonly beautiful in her young womanhood; she was still very handsome when I saw her first, and she always remained a woman of distinguished presence. Unquestionably she was the most cultured and talented of all the Bonapartes; and she was probably one of the most cultured women in France during her time. Her salon was a court in itself. Begun during the reign of Louis Philippe, it had no equal in the nineteenth century for length of ascendancy. For fifty years it was an important institution, the home and centre of Parisian intellect stamped with her own strongly-marked individuality. Her great wealth enabled her to extend unlimited hospitality, and to make her home the meeting-place of the choice spirits of the day . . .[33]

Although she was at home to her friends every evening, her companions differed in type with the days of the week. Sundays she reserved for current invitations and new introductions. Tuesdays were set aside for the reception of official personages, and Wednesdays, for her chosen intimates who were always exclusively artists. The Sunday soirées at the Rue de Courcelles were especially popular, attended by crowds of distinguished men and women, whose names remain familiar to a later generation.[34]

One of the Princess's most regular guests was Maxime Du Camp, who seems to have enjoyed praising La Présidente *chez* La Princesse and reporting back on La Princesse to La Présidente. Other men known to frequent both the *haut monde* and the *demi-monde* in this way – for men, unlike women, could maintain an easy traffic between the two worlds (though the Princess was not particularly delighted when her guests were prepared to forfeit time they could have spent with her by visiting courtesans and kept women) – included Edmond About, Emile Augier, Gustave Flaubert, the painter Jean-Léon Gérôme, Emile de Girardin, the Goncourt brothers, Charles Augustin Sainte-Beuve (who in the 1860s was considered by Princess Mathilde her literary adviser and an intimate friend), the historian, philosopher and critic Hippolyte Taine – and, of course, the ubiquitous Théo.

1 Jean-Jacques Pauvert, *L'Erotisme Second Empire*, Carrère, Paris, 1985, p.115

2 Ibid., p.132

3 Ernest Feydeau, *Théophile Gautier: souvenirs intimes*, E. Plon, Paris, 1874, pp.154–5

4 Théophile Gautier, *Correspondance générale*, Vol.12, 2000, p.164

5 V.C.O. Gréard, *Meissonier, Part II: The Artist's Wisdom*, p.219

6 Pierre de Lano, *L'Amour à Paris sous le Second Empire*, H. Simonis Empis, Paris, 1896, p.8

7 Ernest Feydeau, *Théophile Gautier*, p.167

8 François Porché, *Baudelaire et la Présidente*, Gallimard, Paris, 1959, p.140

9 Ernest Feydeau, *Théophile Gautier*, p.195

10 Théophile Gautier, *Correspondance générale*, Vol.6, 1991, p.89

11 Quoted in Jean Ziegler, *Gautier-Baudelaire: un carré de Dames*, p.88

12 Théophile Gautier, *Correspondance générale*, Vol.4, 1989, pp.9–10

13 Quoted in Jean-Jacques Pauvert, *L'Erotisme Second Empire*, p.103

14 Théophile Gautier, *Correspondance générale*, Vol.4, p.105

15 Ibid., Vol.12, p.172

16 Ibid., Vol.6, p.36

17 Ibid., Vol.12, p.207

18 Ibid., Vol.6, p.97

19 Ibid., p.172

20 See André Billy, *La Présidente et ses amis*, p.47

21 Théophile Gautier, *Correspondance générale*, Vol.5, 1991, p.61

22 Quoted in Jean Ziegler, *Gautier-Baudelaire: un carré de Dames*, pp.100–2

23 Théophile Gautier, *Correspondance générale*, Vol.4, p.507

24 Ibid., p.272

25 Ibid., p.352

26 Ibid., p.353

27 Ibid., Vol.12, p.165

28 Arsene Houssaye, *Les Confessions. Souvenirs d'un demi-siècle 1830–1880*, Vol.5, E. Dentu, Paris, 1891, pp.336 and 338

29 Ibid., p.336

30 *The Journal of Eugène Delacroix*, tr. Walter Pach, Grove Press, New York, 1961, p.461

31 A.J.B. Parent-Duchâtelet, *De la Prostitution dans la ville de Paris*, p.175

32 L. de Hegermann-Lindencrone, *In the Courts of Memory 1858–1875 from Contemporary Letters*, Harper & Brothers, New York and London, 1912, p.68

33 Princess Caroline Murat, *My Memoirs*, Eveleigh Nash, London, 1910, pp.70–1

34 Ibid., p.74

CHAPTER SEVEN

Les Fleurs du mal

D URING THE FOURTEEN or so years of Apollonie Sabatier's liaison with Alfred Mosselman, only one man seems to have seriously disturbed her equilibrium and aroused in her the desire for more than a passing flirtation or 'cavorting on the sofa'. That man was the poet Charles Baudelaire. They had first encountered one another in the early 1840s when Baudelaire was living at the Hôtel Pimodan, and from 1851 he had been a regular guest at the Sunday soirées in the rue Frochot, having been brought there, like so many others, by Théophile Gautier.

Over the next few years Baudelaire, who was a year older than Madame Sabatier, wrote a series of poems inspired by her and sent them to her, one by one, often with a note or letter, always in disguised, cramped handwriting and anonymously. The first of these notes, which accompanied the poem *A une femme trop gaie* (later retitled *A celle qui est trop gaie*) was dated 9 December 1852 and read:

> The person for whom these lines have been written, whether they please or displease her, even if they appear totally ridiculous to her, is very humbly *implored* not to show them to *anyone*. Profound sentiments have a modesty which desires not to be violated. Is not the absence of a signature a symptom of this invincible modesty? He who has written these lines in one of those states of reverie into which he is often plunged by the image of the one who is their object has loved her deeply,

without ever telling her so, and he will *forever* feel for her the
most tender sympathy.[1]

A une femme trop gaie is a curious poem to send to someone who is
'loved deeply'. The title itself contains implied criticism – the woman
is *too* cheerful – and though the narrator of the poem begins by
praising '[her] head, [her] air, [her] every way',[2] by the end of the
fourth stanza the ambivalence of his feelings is starkly declared: 'I . . .
hate you even as I love!'[3] The poet resents the woman's cheerfulness,
her beauty and her liveliness – while simultaneously loving them –
because they contrast too strongly with his own 'apathy', just as do
sunshine and the signs of spring which make him want to destroy a
flower in order to punish the 'insolence' of nature. The poem ends in
masochistic fantasy as the poet expresses the desire to creep up on the
woman when she is asleep, to bruise her breast, to carve a wound in
her 'joyous' flesh and then to infuse his blood between the 'lips' of
this wound. (In the later, published, version of the poem he changed
'blood' to 'venom' and explained that this was meant to signify the
poet's melancholy.)

   This was not the first time that Apollonie had read a poem
addressed to or about herself. Théophile Gautier had published *Poème
de la Femme*[4] in the *Revue des Deux Mondes* on 15 January 1849. That
this poem concerns Apollonie is clear from a stanza which was
omitted from the final version and which reads:

> She resembles thus contorted
> Clésinger's marble statue
> 'The woman bitten by the asp'
> But that art cannot ape.

The Clésinger statue is also indirectly alluded to in a stanza which
Gautier included in the final version:

> Her head stretched out, tilting back;
> Panting, thrusting out her breasts,

> She falls on to the cushions,
> In the arms of her cradling dream.

The whole poem is a pæan to female beauty and sexuality as embodied in this particular woman. A year later another poem, *A une robe rose*, appeared in *L'Artiste*; it begins 'How I like you in this dress/Which so perfectly undresses you' and ends with an expression of unsatisfied desire. Then on 1 February 1853 his poem *Apollonie*, in which the poet rhapsodises about her name, was published in the *Revue de Paris*. So Apollonie was used to being apostrophised in verse, and on receipt of the first anonymous poem and short letter which Baudelaire sent her she may have done no more than smile and put them away in a drawer. It is unlikely that she analysed the poem in depth, or paid much attention to its edge of venom, accepting it simply as another tribute to her beauty and gracious hospitality, taking at face value the 'most tender sympathy' declared in the letter.

On 3 May 1853 Baudelaire sent Apollonie the poem which was to become *Réversibilité* and which at that stage had no title. This poem too is redolent of resentment and, though the poet ends by imploring the prayers of the 'angel full of happiness, joy and light' whom he is addressing, the sense throughout is that he wants this angel to experience anguish instead of gladness, hatred instead of kindness, fevers instead of health, and wrinkles instead of beauty. In other words, he wants his idol to experience some of the pain of the one who idolises her. He also sent in May the poem which begins '*Quand chez les débauchés*' (later given the title *L'Aube spirituelle*) which contains none of the ambivalence of the two earlier poems but which entirely idealises the object of his devotion so that she becomes a 'dear Goddess' and not a woman at all. This poem was sent with a prefatory sentence written in English: 'After a night of pleasure and desolation, all my soul belongs to you.'

Still in May, on Monday the 9th, he sent another poem, beginning '*Une fois, une seule*' and later called *Confession*, along with a letter:

Truly, Madame, I ask a thousand pardons for this idiotic anonymous versifying, which reeks horribly of childishness; but what can I do? I am self-centred like children and invalids. I think about the people I love when I suffer. In general, I think of you in verse, and when the lines have been written, I cannot resist the desire to show them to the person who is their object. At the same time, I hide myself, like someone who is extremely afraid of ridicule. Is there not something essentially comic in love? – particularly for those who have not known it.

But I swear to you that this really is the last time I will expose myself thus; and if my ardent friendship for you lasts as long again as it has already, before I say a word to you about this, we will both be old.

However absurd all this seems to you, believe that there exists a heart which you would be cruel to mock, and where your image lives always.[5]

'*Une fois, une seule . . .*' recalls a time, the only time, when the poet walked with his beloved, her arm resting on his. She talks to him and reveals a more plaintive side of herself than hitherto, speaking of the hard work involved in being a beautiful woman and of her awareness that beauty and love will both come to an end. (In later life Apollonie was to recall to friends a walk arm in arm with Baudelaire along the terrace of the Tuileries gardens beside the Seine one evening.)

There followed a silence of several months, until 7 February 1854, when a further letter accompanied the poem '*Ils marchent devant moi, ces Yeux extraordinaires*' (later to be called *Le Flambeau Vivant*):

I do not believe, Madame, that women in general realise the full extent of their power, be it for good or for evil. Without doubt, it would not be sensible to instruct them all about this. But in your case one risks nothing; your soul is too rich in kindness to leave room for *self-satisfaction* and for cruelty. Besides, you have doubtless been so showered, so saturated with flattery that only one thing can flatter you in future, and that is to learn that you do good – even without knowing it – even when asleep – simply by being alive.

As for this *cowardly anonymity*, what shall I say, what excuse shall I plead, if it is not that my first error necessitates all the others, and that it has become a habit. Imagine, if you like, that sometimes beneath the pressure of an unyielding affliction I cannot find comfort except in the pleasure of writing verses for you, and that afterwards I am obliged to reconcile the innocent desire to show them to you with the horrible fear of displeasing you. – That is what explains *the cowardice*.

Is it not true that you think as I do, – that the most delicious beauty, the most excellent and adorable creature – such as yourself – cannot desire a better compliment than the expression of gratitude for the good she has done?[6]

The accompanying poem apostrophises the beloved's eyes which, the poet declares, save him from 'all the snares and deadly sins'[7] and lead him in the path of the Beautiful. Another poem and letter followed swiftly, on 16 February:

I do not know what women think of the adoration of which they are sometimes the object. Certain people maintain that they must find it absolutely natural, and others that they must laugh at it. They therefore imagine them as either conceited or cynical. But it seems to me that benevolent souls cannot be other than proud and happy at their beneficent action. I do not know whether I will ever be granted the supreme sweetness of talking to you myself of the power which you have acquired over me, and of the perpetual radiation which your image creates in my mind. I am simply happy, for the present, to swear to you again that never was love more disinterested, more ideal, more penetrated with respect than the one I nourish secretly for you, and which I will always hide with the care commanded by this tender respect.[8]

The poem accompanying this letter was '*Que diras-tu ce soir, pauvre âme solitaire?*', in which the poet addresses his own heart and soul, asking what they wish to say to 'the most beautiful, the best, the most dear' one. They reply that they will dedicate their pride to the task of singing her praises, and at the end of the poem the 'phantom' of the beloved is given the following words to utter: 'I am beautiful, and I ordain that for love of me you will love only the Beautiful; I am the guardian Angel, the Muse and the Madonna!'

Monday, 8 May 1854 brought another poem, *A la très-Chère, à la très-belle* (later called *Hymne*), and another letter:

It is a long time, Madame, a really long time since these verses were written. Always the same deplorable habit, reverie and anonymity. Is it the shame of this ridiculous anonymity, or the fear that the verses are bad, that ability has not attained the level of the sentiments, which has made me so hesitant and timid this time? I have no idea. I am so afraid of you, that I have always hidden my name, thinking that an anonymous adoration – clearly ridiculous in the opinion of all those physical worldly boors we could consult on the subject – was, after all, almost innocent, could be no trouble, could disturb nothing, and was infinitely morally superior to a foolish, conceited pursuit, to a direct attack upon a woman who has already placed her affections – and perhaps her duties. Are you not – and I say it with some pride – not only one of the most loved, but also the most deeply respected of all creatures? I want to give you a proof of this. Laugh at it – a lot, if you find it funny – but don't talk about it. Do you not think it natural, simple and human, that a man in love should hate the fortunate lover, the possessor? That he should find him inferior and gross? Well, a while ago, chance had me meet *him*; how can I express to you – without comedy, without making your naughty, always cheerful, face laugh? – how happy I was to find him to be likeable and a man who could please you. My God! do not so many subtleties suggest folly? To conclude, to explain to you my silence and my ardour, an almost religious ardour, I will tell you that when my being is mired in the blackness of its natural spite and stupidity, it dreams profoundly of you. From this stimulating and purifying reverie something good is generally born. You are for me not only the most appealing of women – of all women – but also the dearest and most precious of superstitions. I am an egoist, I make use of you. Here is my miserable bum-wipe. How happy I would be if I could be certain that these high conceptions of love had some chance of being welcomed in a secret corner of your adorable mind! I will never know.

Forgive me, I ask nothing more of you.[9]

The fact that Baudelaire mentions meeting Mosselman in this letter has led one writer, Armand Moss, to speculate that Baudelaire was not, after all, one of the regular guests at the rue Frochot by this time; but he could merely have meant that this was the first time he had had a *tête-à-tête* with Mosselman. It should also be remembered that he was still retaining his disguise, and so might not have wanted Apollonie to realise that he was one of her regular guests. *A la très-Chère, à la très-Belle* or the 'bum-wipe' (*torche-cul*), an expression more in keeping with Gautier's epistolary style and which strikes a jarring note in the midst of these high-minded sentiments, is a hymn of praise to the poet's 'incorruptible love' and marks the completion of this particular phase of Baudelaire's poetic inspiration. It would be more than three years before Madame Sabatier heard from her secret admirer again.

In June 1855 the journal *La Revue des Deux Mondes* published, under the title of *Les Fleurs du mal*, eighteen of Baudelaire's poems, including three of those addressed to Apollonie: *Réversibilité, Confession* and *L'Aube spirituelle*. There could therefore have been no further genuine question of anonymity. There were no developments, however: Apollonie's life continued entirely as before, though she was seeing rather less of Baudelaire as he was no longer living nearby in the rue Pigalle but was leading a nomadic existence, moving from hotel to hotel partly in order to evade his creditors.

The complete collection of *Les Fleurs du mal* was published two years later, on 25 June 1857. On 16 July it was impounded at the printer's in Alençon, and both Baudelaire and his editor, Poulet-Malassis, were charged with offending public and religious morals. On Tuesday, 18 August, two days before the trial was to take place, Baudelaire sent Apollonie a special copy of the book, printed on laid paper, bound in green half morocco, and with the words '*A la Très belle, à la Très bonne, à la Très Chère*' inscribed on the fly-leaf, along with the following letter:

Dear Madame

You didn't believe for one moment, did you, that I could have forgotten you? I have been keeping a special copy for you since it was published, and if it is clothed in a costume so unworthy of you, it is not my fault, but that of my binder, from whom I had ordered something far more spiritual.

Would you believe that the wretches (I speak of the examining magistrate, the prosecutor etc.) have dared to condemn, along with other passages, two of the pieces written for my dear Idol (*Tout entière* and *A Celle qui est trop gaie*)? This last is the one which the venerable Sainte-Beuve declares the best in the volume.

This is the first time I have written to you in my real hand-writing. If I were not overwhelmed with business and corre-spondence (the hearing is the day after tomorrow), I would use this occasion to ask your forgiveness for so much folly and childishness. But in any case, have you not taken sufficient revenge, especially through your little sister? Oh, the little monster! She horrified me one day when we met and she burst out laughing in my face and said: *are you still in love with my sister, and are you still writing her those wonderful letters?* I realised, first, that when I had wanted to hide myself, I had not made a very good job of it and, secondly, that beneath your charming face, you conceal a not very charitable soul. Lechers are *in love*, but poets are *idolatrous*, and I think your sister is not of the sort to understand eternal things.

Allow me then, at the risk of entertaining you also, to renew those protestations which so entertained that little fool. Imagine an amalgam of reverie, liking and respect, with a thousand serious childishnesses, and you will have an inkling of the very sincere something which I do not feel able to define any better.

To forget you is impossible. Poets are said to have existed who have lived their whole lives with their eyes fixed on one cherished image. In fact I believe (though I am too biased) *that fidelity is one of the signs of genius.*

You are more than an ideal and cherished image, you are my *superstition.* When I do something really stupid, I say to myself: *My God! if only she knew!* When I do something good, I say to myself: *This brings me closer to her – in spirit.*

And the last time that I had the happiness (despite my own best efforts) to meet you! – for you do not know how careful I am to avoid you! – I said to myself: how remarkable it would be if this carriage was waiting for her, perhaps I had better go another way. And then: *Good evening, sir!* I went off, repeating all the way: *Good evening, sir!* trying to imitate your voice.

I saw my judges last Thursday. They are not merely not handsome, they are abominably ugly; and their souls no doubt resemble their faces.

Flaubert had the Empress on his side. I am lacking a woman. And then a few days ago, the bizarre thought took hold of me that perhaps you could, through certain relationships and maybe complicated channels, get a word of sense into one of those dense heads.

The hearing is for the day after tomorrow, Thursday morning . . . [details of the judges are included here]

But I want to put all these trivialities on one side.

Remember that someone is thinking of you, that there is nothing trivial about his thought, and that he bears a bit of a grudge against you for your malicious *high spirits.*

I beg you most ardently to keep to yourself in future all that I may confide in you. You are my constant Companion, and my Secret. It is this intimacy, in which I have been playing opposite myself for so long, which has made me bold enough to use such a familiar tone.

Farewell, dear Madame, I kiss your hands with all my Devotion.

Charles Baudelaire

All the verses between page 84 and page 105 belong to you.[10]

This last remark of Baudelaire's assigns some further poems to Apollonie in addition to the ones he had already sent her: *Tout entière, Harmonie du soir* and *Le Flacon*. His reference to 'certain relationships and maybe complicated channels' through which she might be able to influence the judges probably referred to Alfred Mosselman's links with Auguste de Morny. Unfortunately this was the worst possible time to ask Mosselman to intercede with Morny, since the two men had fallen out at the beginning of this year over Morny's callous dropping of Mosselman's sister, the Countess Le Hon, on the occasion of his marriage to a Russian princess. Apollonie may nevertheless have succeeded in getting an introduction to one of the judges, De Belleyme – possibly through Charles Jalabert, who was painting a portrait of the judge at this time – but, if so, nothing came of her intervention. At the trial on 20 August the charge of religious immorality was dropped but that of offending public morals was upheld. Baudelaire was fined three hundred francs, but this was subsequently reduced to fifty after the direct intervention of the Empress. Poulet-Malassis was fined two hundred francs and ordered to delete six poems judged to contain 'obscene or immoral passages or expressions'.

Baudelaire's letter of 18 August drew, for the first time, a response from Apollonie. (She could hardly have responded to the earlier letters as she did not officially know where they came from.) The sequence of events is difficult to establish with certainty, as the letters that Apollonie wrote to Baudelaire have not been preserved in their entirety. A fragment remains of a reply she wrote to him on 29 August, from which it can be inferred that they had met on the previous Thursday, the 27th. Prior to that meeting, Apollonie had been agitated:

Today I am calmer. I have been more aware of the influence of our Thursday evening. I can tell you, without you taxing me with exaggeration, that I am the happiest of women, that I have never been more aware that I love you, that I have never seen you more handsome, more adorable – quite simply, my divine friend. You can strut about, if that pleases you, but don't go and look at yourself, for, whatever you do, you will never manage to give yourself the expression which I saw on you for a second. Now, whatever happens, I will see you always thus, this is the Charles that I love; you may with impunity tighten your lips and draw together your eyebrows without me worrying, I will close my eyes and I will see the other you . . .[11]

On 31 August Charles wrote again to Apollonie, quoting (in italics) certain phrases from a letter she had written to him (perhaps the same one as that from which the fragment quoted above remains) which make it clear that, in writing at least, she had offered herself to him. It is also clear from this letter that they had met on the previous evening as well:

I have torn up this torrent of childishness piled on my table. I did not find it serious enough for you, dear beloved. I take up your two letters again, and write a new reply.

I need a little courage for that; for my nerves are giving me great pain, enough to make me cry out, and I woke up with the inexplicable moral uneasiness which I had when I left you yesterday evening.

. . . *absolute lack of modesty.*

That makes you even dearer to me.

It seems to me that I have belonged to you since the first day I saw you. You will make of that what you will, but I am yours heart, soul and body.

I urge you to keep this letter hidden, unhappy woman! – *Do you really know what you are saying?* There are people whose job it is to put in prison those who do not pay their bills of exchange; but no one punishes the violation of pledges of friendship and love.

I said to you yesterday: You will forget me; you will betray me; the one who amuses you now will end by boring you. And today I add: it is only he who, like an imbecile, takes seriously the things of the soul who will suffer. You see, my beautiful darling, that I have *odious* prejudices where women are concerned. In short, I do not have *faith*. You have a beautiful soul but, all things considered, it is female.

Look how over the course of a few days our situation has been shattered. First, we are both possessed by the fear of grieving an honest man who is fortunate enough still to be in love.

Then we fear our own storm, because we know (I especially) that there are difficult knots to untie.

And finally, just a few days ago, you were a divinity, which is so comfortable, so beautiful, so inviolable. And now you're a woman. And if I'm unfortunate enough to acquire the right to be jealous! oh! what horror in even thinking of it! for with a person such as you, whose eyes are full of smiles and charm for everyone, one would suffer martyrdom.

The second letter bears a seal whose solemnity would please me if I were really sure that you understood it. *Never meet or never part!* [original in English] That means for certain that it would be much better never to have met, but that having met, one should not part. On a letter of farewell, this seal would be very droll.

In the end, let whatever will happen, happen. I am something of a fatalist. But what I know for sure is that I have a horror of passion – because I know it, with all its ignominies; and now the beloved image which dominated all the fortunes of life has become too seductive.

I dare not reread this letter too much; I would perhaps be obliged to change it; for I greatly fear distressing you; it seems to me that I must have let something of the unpleasant side of my character show through.

I hate the thought of making you go to that dirty rue J.-J.-Rousseau. For I have plenty of other things to say to you. So you must write to tell me a way.

As for our little project, if it becomes possible, let me know a few days in advance.

Farewell, dear beloved; I'm a little cross with you for being too charming. Just remember that when I carry away the scent of your arms and your hair, I also carry away the desire to return to them. But what an unbearable obsession!

Charles

I will in fact take this myself to the rue J.-J.-Rousseau, in case you go there today. That way it will reach you sooner.[12]

The rue Jean-Jacques-Rousseau was the location of the central post office, from which letters could be collected. Armand Duval in *La Dame aux camélias* also makes use of it.

What remains of Apollonie's reply to the above letter clearly shows how much this whole exchange is hurting her:

Look, dear, do you want me to tell you what I think, a cruel thought which hurts me greatly? It is that you do not love me. That is why you have these fears, these hesitations to contract a liaison which, in such conditions, would become a source of annoyance for you and a continual torment for me. Do I not have the proof of this in a sentence from your letter? It is so explicit that it makes my blood run cold. *In short, I do not have faith*. You do not have faith! But in that case you lack love. What can one say to that? Is it not clarity itself? Oh my God! How this idea makes me suffer and how I would like to weep on your breast! I feel as though that would comfort me. Be that as it may, I will not change my mind about our meeting tomorrow. I want to see you, if only to try out my role of friend. Oh why did you seek to see me again?

Your very unhappy friend[13]

A few days later, after Charles had been trying to avoid a further meeting, Apollonie wrote again:

What comedy or rather what drama are we playing? For my mind does not know what conjectures to draw and I will not hide from you that I am very anxious. Your conduct has been so strange for some days, that I no longer understand anything. It is much too subtle for a clumsy creature of my calibre. Enlighten me, my friend, I ask only to understand what deathly chill has blown out this beautiful flame. Is it simply the effect of wise reflections? They have come rather late. Alas! is it not all my fault? I should have been grave and thoughtful when you came to me. But what do you want? When the mouth trembles and the heart beats, sensible thoughts fly away . . .

I am not in the habit of criticising what my friends do. It seems that you are terribly afraid of finding yourself alone with me. That is however so unnecessary! You can do what you like about it. When this whim has passed, write or come to me. I am indulgent, and I will forgive you for the pain you are causing me.

I cannot resist the desire to say a few words to you about our quarrel. I had told myself that my conduct should be entirely dignified, but before a whole day has passed my heart is already lacking the strength and besides, Charles, my anger is entirely legitimate! What am I supposed to think when I see you flee my caresses, if not that you are thinking about that other one, whose soul and dark face come to place themselves between us? In the end, I feel humiliated and let down. If I did not respect myself too much, I would insult you. I would like to see you suffer. For I am burning with jealousy, and reason is not possible in such moments. Oh, dear friend, I hope you will never suffer from it.

What a night I have spent and how much I have cursed this cruel love!

I have waited for you all day. . . . In case you come to my house on a whim tomorrow, I should warn you that I will only be in from one to three o'clock, or, in the evening, from eight until midnight.

Good day, my Charles. How is what remains of your heart? Mine is calmer. I have reasoned with it firmly in order not to bore you too much with its weaknesses. You'll see! I will learn how to make it descend to the temperature you desire. I will definitely suffer, but to please you, I will resign myself to bearing all possible sorrows.[14]

On this (incomplete) correspondence a vast edifice of speculation and commentary has been constructed. It has been asserted that Charles and Apollonie slept together at least once (some have even assumed that the 'rue J.-J.-Rousseau' referred to a seedy hotel rather than to a post office)[15] and there are those who have asserted that the relationship collapsed because Baudelaire was impotent.[16] There is no evidence that this latter was the case, and the only evidence for the existence of a physical relationship of any kind, however brief, lies in certain phrases such as Charles's reference to 'the scent of your arms and your hair' and Apollonie's protests in her final letter about Charles now 'fleeing her embraces'. She herself attributes this rejection, at least in part, to his involvement with another woman, Jeanne Duval, a mulatto actress with whom he had been involved, on and off, since 1843 when he had encountered her playing a *soubrette* role in a small theatre on the Left Bank. (For years Apollonie kept a portrait of Jeanne drawn by Baudelaire; she hid it in her copy of *Les Fleurs du mal* and wrote underneath it 'His ideal!') Yet she also admits that what is going on is incomprehensible to her, and here she gets to the nub of the problem – or at least of one of the problems, for Baudelaire's misogyny is another powerful force which cannot be ignored.

The poems that Baudelaire sent to Madame Sabatier between

December 1852 and May 1854 were precisely that – poems. They were formal, stylised, worked on until they were complete in every respect, in rhyme, rhythm and imagery. One cannot assume that the 'I' of the poem is the living, flesh-and-blood Monsieur Charles Baudelaire himself, even though, for ease of expression, one talks about 'the poet' saying this or that. Likewise, one cannot make too close an identification between the 'you' of a poem and an actual woman, between Apollonie Sabatier and the muse into which Baudelaire transformed her. However, undercutting that sense of distance, that stylisation, were the accompanying letters which appear to be saying, if at times ambiguously, more than 'this is the image I have made out of my perception of you' or 'this is how my poems are made' – to be saying, at least between the lines, 'I love you.' That, in any event, judging from her subsequent reaction, is how Apollonie read them, and one can hardly blame her for it.

That sad question in one of her letters – 'Oh why did you seek to see me again?' – is the cry of a woman who has suffered in the past and then recovered from her suffering. It is a protest at having a wound reopened. It suggests that she had believed herself to be in love with the poet who wrote such strangely passionate letters and poems to her in 1853 and 1854, who refused to reveal himself even though she had realised who he was, who was therefore not inviting any response from her and who, she presumed, would continue to love her and thus to write to her. Then the letters and the poems had stopped arriving. For a while she would have gone on expecting them – there had been a fairly lengthy gap before – but eventually she must have realised there would be no more. She continued to say nothing to their author, not even when some of the poems were published – apart from, according to Baudelaire, 'Good evening, sir!' – but felt some degree of abandonment or, at the very least, wonder as to why such ardour had apparently ceased. (It has been suggested that the poems came to an end because Baudelaire, while still attached in some way to Jeanne Duval, was in the process of taking up with another woman, Marie Daubrun, an actress who was also the mistress of Théodore de Banville. It may also simply have been the case that the poems on this particular theme, with this particular inspiration, had, to the poet's mind, been satisfactorily completed.)

And then, three years later, there is suddenly another letter, with renewed protestations of love, and actually signed. Apollonie did not take the time to dissect this letter in a literary critical manner, to detect all its ambiguities or to consider whether his motives were merely that he wanted her to intervene in his trial. Instead she thought, 'Charles does still love me after all, and now that he has revealed himself, I can tell him that I love him too.' Her response to him suggests that she thought he would now become her *amant de cœur*. The horror this response inspired in the poet is perfectly clear in his letter of 31 August, even though it is combined with a reluctance to abandon his ideal, unfleshly love and hence a desire not to lose the real woman completely. So he appears to be hanging on to her, wanting to make plans for some future 'project' together, while at the same time not being able to respond to the love she is offering – which would involve loving the woman and not just the image he had created for his own use.

Apollonie misread the situation partly through not understanding the complicated workings of a poet's mind – through never having read the letters carefully enough – and partly through attributing higher motives to Baudelaire's renewed correspondence with her than were actually in operation. She was also a romantic who liked the idea of this hitherto secret love, which she interpreted according to her own romantic notions. But, in addition to these misunderstandings, there is the convoluted nature of Baudelaire's feelings about women. His ambivalence is at its starkest in his relation to Apollonie: he loves and he hates, he adores the female idol yet the woman herself disgusts him. One phrase in particular in his letter of 31 August is brutally dismissive – '*Te voilà femme maintenant*' ('. . . just a few days ago, you were a divinity . . . *And now you're a woman.*') Several reasons have been advanced for Baudelaire's misogyny, including his complicated relationship with his mother by whom he felt abandoned when she married his stepfather, General Aupick, and it has been noted that his relationship with Jeanne Duval also revolved around his attraction to what simultaneously revolted him. (Jeanne, to whom Baudelaire was irresistibly physically attracted, mocked his work, argued with him, poisoned his cat and frequently took other lovers.) In a sense, his relationship with Apollonie was a mirror image of his relationship with Jeanne. In Jeanne's case, he is drawn towards what he loathes, whereas with Apollonie he finds himself loathing that towards which he is drawn. That enduring poetry should have been produced out of this conflict may be some consolation in an abstract sense, but can have been little more than a source of bewilderment to the women concerned.

The ambivalent, dualistic, even schizophrenic nature of Baudelaire's feelings about women is apparent from his essay published in 1863, *The Painter of Modern Life*, in the section entitled 'Woman'. He writes of woman as the Being for whom, but especially through whom, artists and poets create their work; that she is not merely the feminine gender of man but is 'rather a divinity, a star that presides over all the parturitions of the male brain'.[17] He goes on to say: 'She is a sort of idol – stupid, maybe, but dazzling'[18] – and he also seems to prefer his idols clothed, liking 'the muslins, the gauzes and the great, iridescent clouds of the stuffs that envelop her'.[19] In this essay Baudelaire is a poet writing about an artist, Constantin Guys, and trying to give some explanation of the sources of creativity in modern life; and so, as in his poetry, he is treating woman as image rather than reality, and it would be to misread him as much as Apollonie did to reduce what he writes here to a simple tract of his 'views on women'. But in an earlier essay or, rather, collection of aphorisms, *My Heart Laid Bare*, his fundamental misogyny comes across more baldly:

Woman is the opposite of the Dandy. That is why she should be regarded with disgust.

Woman is hungry, and she wants to eat; thirsty, and she wants to drink.

She feels randy, and she wants to be————.

Fine characteristics!

Woman is 'natural' – that is to say, abominable.

Moreover, she is always vulgar – that is to say, the opposite of the Dandy.[20]

The *pièce de résistance* of this catalogue of misogynistic aphorisms is: 'I have always been amazed that women are allowed to enter churches. What sort of conversations can *they* have with God?'[21]

Baudelaire's attitude towards women, though extreme and blatantly expressed, was not particularly unusual for his time and place. Some of Meissonier's comments about the nature of the relationship between men and women are only more courteously phrased versions of the same contempt. He considered, for instance, that 'Man should educate woman, and form her nature from the very outset.'[22] And the Goncourt brothers declared that they regarded women – apart from those with a great deal of education – as evil and stupid animals, fit only for breeding.[23] Most men, however, managed somehow to balance their scorn and their adoration, to enjoy showing off their extravagantly dressed wives and mistresses at the same time as inwardly despising them – or else they managed the balance by worshipping their wives and despising their mistresses. Baudelaire could not achieve this balance and, when Apollonie forced him to realise that his idol was also a woman, she inadvertently destroyed the possibility of any further serious relationship between them.

Following the crisis, Baudelaire's attendance at the Sunday soirées became patchy as he continually found excuses not to be present. He had in any event not been a regular visitor for some time. But he could never entirely relinquish his imaginary muse, and from time to time would send her presents. On Tuesday, 8 September he sent her a note about seats for *King Lear*, and another one on the same subject two days later. On Sunday the 13th he sent a note excusing himself from dinner, and on Friday the 25th he wrote to her about an inkwell he had bought for her (which he admitted looked rather better in the shop window than up close). On 17 November he sent her another note, with some books. The following year, on Sunday, 3 January, he was still excusing himself from dinner. On Tuesday the 12th he wrote to her about Mosselman having caught sight of him, looking rather ill. On Sunday, 2 May he again sent her a note with a book. Two years later, on 15 May 1860, he published in *La Revue contemporaine* a new poem, *Semper Eadem*, also inspired by Apollonie, in which he seems to acknowledge that his feelings for her have been based on a lie, but a lie with which he nevertheless wants to intoxicate himself. There is even a suggestion of resentment that she will not allow him to remain in his state of dream. In fact, at the height of this saga Apollonie was as carried away by a dream as was Charles, imagining him to be quite other than he was, believing that he loved her in a way that could find fulfilment in an ordinary sexual liaison. They were both behaving as Apollonie describes in her first letter to him – closing their eyes and seeing 'the other you', the other they each desired to see and not the reality at all.

Perhaps Baudelaire had Apollonie in mind when he wrote of the relations between the sexes in his notes entitled *Years in Brussels*: 'A matter in which God has shown an infinite cunning is in contriving two creatures so deeply strange to one another that every step they take in their mutual dealings may be a false one.'[24]

1 Baudelaire, *Correspondance*, ed. Claude Pichois, Vol.1, Gallimard, Paris, 1973, p.205

2 Charles Baudelaire, *The Flowers of Evil*, tr. James McGowan, OUP, Oxford, 1998, p.87

3 Ibid., p.89

4 Théophile Gautier, *Emaux et camées*, ed. Claudine Gothot-Mersch, Gallimard, Paris, 1981, pp.29–30

5 Baudelaire, *Correspondance*, Vol.1, p.225

6 Ibid., p.266

7 Charles Baudelaire, *The Flowers of Evil*, p.87

8 Baudelaire, *Correspondance*, Vol.1, p.267

9 Ibid., pp.275–6

10 Ibid., pp.421–3

11 Quoted in André Billy, *La Présidente et ses amis*, pp.131–2

12 Baudelaire, *Correspondance*, Vol.1, pp.425–6

13 Quoted in André Billy, *La Présidente et ses amis*, pp. 132–3

14 Ibid., pp.133–5

15 E.g. François Porché, *Baudelaire et la Présidente*, p.214 and Louis Mermaz, *Madame Sabatier*, p.177

16 E.g. François Porché, *Baudelaire et la Présidente*, pp.215–19

17 Charles Baudelaire, *My Heart Laid Bare, and Other Prose Writings*, tr. Norman Cameron, Weidenfeld & Nicolson, London, 1950, p.59

18 Ibid.

19 Ibid., p.60

20 Ibid., p.176

21 Ibid., p.191

22 V.C.O. Gréard, *Meissonier, Part II: The artist's wisdom*, p.181

23 Robert Baldick (ed. and tr.), *Pages from the Goncourt Journal*, OUP, London/ New York/Toronto, 1962, p.18

24 Charles Baudelaire, *My Heart Laid Bare, and Other Prose Writings*, p.217

CHAPTER EIGHT

Rebuilding

N APOLEON III WILL always be remembered for the great rebuilding project he and his Prefect of the Seine, Baron Haussmann, put into operation: it was designed to transform Paris into a modern capital city to rival London, which the Emperor had come to know well during his time of exile. A programme of public works and an alliance of government and private enterprise transformed the infrastructure of streets, drains, sewers and water supply, and the physiognomy of Paris was permanently altered by the creation of new arteries, buildings and parks.

Baron Haussmann and the Emperor worked closely on this great project of transformation, meeting on an almost daily basis. Haussmann styled himself *artiste démolisseur*, and in the creation of his vision he cleared away much of medieval Paris. He was a devotee of the straight line and prepared to demolish anything which got in the way of it. Five new bridges were built over the Seine – the Pont Napoléon (now the Pont National), the Pont de la Gare (now the Pont de Bercy), the Pont du Point du Jour (now the Pont d'Auteuil), the Pont de l'Alma and the Pont de Solférino – and six others were rebuilt. A number of monumental buildings were erected, including four major theatres, fifteen churches, seventy schools, half a dozen town halls (*mairies*), two major railway stations (the Gares du Nord and d'Austerlitz) and six huge barracks (including the Prefecture of Police). Perhaps the most ambitious scheme was the massive expropriation and demolition of property on the Ile de la Cité and the erection of the new public edifices which reduced the population there from fifteen thousand to five thousand and changed the heart of the city.

One of the greatest improvements designed by Haussmann was the introduction of a new and elaborate sewerage system, for which Paris became famed, and which largely ended the outbreaks of cholera which had regularly decimated the population. The provision of new and improved open spaces represented another aspect of the trans-formation of the city, enhancing it as a place of relaxation and enjoyment as well as of work. The development of the Bois de Boulogne was one of the Emperor's pet projects, inspired by his fond memories of Hyde Park. Work began on it during the spring of 1853, even before Haussmann's appointment in June of that year; the two lakes, the roadway around them and the adjoining lawns had been completed by 1854, the Longchamp racecourse was inaugurated in April 1857 and the Bois had assumed its present aspect by 1858. Work also commenced in the late 1850s on the Bois de Vincennes, near a more crowded part of Paris. Occasionally during the rebuilding process trees were transplanted from one place to another; in 1859, for example, a number of sixty-year-old chestnut trees were removed from the neighbourhood of the Entrepôt des Vins in order to make way for the new boulevard Saint-Germain, and were replanted in the Champs Elysées.

There was a negative side to the monumental building works, in that thousands of poorer people were pushed out to the edges of the city as their old houses were demolished and they were unable to afford the higher rents of the new properties constructed in their place. La Chroniqueuse recorded in 1859 that fifth-floor apartments which had previously cost sixty to seventy pounds a year to rent were now priced at a hundred and sixty to two hundred pounds and that, as a consequence, many English people were also now leaving.[1] The bourgeoisie had already moved out of the central areas, seeking healthier and more salubrious living space on the outskirts. The problems were exacerbated by the growth in the population of Paris, itself partly a result of the influx of artisans and labourers to work on the rebuilding project. Permanent emigration from the countryside to Paris increased dramatically throughout the second half of the century and the capital gained 121,000 inhabitants between the years of 1851 and 1856 alone,[2] but an administration preoccupied with buildings for the wealthy offered very few incentives for the provision of working-class housing. The gap between rich and poor widened considerably during this period of apparent prosperity, and Haussmann's splendid façades hid an appalling world of slums and tenements. Orleanist and Republican opposition tried to exploit the discontent arising from these negative aspects of the rebuilding of Paris, but they met with little success until towards the end of the 1860s, when Haussmann's unorthodox financial methods, which involved the creation of a hidden debt of about half a billion francs and a complicated system of deferred payments, came to light.

This was an age of enormous expansion: of communication, through the railway system, telegraph lines and shipbuilding; of scientific development, including the work of Louis Pasteur, and advances in fields as diverse as aluminium and margarine manufacture. Gaslight, which had gradually been replacing oil lighting throughout Paris in the 1840s, was viewed, along with the railway, as a symbol of human and industrial progress. By the 1850s three thousand new gas lamps had been installed in the streets, and the boulevards were fully gaslit by 1857. Many streets were lit all night. Electric lighting was tried out in the Tuileries gardens for the first time in May 1859. There was a sense of rapid progress, of the constant discovery of new things and new experiences to savour – as well as the *ennui* associated with the overloaded, jaded palate.

Those unable to afford the high rents may have been leaving Paris or moving to the outskirts, but meanwhile the city was acting as a magnet for foreign or provincial visitors with money to burn. As La Chroniqueuse reported in November 1859:

They are all here – England, Russia, Austria, Germany, Italy, Spain, in fact, all the world is represented in a *réunion* in the *salons* of our *élite*; and wealth, that great ruler of us all, lends its aid to magnify and decorate this assemblage of the great and the powerful of all lands. A Parisian *salon* cannot be equalled in this respect, for Paris is the centre of fashion. Here the Goddess of Pleasure has erected her temple, and here must come her worshippers.[3]

Two world fairs were held in Paris during the Second Empire, which did much to advertise the city to the world and to encourage this influx of visitors. The first of these, the Paris Universal Exposition of 1855, was designed to commemorate forty years of peace in Europe since Waterloo as well as to demonstrate that Paris was at least the equal of London where, four years previously, the Crystal Palace Exhibition had inaugurated a series of world fairs. The Paris Exposition, which was opened by Napoleon III and his cousin Prince Napoleon on 15 May, incorporated the fine arts as well as agriculture and industry. The exhibition was financed by the government and had been planned by an imperial commission under the general supervision of Prince Napoleon who, despite being away fighting in the Crimea from April 1854 to February 1855, proved an able and energetic administrator. Most of the leading lights in its planning were heavily influenced by the doctrines of Saint-Simon, with his emphasis on the transformation of society and the improvement of the lot of the masses through the development of science and industry under government sponsorship.

The main body of the Exposition was housed in the specially built Palais de l'Industrie on the site now covered by the Rond Point of the Champs Elysées, while the fine arts exhibits were displayed in the separate Palais des Beaux Arts, built in the French Renaissance style by Hector Lefuel in the avenue Montaigne. In the Rotonde du Panorama, built in 1838 and situated between the Seine and the Palais de l'Industrie, to which it was linked by a walkway, were displayed the imperial jewels and examples of decorative art from the imperial residences. The Palais de l'Industrie itself, which was not quite as large as the Crystal Palace, was one of the first buildings in Paris to be constructed largely of iron and glass, though it was also given a stone facing. It was inadequately ventilated, which led to some discomfort during the hot summer of 1855, despite the use of muslin screens.

There were twenty-four thousand exhibitors (some eleven thousand of whom were French) from thirty-four countries. The original intention to celebrate forty years of peace had been overturned by the Crimean War – France and England had declared war on Russia on 27 March 1854 – but Russia was nevertheless invited to participate. The offer was declined, but Russian traders were issued with passes and Russian officers who were prisoners of war in France were allowed to attend on their word of honour that they would not try to escape. And in August Queen Victoria, along with Prince Albert and two of their children, visited Paris, staying for nine days as the guests of the Emperor and Empress. As allies against Russia, England and France were enjoying their best relations in years, and crowds lined the boulevards to cheer the Queen, who, in addition to visiting the Exposition, explored some of the other pleasures Paris had to offer: 'The Queen, Prince Albert and their children drove around Paris in a hackney carriage and in the strictest incognito; they made purchases in several shops.'[4]

Shops had been developing at a great pace, a development in line with the epoch's emphasis on the value of appearances and material possessions. One of the world's first modern department stores and the quintessential example of this phenomenon, the Bon Marché, was founded by Aristide Boucicaut, the son of a hatter who had arrived in Paris in 1835. He had initially found employment at the Petit Saint-Thomas store, where he gained the reputation of being a brilliant buyer and seller. Retiring in 1852, he used his savings to enter into partnership with the owner of what was then a tiny shop, Au Bon Marché, at the corner of the rue de Sèvres and the rue du Bac. Over the next eleven years he introduced all the characteristic features of what would come to be the modern shopping experience, including entry without obligation to buy, the marking of prices, the right of return and refund, and the offering of a great variety of merchandise seductively displayed in the relevant departments. Another large store, catering for a wealthier clientèle than that of the Bon Marché, was the Grand Magasin du Louvre; opened in July 1855, it took up the whole ground floor of the Hôtel du Louvre, which had been especially constructed in the place du Palais Royal in preparation for the Exposition. Luxuriously appointed, with salons and a buffet, the store eventually took over the entire premises and the hotel moved to a site across the street.

Visitors to Paris could also enjoy the many theatres and several opera houses which each had their distinct characteristics. Three of the opera houses – the Opéra, the Théâtre Lyrique and the Opéra Comique – presented works in French, while the Théâtre Italien was so called because the performances there were given in Italian. The Opéra Comique catered particularly for the bourgeoisie, the Théâtre Lyrique for working people and artists, while the Opéra's clientèle were primarily members of the aristocracy and the intellectual élite. Particularly associated with the Second Empire are the operettas of Jacques Offenbach, who opened his Bouffes Parisiens on 5 July 1855 in the small theatre he had discovered and renovated, with the patronage of Prince Napoleon and Auguste de Morny, on the Champs Elysées. The programme for the first night included a musical farce by Offenbach himself, themes from Rossini, and a romantic idyll and prologue by Ludovic Halévy, who subsequently worked closely with Offenbach as a librettist.

The Exposition was officially closed by the Emperor on 15 November. Forty thousand people attended the closing ceremony at which Berlioz conducted his cantata L'Impériale with twelve thousand performers, Prince Napoleon bestowed ten thousand awards, and Napoleon III decorated forty artists, including thirteen foreigners, with the Legion of Honour. The Exposition had summarised many of the dominant ideas of the nineteenth century: the belief in an indefinite material and moral progress, the assumption that the development of science and industry would bring wisdom and happiness, and hope for the rapprochement of classes and peace in Europe. The Paris Exposition in its totality had been almost twice the size of its London predecessor, and some half a million foreign and provincial visitors were thus introduced to the splendours of the Empire and to a Paris whose transformation at the hands of Napoleon III and his Prefect of the Seine was well under way.

In the mid-1850s Napoleon III's fortunes were at their highest. The Crimean War had ended in victory for the French and British on 18 January 1856 and two months later, early on the morning of Sunday, 16 March, the birth of Napoleon and Eugénie's son, to be known as the Prince Imperial, was announced by a hundred and one cannon salvos. He was baptised in Notre Dame on 14 June. The tapestries on the wall were embroidered with golden bees, the Napoleonic symbol, and a representative of the Pope performed the ceremony.

During this time of imperial confidence, the fortunes of business-men and entrepreneurs such as Alfred Mosselman also flourished, and he continued to maintain Apollonie Sabatier in her apartment in the rue Frochot. Had he wanted to, he could have married her, as his wife died in July 1856, at the age of only forty-two, at her house in Viroflay. According to her death certificate, Alfred's address at the time was 6 passage Sandrié in Paris; the couple had been living apart for several years.

Though by virtue of her position as Alfred's mistress Apollonie belonged firmly to the *demi-monde*, her lifestyle was quite different from that of a great courtesan. She lacked for nothing, since all the physical comforts she needed were provided for her by Alfred – she had plenty of money for clothes, her apartment was furnished with taste and the food she served was excellent. But there was no sense of her being 'on the make', of staying with him for the sake of money, or of playing him off against other lovers to increase her revenue. She did not even own a carriage, but went by hired cab whenever Alfred did not provide a means of transport for her. Her only luxury items were paintings, sculptures and other ornaments, given to her either by Alfred or by the artists themselves. And apart from the possible exception of Baudelaire, and despite all the bawdy talk, Apollonie did not dispense her sexual favours elsewhere during the time of her lengthy liaison with Alfred.

The second half of the 1850s saw significant developments in the life of her sister Bébé. In 1854 she had become involved with a young cavalry officer, Ulric Fallet, who was five years older than her, and on

5 July of that year he officially recognised her little girl, Jeanne, as his own. This was his first step in uniting himself with Bébé (now usually called Adèle), whom he could not yet marry because of his status as an officer in the Imperial Guard. (Adèle's story at this time bears an uncanny resemblance to that of her mother before her.) For the next ten years they lived together without being married, during which time they produced four children. Their first son, whose date of birth is unknown, died before 1858. In the spring of that year Ulric took Adèle with him to Egypt when he was posted there on a military mission. In two letters to her sister, whom she addresses as '*ma chère Ananas*' ('my dear Pineapple'), Adèle writes of her pain at not being able to be presented by Ulric as his legitimate wife. On 23 March 1859 Adèle gave birth to a second son in Paris, who also died at only a few months old. (Maxime Du Camp wrote a letter of condolence to Apollonie about this, lamenting poor Bébé's 'bad luck' with her sons.)[5] Their next two children survived, and Ulric and Adèle were finally married on 2 July 1864. They were rarely in France, as Ulric was generally serving abroad.

Apollonie was also closely involved with other members of her family, her mother and her two brothers, Alexandre and Louis; the latter was a house painter, while Alexandre was a sailor. In 1854 Alexandre was diagnosed as a consumptive and could no longer go to sea. He came to live at 9 rue Neuve-Bréda, very near the rue Frochot, and Apollonie did her best to look after him. On the advice of Julien Turgan she consulted a Dr Cabarrus, a homeopathic doctor specialising in illnesses of the respiratory tract. He had an excellent reputation, particularly among singers and literary men, and immediately responded to Apollonie's request for help. He prescribed various potions for Alexandre and refused all payment (which suggests the appeal Apollonie held for men, and how they desired to do her favours). But it turned out to be too late to help Alexandre, whose condition deteriorated rapidly. He was taken to his mother's house, which at that time was in the village of Montfermeil, a few miles to the east of Paris, where he died in June at the age of thirty-one. Apollonie had been very fond of him, and she was much distressed.

Théophile Gautier continued to write to Apollonie in his usual tone, a notable letter being the long one he sent her from St Petersburg on 10 January 1859:

> Next to my little nest and my brood, the only thing that I miss about Paris is your sparkling laugh and your gaiety shining through the intellectual bacchanalia of Sunday. I miss also the aromatic sachet, more fragrant than Solomon's perfume mountains, hidden beneath your divine armpit, and your back of Paros mica against which I rub myself with the secret desires of a luxuriating cat. I think about it often, and sometimes I think about it with only one hand; the other wanders, and the altar of memory receives the libations of solitude . . .
>
> Whether or not you tickle in my honour the little pink clitoris nestling in gold and fleece, I will love you just the same, light of my eyes, smile of my lips, caress of my soul . . .[6]

Gustave Flaubert had also been in the habit of writing flirtatious letters to Apollonie for many years, finding in her an outlet for some otherwise repressed urge to engage in a rather schoolboyish lubricity. At times he seems almost to have indulged in a fantasy lesbian relationship with her, in which he not only made sapphic allusions but attributed female characteristics to his own anatomy. In the summer of 1859, for instance, he wrote her a letter[7] full of sexual innuendo in which he pictures her swimming in the Seine, the river simulating the act of love beneath her like a 'tribade' (from the Greek *tribein*, 'to rub', and used at the time for 'lesbian', as seen in the work of Parent-Duchâtelet), and wishing that he could himself be that river. Later in the same year he writes[8] that he has had so little sexual activity of late that, were he not in the habit of washing himself every day, his virginity would grow back, the membrane re-forming. He also reveals himself as a foot fetishist, longing to make 'obscene caresses'[9] in the eyelets of Apollonie's boots. (He was, at the time of writing, about to turn thirty-eight, being just a little older than Apollonie herself.)

Then, some time in the spring or summer of 1860, everything changed, for Alfred Mosselman left Apollonie. All appeared to be as usual at the end of January, when a letter from Théo to Maxime Du Camp mentioned that La Présidente and 'Macarouille' would be dining with him on the following Tuesday.[10] But on 31 March, in a letter to Gustave Flaubert, Louis Bouilhet mentions trouble between Alfred and Apollonie, and laments the likely repercussions for himself and his friends, commenting that Apollonie's salon is the only agreeable place in Paris.[11]

One of the reasons, possibly the main reason, for the break-up was Alfred's infidelity and his affair with a woman eighteen years Apollonie's junior, one Laurentine Bernage. Apollonie was by this time thirty-eight years old and, though still attractive, not quite the same proposition as a mistress as she had been at twenty-four. The Mosselman family finances may also have been going through a difficult patch. Whatever the reasons for the ending of the liaison, Alfred did not intend to abandon Apollonie entirely, offering her a not inconsiderable allowance of six thousand francs a year. She, however, refused it, and in so doing demonstrated again how different she was from the run of kept women in Paris. Her pride was hurt, and more than her pride. She had been very happy with Alfred, and her relationship with him had also meant that she was surrounded by many friends. If she had thought about the future at all – and she had a tendency to take life as it came, living only from day to day – she had imagined that her relationship with Alfred would continue indefinitely. Apollonie had never pressed him for marriage, assuming that the terms of their relationship made it unnecessary as well as unlikely. She appears to have thought that they were committed to one another, despite the absence of legal bonds, and his desertion came as a complete shock: her world was turned upside down. The break was total, and meant that Alfred no longer saw their mutual friends, as is clear from a letter he wrote to Théo in June 1864:

Since I no longer have the opportunity, as in the past, of seeing you and hearing you talk of everything with so much charm, I want at least to tell you that the memory has remained with me of many things which serious people would be very embarrassed to remember.

I hope not to die before being able to read your admittance speech to the Academy; I will do my utmost to go and hear you.

Remember me to your daughters who I hear are tall, beautiful and clever.

My respects to Ernesta, my friendship to you

A. Mosselman[12]

Rather than accept money from a man who had rejected her emotionally and sexually, Apollonie, with her usual aplomb and determination to make the best of things – she had shown her resilience in her recovery from the Baudelaire incident – resolved to support herself. The means she chose was the painting and repairing of miniatures, a very popular genre of the period and one in which she had previously been instructed by Ernest Meissonier; he had been sufficiently impressed by her artistic abilities to allow her to share his studio on her frequent visits to his and Emma's house at Poissy during the 1850s, where he had also painted her on numerous occasions. (Meissonier rarely painted women, but he enjoyed using Apollonie as a model; not only was she beautiful, but she was also patient and good company during sittings.) The quality of her work and the recommendations of her friends meant that she was able to make a small living in this way, but it never amounted to a great deal. She had some success, nevertheless, and even had four small oil portraits accepted for exhibition in the Salon of 1861. Du Camp gave them a positive mention in his review of that year's Salon, while he is dismissive of most of the other portraits exhibited.[13]

For the first few months after the rupture life at the rue Frochot carried on much as normal, the only difference at the Sunday soirées being the absence of Alfred. Before long, however, Apollonie's reduced financial circumstances began to take effect. She realised that she needed both to reduce her expenditure considerably and to sell much of what she had acquired during her years with Alfred. On

13 December 1861 a sale was held of her ornaments and valuables at the Salle des Ventes; Maxime Du Camp mentioned in a letter to Flaubert that he had spent the whole day there.[14] (Flaubert had continued his sexual banter with Apollonie during that year, having written on 31 January that he would love to see her 'new moon' – that is, her naked bottom; he writes that he would cover it with kisses, eat it and let himself expire upon it.)[15] Among the items for sale were the Clésinger bust and the Falconet *Venus*, which Apollonie particularly hated having to relinquish. They also included Meissonier's *Polichinelle* which he had himself, at Apollonie's request, removed from her door panel, and made the necessary adjustments to enable it to be sold as a separate painting. All Apollonie decided to keep was the portrait by Ricard and a few other works by her friends. The sale raised some forty-three thousand francs.

The letter from Du Camp to Flaubert on 13 December 1861 contains more news of Apollonie than a simple account of the sale; he tells his friend with some glee: 'I've seen La Présidente who has taken up with a young 22-year-old composer who makes up in love what he can't give her in money . . .'[16] This young man was Elie Miriam Delaborde, a pianist who was also the illegitimate (though unacknowledged) son of the eccentric and reclusive composer Charles Valentin Alkan, a friend of Chopin and others in the circle of George Sand. Elie Miriam had been born in Paris on 8 February 1839 and was therefore indeed twenty-two in 1861 – seventeen years younger than Apollonie.

No one knows why Elie Miriam took or was given the surname 'Delaborde', though there may have been a connection with the George Sand circle as this was the maiden name of Sand's mother. Delaborde's own mother was Lina Eraîm Miriam, a *rentière* ('woman of independent means') living in Paris. She may have been a pupil of Alkan's, she was of high social standing and she was already married. The period of Elie Miriam's birth and early childhood coincides with Alkan's first extended absence from the concert platform, which was to last for six years. Lina Eraîm is cited in Alkan's will, which is the only known official intimation that he had anything to do with her.

From a legal point of view Elie Miriam seems never to have existed, though he pursued a distinguished musical and artistic career and led a highly colourful private life. Like his father, he favoured the *pédalier* (a piano with a pedal board attached) and he was also a composer. In contrast to Alkan, however, his character was extrovert and urbane; he toured widely as a virtuoso, he painted a little and counted both Manet and Bizet (with whom he shared a passion for swimming and possibly also for Bizet's wife) among his friends. Apollonie was involved in helping to launch his career, and they may have spent some time together in Italy, in a villa owned by the Marquess Raimondi in Mosino, near the city of Villa Guardia.

However enjoyable her liaison with this young man, it could do nothing to improve her financial position and in 1862 Apollonie moved into a smaller, four-room apartment in the rue de la Faisanderie, near the Porte Dauphine entrance to the Bois de Boulogne. This was a newly built area which had rapidly become rather fashionable. The apartment was a little dark for her taste but she still managed to make it attractive and, as recorded by Théo's daughter, Judith, she did her own cooking there while singing to herself.[17] The rent for this apartment was five hundred and fifty francs a year, as compared to twelve hundred francs for the rue Frochot. Flaubert wrote her a sympathetic letter during that year, counselling her against despair and reminding her that one never knows what will happen next – such an attitude helps one to sleep, and the wind may change during the night.[18]

Few of the friends whom Apollonie had entertained in more prosperous times visited her with anything like such regularity now that she was in straitened circumstances. Several of them found the conviviality they had previously enjoyed in the rue Frochot in a new institution, the *dîners Magny*, an exclusively male dining club inaugurated in November 1862 which met on alternate Mondays at Magny's restaurant in the rue Contrescarpe Dauphine. One might have imagined that the men who had enjoyed flirting with and writing suggestive letters to Apollonie over many years would have been only too ready to translate their words into actions once Alfred

Mosselman had ceased to be her protector; instead Mosselman's absence removed the safety net from these men's transactions with her and, if anything, most of them avoided her company now that she was free to respond to them (another indication, perhaps, that Baudelaire's reactions were not so very unusual). But one man from the old days did venture on a more complete relationship with her at this period, and that was the Englishman Richard Wallace.

Richard was the illegitimate son of the fourth Marquess of Hertford, though Lord Hertford never acknowledged his paternity during his lifetime. (In this way his situation is remarkably parallel to that of Elie Miriam Delaborde vis-à-vis Alkan, and one wonders whether Apollonie was particularly drawn to men whose fathers would not acknowledge them, just as the Viscount Louis Harmand d'Abancourt had never acknowledged her.) Her new companion was born Richard Jackson, and changed his name to Wallace (his mother's maiden name) in 1842, when the fourth Marquess attained to the title and made Richard his secretary. The two men worked together closely at the Marquess's chosen profession of art collector, Richard living with him either at his apartment in the rue Lafitte or at his small château of Bagatelle in the Bois de Boulogne. (According to the Goncourt brothers, one of the fourth Marquess's claims to fame was that it was he who dubbed the area of the main boulevards between the Maison d'Or, the Opéra in the rue Le Peletier, the Café Anglais and Tortoni's 'the clitoris of Paris'.)

It was Richard Wallace, acting on behalf of Lord Hertford, who purchased Meissonier's *Polichinelle* at the sale in December 1861. He and Apollonie had known each other since the Hôtel Pimodan days, when Richard had been a member of the bohemian circle which used to gather there, and it has even been suggested that they had first had an affair in 1844. The evidence for this supposition rests on a document written by Apollonie to Richard between 1871 and 1874, part of which is preserved in the manuscripts department of the Bibliothèque Nationale. Entitled *Souvenirs de ma mère* (Memories of My Mother), it reads as follows:

It is in our blood, my mother's and mine, to be devoted to the people of your nation for my mother saved the lives of two of your compatriots.

The first time, she was twelve or thirteen years old. I believe it was during the battle of Fleurus.[19] She was very well liked by a nice old surgeon who, seeing how good she was at bandaging the wounded, took her with him to do the dressings while he operated. One day, a young English officer was brought in, as handsome as an angel. His shoulder had been shattered by a bullet. The little girl took a liking to him and wanted to take special care of him, which provoked the reproaches of the old doctor who, not having enough people to tend all the unfortunate wounded men with which the house was teeming, would not permit her to spend more time on this one than on the rest. But, drawn by some mysterious need of her heart, she didn't want to leave him day or night. On the second day, she saw her invalid was worse; his shoulder was terribly swollen. It seemed perfectly natural to her to probe the wound, feel the hard body of the bullet and extract it. She had seen this operation performed so many times before! In short, by dint of loving care, she managed to save him. As he was a prisoner of war, he was put on a cart to be taken away. The little girl surrounded him with as much hay as possible to lessen the jolts of the vehicle, then the poor wounded man took her hand, pressed it to his heart and mouth, said her name, the only word of French he knew, putting into his expression all the loving acknowledgment he felt, and then they separated. The little girl wept for her invalid but, at heart, she was happy to have saved him. I have always wanted to tell you this little story which moved me to tears, but then, as I had so little time in which to look at you, I concerned myself solely with that and forgot my little stories.

The other one took place in the rue des Dames, in Batignolles, where my mother was living. She was by the window. Suddenly a man dashed into the street. He was as

white as a corpse. He had been pursued all the way from the
Gare Saint-Lazare by French workers armed with shovels and
sticks, intent on killing him. She rushed out and took the
wounded man, a poor English mechanic, almost by force as
he didn't quite know whether she intended to save him or hand
him over, hid him in her house and comforted him. Then she
went outside and misled the madmen by telling them that she
had seen the man running away through the gardens. It seems
that at this time French workers had sworn to kill any foreign
worker brought in amongst them. This was in 1844. Do you
remember that year, my friend? For me, it is present in my
thoughts as though it were yesterday.[20]

This document is of interest for the flavour it gives of Apollonie's
rather sentimental nature, but it seems slim evidence on which to
posit an affair between herself and Richard Wallace in 1844, even
though she does remind him of that year with affection. She could by
invoking this date simply be recalling a time when they were both
young – Richard was four years older than Apollonie – and enjoying
the company of friends and stimulus of new ideas. Whether or not
this relationship amounted to more than friendship at that early stage,
they were likely to have encountered one another at various times
over the years. Richard, for instance, was a regular visitor to the
Meissoniers' house at Poissy, as were Apollonie and Alfred Mosselman. On occasion he may also have attended her Sunday salon. And
when Apollonie was preparing for her sale in December 1861,
Richard would have been the ideal man to turn to for advice, as
he was eminently placed to know what was likely to fetch a good
price in the art collecting world.

At some time in the early 1860s Apollonie and Richard travelled
together to the Isle of Wight on Richard's grandmother's yacht (even
though Apollonie never greatly enjoyed travelling, disliking the
separation from material comforts and her bathroom). In addition
they made a trip to Belgium and Holland to visit the museums there,
and they may also have stayed in Italy together. During this period

Richard could live comfortably on the salary he received from the Marquess of Hertford, though he was by no means wealthy in his own right. He and Apollonie did not enjoy an exclusive relationship, as Richard also had a long-term mistress, Amélie Castelnau, who worked in a *parfumerie* and by whom he had had a son in 1840. To what extent Apollonie was seeing Elie Miriam Delaborde at the same time as Richard Wallace, or for how long either liaison lasted, is impossible to determine, but a note in the margin of the Wallace Collection's copy of a book by Bernard Falk called *Old Q's Daughter* ('Old Q' was the fourth Duke of Queensbury and believed himself to be the father of the third Marquess of Hertford's wife) asserts that Richard Wallace would have married Apollonie but cut short his relations with her because of an escapade she had with an artist in Italy. The note was written by Robert Cecil, Assistant to the Director of the Wallace Collection from 1946 to 1979, and states that this information came from D.S. MacColl, Keeper of the Collection from 1911 to 1924, who was married to a granddaughter of Adèle (Bébé) Sabatier.[21] Whether this 'artist' was Elie Miriam Delaborde or some other man is unclear. What is clear is that Apollonie never again settled into a semi-permanent relationship of the type she had enjoyed with Alfred Mosselman.

When in Paris she continued to entertain, though on a much reduced scale, and she was also a regular guest at Théophile Gautier's house in Neuilly. The Goncourt brothers, who had first met her at the rue Frochot and subsequently at Théo's birthday party on 31 August 1862, encountered her again on the evening of 16 April 1864 and wrote on their return home their famous description of her as a '*vivandière de faunes*', literally a 'sutler of fauns, or satyrs' and sometimes translated as a 'camp-follower for fauns'.[22] This is a phrase which has been often repeated but never adequately explained; possibly the Goncourts were not entirely clear themselves what they meant by it. They excelled throughout their lives at denigrating the people around them, and this insult they dreamt up for Apollonie is also insulting to the men she had entertained throughout her life thus far, the supposed 'fauns', who were also supposed to be friends, or at least acquaintances, of the Goncourt brothers. In addition they declared her to be rather common, with a coarse manner.[23] This may have referred to her liking for, or at least acceptance of, lewd talk. When this volume of their Journal was published and Apollonie read it, she exclaimed, 'So that's what happens when you invite people to your house!' and threw it on the fire.

In 1866 Apollonie left her ground-floor apartment in the rue de la Faisanderie and moved into a newly constructed building at 5 rue Pergolèse, near the Porte Maillot. The annual rent there was eight hundred and fifty francs, which suggests she was managing her finances rather well to be able to afford to move. In the same year she needed to call upon all her customary tact in managing her relationships with Théophile Gautier and Ernesta Grisi, both friends she valued deeply, when Théo suddenly left Ernesta around the time of their daughter Judith's marriage to Catulle Mendès, a marriage about which he had the deepest forebodings. Apollonie continued to maintain close contact with members of her family, receiving frequent visits from Bébé's daughter Jeanne who had settled in Paris on her marriage to a doctor called Emile Zabé. She also saw her old friend Elisa de Lucenay – she of the bangles and cigarettes – nearly every day. Elisa had married Jean-Baptiste Bressant, a well-known member of the Comédie Française, and the couple lived at 53 rue Spontini, just the other side of the avenue de l'Impératrice from Apollonie's address. Unfortunately, after having been persuaded by Bébé to invest in a shipping business in 1865, Apollonie lost much of the proceeds of her auction two years later when the business collapsed as a result of France's ill-fated intervention in Mexico. (This had involved the attempt to place a Habsburg prince, Maximilian, on the throne, and ultimately led to a humiliating withdrawal by French troops and the execution of Maximilian.) The collapse left Apollonie in considerable financial difficulty, and at one point she had to ask Meissonier for a loan of a thousand francs. He proferred it without hesitation; Gustave Ricard also willingly lent her money.

In 1867 Alfred Mosselman died, at the age of fifty-seven. He and Apollonie had not met again since the break-up. Charles Baudelaire also died in 1867, of syphilis. Contrary to some romantic reports,[24] Apollonie was not with him when he died on 31 August; she was in Como, either with Richard Wallace or with some other lover.

1 La Chroniqueuse, *Photographs of Paris Life*, pp.149–50

2 See Kristin Ross, 'Shopping' in Emile Zola, *The Ladies' Paradise*, University of California Press, Berkeley/Los Angeles/Oxford, 1992

3 Chroniqueuse, *Photographs of Paris Life*, p.173

4 Comte Horace de Viel Castel, *Mémoires sur le règne de Napoléon III (1851–1864)*, Vol.3, p.179

5 Quoted in André Billy, *La Présidente et ses amis*, p.185

6 Jean-Jacques Pauvert, *L'Erotisme Second Empire*, pp.170–1

7 Ibid., pp.31–2

8 Ibid., p.62

9 Ibid., p.63

10 Théophile Gautier, *Correspondance générale*, Vol.7, 1992, p.210

11 Gustave Flaubert, *Correspondance générale*, Vol.III, 1991, p.904

12 Théophile Gautier, *Correspondance générale*, Vol.8, 1993, p.313

13 Maxime Du Camp, *Le Salon de 1861*, A. Bourdilliat & Cie, Paris, 1861, pp.166–7

14 Gustave Flaubert, *Correspondance*, Vol.III, p.842

15 Ibid., p.143

16 Ibid., p.842

17 Judith Gautier, *Le Collier des jours. Le Second Rang du collier*, Félix Luven, Paris, 1909, p.184

18 Gustave Flaubert, *Correspondance*, Vol.III, pp.218–19

19 More commonly known as the battle of Ligny, this took place on 16 June 1815

20 BNF, Département des manuscrits, dossiers de Jacques Crépet et Jean Ziegler

21 From letter of 3 January 1997 from Robert Wenley of Wallace Collection to Gérard de Senneville, copy in Wallace Collection's file on Madame Sabatier

22 Robert Baldick (ed. and tr.), *Pages from the Goncourt Journal*, p.98

23 Ibid.

24 See Léon Séché, *La Jeunesse dorée sous Louis-Philippe*, Mercure de France, Paris, 1910, pp.293–4

CHAPTER NINE

The Hôtel Païva

W HEN BLANCHE DE Païva was not receiving a wealthy client
at her *rez-de-chaussée* in the place Saint-Georges, she would be
discussing her business investments with an adviser, purchasing some
new item of jewellery (precious stones and jewels being one of her
passions) or preparing herself for an evening at the theatre. In her case,
this usually meant the Opéra (where she hired a box for every
Monday and Wednesday) or the Théâtre Italien; she scorned the
more low-brow entertainments of opéra bouffe or light comedy. She
was particularly fond of the operas of Verdi and never missed a
première of his, so would have been present at the Théâtre Italien on
23 December 1854 for *Il Trovatore*, at the Théâtre Lyrique on 24
December 1863 for *Rigoletto* and at the same theatre on 27 October
1864 for *La Traviata*, the opera based on *La Dame aux camélias*. She
would always be accompanied by one of her entourage, such as
Théophile Gautier, Jules Lecomte or the famous music critic Pier
Angelo Fiorentino, and on entering her box would cause a sensation
by the luxury of her attire.

Throughout the Second Empire the Opéra remained in its old
building on the rue Le Peletier, joined to the boulevard des Italiens
by a covered passageway. Facilities and seating were far from
adequate, though the company was regarded as one of the best in
the world. The Emperor was not himself passionately fond of music,
but did attend fairly often as a ceremonial gesture; he realised,
however, that a new and splendid opera house would increase
national prestige and enhance his new city. Accordingly a competi-

tion was held in 1860 for the design of a new house, and it was won
by a young architect called Charles Garnier. His creation, the first
stone of which was laid in July 1862 but which was not completed
until 1875, encapsulates the baroque style which he called 'Napoleon
III' and which was essentially a mélange of styles from every era,
elaborate, imitative and ostentatious.

Blanche had hoped that her marriage to the Marquess de Païva
would lift her out of the ranks of courtesans and into the sphere of
respectability, but in order to leave her profession behind she needed
a regular income from other sources. Her investments went some
way to providing it, but she needed to keep increasing them in order
to fund her desired way of life, and that meant continuing to accept
clients (and charging them very high fees for her services). Wealth
was a prerequisite; no man could even think of propositioning La
Païva if he were not extremely rich, and the difficulty of obtaining
her favours gave rise to legends. There was the story, for instance, of a
young man whom Emile Bergerat claims[1] to have been Adolphe
Gaiffe, a friend of Baudelaire's and Gautier's whose family fortunes
had known better days; Viel Castel narrates the tale irresistibly, in the
style of a fairy story:

One of these suitors, at the end of his tether, told her bluntly that
he was determined to sleep with her; he said it to her, and wrote
so well and so often that one morning she took him aside and
spoke to him as follows:

'You really want to sleep with me, you've set your heart on it
and it's become your *idée fixe*; we must therefore get it over
with, so that we can have some peace with one another
afterwards. What can you offer me? You are poor, you possess
bonds to the value of thirty thousand *livres*; I love money, I can
never get enough of it, yet I still have more than you; I want to
make you buy the favour you request – do you have ten
thousand francs?'

'No,' replied the petitioner.

'You have answered well, because if you had said that you did possess ten thousand, I would have asked you for twenty. But as you do not have ten thousand francs, bring me that amount; we will burn it, and I will be all yours for as long as this fire of ten thousand francs lasts.'

The lover bowed and said:

'Until tomorrow, marchioness.'

The next day the marchioness, seated on the couch in her boudoir, was emblazoned at her most coquettish; a marble pedestal table, like an antique altar, seemed to await a victim; the air was perfumed, and daylight barely penetrated the thick curtains which draped the windows.

The lover, decorated not with pennants but with twelve thousand-franc notes drawn on the bank of France – for he had desired to render his sacrifice the more complete – approached the goddess.

La Païva, without changing her position and with the smile and expression of an amorous viper, felt the twelve thousand francs, found them adorable and, arranging them on the marble table-top in such a way that they would burn one after the other, set fire to the first.

The young man flew at once into La Païva's arms and, dispensing with preliminaries, attained his goal immediately, profiting from his good fortune in the manner of a man who knows the value of time.

The notes were burnt up; the satisfied lover and the smiling Païva, rumpled and mocking, found themselves face to face and, while they were adjusting their clothing, the knight, in response to the courtesan's scornful glances, said to her:

'You poor thing, I've made a fool of you; my friend Aguado did such a good job of photographing the notes that you were taken in.'

At these words, La Païva sprang like a panther towards the imprudent man. Neither Camilla nor Hermione in their rages could compare with the anger of the duped courtesan. Had it not been for the court of assizes, she would have stabbed or

strangled the insolent man. As it was, she had to make do with
stabs of the tongue in place of the dagger; with them she was
unstinting, bombarding with terms of abuse the satisfied one
who was no longer a lover, and who brushed the dust from his
knees as he left.[2]

Such a reaction from La Païva accords with what would have been
expected of such a woman by anyone familiar with Parent-Duchâtelet's descriptions: 'Anger is a frequent emotion in these women
who, in such a state, display a truly remarkable energy of body and
soul: they produce a flood of words which, by their nature and
originality of expression, result in an eloquence which belongs only
to this class.'[3] Whatever the truth concealed in this story, such
encounters were rendered unnecessary by the arrival in Blanche's
life of one man, eleven years her junior: the Count Guido Henckel
von Donnersmarck.

He was descended from a very old family from Upper Silesia, one
of the most ardent centres of Prussian nationalism and, in the
nineteenth century, a very rich mining area. The property of the
Henckels covered many thousands of acres, consisting of vast forests
and agricultural land but also – and more importantly as regards their
wealth – mines and factories. The family's main residence was the
castle of Neudeck, in Tarnowitz, on the border of Poland and Silesia;
it was a fortress castle, complete with dungeon, moat and ramparts,
and it had belonged to them since 1623. The family motto was
Memento vivere ('Remember to live').

Guido, born in 1830, was the youngest child of a family of four –
two boys and two girls. His father, a difficult man, disliked both his
daughters and gave all his affection to his elder son, a delicate boy. In
1847 Guido obtained permission to visit Paris, in the company of an
old family servant who was French by birth. He was still there in 1848
at the outbreak of the February Revolution; Tarnowitz was not
spared the repercussions which spread throughout most of Europe,
and the peasants and workers there staged a revolt. Guido's father,
who was most disturbed by these developments, was then struck by

the additional blow of his elder son's death. At this point he decided to hand over the running of his business interests to Guido, who was accordingly recalled from Paris. When he arrived at Neudeck he found a crowd of demonstrators surrounding the castle, preventing the family from leaving. He passed this first test of his management ability with flying colours, talking to the protestors until they agreed to withdraw.

This accomplished, he dedicated himself to the running of the family business, undertaking a major overhaul of all its enterprises. He travelled far more than had his predecessors, both to acquire new ideas and for public relations purposes. He tended to spend the summer in Tarnowitz while the winter would find him in Berlin, moving in court and political circles, hearing much and giving away little, always with an eye to defending his own interests. His business activities also brought him into contact with French and Belgian entrepreneurs. In particular, he formed an association with the largest producer of zinc in the world – the Belgian company of Vieille Montagne, the family business of Alfred Mosselman.

As a young man, Guido was considered very handsome. He had a long face and large eyes, and bore himself in an aristocratic manner, with more the air of a romantic poet than that of a businessman.

This, then, was the man La Païva encountered in the mid-1850s, when she was just over thirty-five years old. He was introduced to her by Bamberg, the Prussian consul in Paris, who sometimes dined in the place Saint-Georges. Blanche and Guido immediately struck up a rapport. They were united by a love of money and a passion for its pursuit, but there was far more to it than that. Guido was fascinated by Blanche, and he would talk about her with ardour until his death. He loved everything about her: her appearance, her manners, her wit, her ease in society, her sexual knowledge and her business acumen. How much the fascination was reciprocated is an open question. There are those – both contemporary and later commentators[4] – who are convinced that Blanche was incapable of love, that self-interest was the only motivating force in her life. Others[5] are convinced that for Guido Henckel von Donnersmarck she experienced genuine, long-lasting passion. What is certainly clear is that her liaison with Guido was exclusive, and ended the necessity for her ever to receive another client. His business affairs also provided her with an interest and purpose in life which may previously have been lacking; together they formed a real partnership and became one of the most well-known couples in Second Empire Paris. And it seemed that, as far as Guido was concerned, Blanche had no past.

After meeting Blanche Guido began to travel regularly between Paris and Neudeck, where he placed directors to run the business during his absences. And money flowed into the place Saint-Georges, where he took up residence with Blanche. She was gradually introduced by Guido into the running of his business affairs; he was surprised and delighted by how quickly she learnt how it all worked and what the problems and pitfalls were, and by her ability to suggest ways forward. The experience she had gained in the management of her own finances – and the hard lessons she had learnt through her disastrous attempts to manage, or undermine, Henri Herz's business interests – now bore fruit. She was also able to extend Guido's acquaintance with all the pleasures of Paris, and played a valuable role in helping him acquire an edge of sophistication and a sense of *savoir faire*.

In 1857 Viel Castel wrote of this unlikely couple:

La Païva is at least forty years old, she is painted and powdered like an old tightrope walker, she has slept with everyone, yet her German is thirty-six at the most.

La Païva's bedroom must conceal mysteries which alone hold the key to these extravagances of immorality.[6]

The actual ages of the couple at the time of Viel Castel's entry in his diary were thirty-eight and twenty-seven. This age gap was Blanche's principal worry at the time she took up with Guido, and she took steps to disguise it, convincing him – and the authorities – that she had been born in 1826 (which would have made her ten years old at the time of her first marriage and eleven at the birth of her son).

Guido never questioned this assertion, always believing that she was only four years older than he was.

On 11 July 1855 Blanche de Païva had purchased, for the sum of 406,640 francs, a plot of ground situated at 25 avenue des Champs Elysées. This had become a particularly fashionable area to live in, eclipsing the old faubourg Saint-Germain. Other people who acquired land on or around the Champs Elysées included Prince Napoleon, who had a neo-Pompeian palace built for himself which was officially opened on 15 January 1860 (Théophile Gautier composed a special prologue for the occasion); Emile de Girardin, who chose to build in the Roman style; the Count de Quinsonas, who went for a Gothic castle; and Jules de Lesseps, who had a Tunisian château constructed. Blanche intended to build a *hôtel* to rival all these in magnificence. The plot having been acquired, and Henckel von Donnersmarck ready to finance Blanche's great project, she looked around for a suitable architect to realise her vision. She found him in Pierre Manguin, who was a little over forty years old when he was put in touch with her at her request. She had noticed his work at the Universal Exposition of 1855.

The work of designing, building, decorating and furnishing what became known as the Hôtel Païva took ten years to complete. Blanche was closely involved in the process from the beginning, absorbing architectural principles from Manguin with her habitual ease of assimilation. The marble and onyx were carved on site, as though the building under construction were a medieval cathedral rather than a nineteenth-century private mansion. In consultation with Manguin, Blanche chose the artists and craftsmen she wanted to work on each aspect of her magnificent dwelling. She was not interested in collecting antique objects but in commissioning new ones, and thus became a significant patron to a number of artists just embarking on their careers. To paint the ceiling in the main drawing room, the *grand salon*, she selected Paul Baudry, who had won the Prix de Rome in 1850. The son of a shoemaker from La Roche-sur-Yon, he had received a scholarship enabling him to study at the Ecole des Beaux Arts but had known poverty and even wretchedness. On his return from Rome he had attained some success but not enough to make him very well known. La Païva's commission gave him a chance to make his reputation; he went on to paint the foyer of Garnier's new Opéra. Dalou, the artist chosen by La Païva to produce the sculptures which would occupy the corners of the *grand salon*, had only just ceased to be a student when she commissioned him. He was living in poor accommodation in the rue Gît-le-Cœur, with barely enough money to afford to eat every day. The commission from La Païva transformed his life: she not only provided a showcase for his talents but paid her artists well.

By the final months of the great project Blanche was growing impatient, longing to move in. She would arrive on horseback most afternoons, after her ride in the Bois, to measure progress and encourage – or bully – the workers.

The result was dazzling, overwhelming, its ostentation entirely in keeping with the spirit of the age. Baudry's ceiling in the *grand salon*, whose five tall windows overlooked the Champs Elysées, showed Day chasing away Night; the model for Night was said to be La Païva herself.[7] One of the statues gracing the huge fireplace of red and white marble was also taken to be a representation of the mistress of the house. The other drawing rooms were hung with crimson damask, specially woven at Lyons at vast expense. There was a *salon des griffons* containing a black marble fireplace, and a music room boasting *médaillons* by Picou. Throughout the whole house there was a profusion of gold, ornamentation, hangings, statues and paintings. The dining room looked out on to an inner courtyard, and bore an inscription on the wall: '*Mange ce qui est bon, bois ce qui est clair, et ne parle que de ce qui est vrai*' ('Eat what is good, drink what is clear, and only talk of what is true.') This room had four double doors decorated by the painter Ranvier with pastoral and hunting motifs and was dominated by a fresco on the ceiling, painted by Dalou, of Diana asleep on a stag. The staircase (adorned with statues of Virgil, Petrarch and Dante) and the bath were made of onyx. The first floor housed La Païva's bathroom, bedroom and boudoir, as well as a room for Henckel von Donnersmarck. La Païva's bed, inlaid with rare woods and ivory, stood in an alcove below a ceiling on which was portrayed Aurora, goddess of the dawn. Each item of furniture was a masterpiece in itself – such as the sideboard in the dining room, with its friezes reminiscent of della Robbia's singers.

Blanche de Païva and Guido Henckel von Donnersmarck finally moved into their new abode in 1866, though the finishing touches were not completed until two years later when all the items of furniture were finally installed (this was because some of the items they had commissioned were on display in the Universal Exposition of 1867). Here La Païva continued to hold her twice-weekly dinners, lavishing hospitality on the chosen few. The reputation of her *hôtel* was enhanced by the fact that very few people ever saw inside it during the time she lived there. Paul Baudry even had difficulty persuading her to admit the jury for the Emperor's prize to see his paintings, judging from a letter he wrote in desperation to Théophile Gautier in May 1869.[8] It was partly in order to avoid rejection and a reminder of her past life that Blanche limited her invitations to the select group of her friends; no respectable woman from the *haut monde*, for instance, would deign to set foot inside the showy residence of a famous courtesan even if she was now an ex-courtesan, and Blanche pragmatically took the view that it was preferable to reject than to be rejected. She also preferred to invite only those people she found amusing, enlightening or useful. The effect of the restricted admittance to the Hôtel Païva was to produce an aura of fascination around the building, as though it were the magical palace of an enchantress – or of a witch. Fabulous stories abounded; it was said, for instance, that La Païva's bed was flanked by two enormous safes, for her money and her jewels.

There was even a story put around that the Emperor turned up one day, overcome by curiosity to see inside the famous *hôtel*. This was supposed to have taken place after a celebrated incident at the Théâtre Italien, where La Païva had managed to hire the stage box directly opposite the imperial box. On this particular occasion the Emperor remarked to his aide de camp that he wished the Empress were equipped with a Japanese screen like the one La Païva was using to shield her eyes from the glare and heat of the footlights. This remark was unwisely conveyed to Blanche who, never one to miss an opportunity, promptly had her screen sent round to the imperial box. The Empress disdained even to notice it, which *hauteur* rather embarrassed, so it was said, the Emperor. Arsène Houssaye takes up the tale:

> A few days later, when the marchioness was alone in her *hôtel*, one of her manservants brought her a card inside an envelope from a gentleman who had declined to give his name and who wished to see Mme de Païva. She tore open the envelope and read the handwritten name: 'Napoleon III'.
>
> As nothing ever astonished her, she went forward nonchalantly to meet the Emperor, who offered her his fist, in the manner of Louis XIV, in order to conduct her into the drawing room. He was curious to see at last this *hôtel* of which the whole world was talking, although no one apart from the marchioness's twenty-four friends had set foot inside it.
>
> He was no great connoisseur, but he marvelled in front of everything at the exquisite taste of the mistress of the house. He insisted on climbing the onyx staircase. On the first floor, he was no less enchanted by all the furnishings, all the works of art, directing admiring glances everywhere, including at the marchioness who, as always, was covered in jewels like a reliquary.[9]

This was still not the end of the story. A few days later, after midnight at the Friday dinner party, while the hostess and her ten guests were partaking of tea and iced coffee, a servant suddenly announced portentously: 'His Majesty the Emperor!' Everyone stood to attention in amazed silence, as La Païva stepped forward to greet the illustrious visitor. According to Houssaye, 'Napoleon III stretched out his hands like Jesus stilling the waves',[10] and asked for the discussion to continue as before. Unsurprisingly, however, conversation now became stilted though the Emperor kept showering compliments on various of the guests, including Gautier and Dela-croix. He then spent some time staring at the ceiling and twiddling the ends of his famous moustache. Then finally he began to complain about how annoying life was at the Tuileries, at which point, says Houssaye, 'we recognised Vivier, king of the comedians, the spitting image of Napoleon III'.[11]

La Païva was said never to have forgiven Vivier for this trick; incapable of laughing at her own expense, and desiring that no one should better her in ostentatious display, she hated being either deceived or upstaged. The Emperor, on the other hand, was believed to have been amused when he heard about it and soon afterwards Vivier, who was also a famous horn player, was deco-rated. Whether it was the actor or the Emperor who made the first visit has never been clarified; Houssaye implies[12] that it was indeed the Emperor, but then he is rarely to be trusted when it comes to matters of fact. That the court was aware of Blanche de Païva and her magnificent *hôtel* is clear from the memoirs of Princess Murat, who writes that La Païva's 'establishment in the Champs Elysées, where none but men were admitted, was kept up with the most insolent luxury'.[13] It is the word 'insolent' which is the most telling here, suggesting that high society was by no means indifferent to the activities and self-display of the ex-courtesan which was such an effective parody of their own.

The life of the court featured its own cycle of entertainments. Annually between the New Year and the beginning of Lent, the Emperor and Empress would give four grand balls to which several thousand guests would be invited. A great object for the occasional visitor would be to make his or her way into the *Salle des Maréchaux*, in which the imperial quadrille was danced. La Chroniqueuse conveys an idea of the brilliance of these occasions in her report of the ball given on 11 January 1860:

The skilful arrangement of the mirrors in the apartment, which reflected a hundred-fold the persons and objects contained therein; the brilliant lights which made the diamonds of the ladies sparkle and glow like very fire upon the snowy bosoms of the fair wearers; the many and various uniforms; and, last of all, the exquisite court costume worn by the French gentlemen, made one of the grandest *coups-d-œil* that can possibly be imagined.[14]

During carnival time there was usually a fancy dress ball held at the Tuileries, to which invitations would be restricted to those who had previously been presented at court. There they would dance to the music of Waldteufel, Strauss and Offenbach.

During Lent there was no dancing, but there were four concerts, organised by the court chamberlain Bacciochi and the composer Auber, chapel master at the Tuileries. The court spent the spring and most of the summer in the great châteaus of Fontainebleau and Saint-Cloud, the latter often used for entertaining royal visitors from abroad. In the summer they would move to Biarritz near the Spanish border for a few weeks of informality at the Villa Eugénie, a small retreat Napoleon III had built for the Empress.

From 1856, in late October or early November the focus would shift to Compiègne, some fifty miles north of Paris near a beautiful forest famous for its game. The court would remain there for a month to six weeks. Invitations to Compiègne were greatly prized; several hundred guests selected by the Empress from various classes and professions, including artists, would be invited for four days at a time (known as a *série*), and a special train ran from the Gare du Nord at 2.33pm to take them. Once at Compiègne, the entertainment was both plentiful and compulsory. In addition to hunting, guests were expected to play charades, dress up and perform in plays, as well as sparkle in conversation at every meal-time, all in the presence of the imperial couple. The expense could also be daunting, as the women were expected to wear new outfits twice a day, while the men had to appear for dinner in court dress.

Though no acknowledged *demi-mondaine* would ever find her way to Compiègne, it was not unknown for the Emperor to invite his mistresses there, particularly if, like the Countess Walewska, they were married to some other member of the establishment. (Her husband, Count Walewski, was an illegitimate son of Napoleon I.) The Emperor had several mistresses during the course of his marriage as well as many more casual sexual encounters with women procured for him by Count Bacciochi. Prior to his marriage he had already fathered several illegitimate sons, and had enjoyed a liaison of many years' standing with an English woman known to posterity as 'Miss Howard'. One of his longer-term mistresses during the 1860s was Marguerite Bellanger, whose original name was Julie Lebœuf. After working as a hotel chambermaid in Boulogne she had run off to join a circus, becoming an acrobat and a bareback rider. The Emperor, who had first encountered her at Saint-Cloud where she had been brought to the imperial hunt as the guest of a young army officer, was particularly impressed by her ability to do a variety of things while standing on her hands. He bought her a house on the rue des Vignes in Passy, but pensioned her off in 1866 with a Prussian husband and a house in the country.

In the grand house on the Champs Elysées it was said to be very cold (despite the efficient and innovatory central heating system which was still working well in 2001) and Blanche was supposed to like having her hair done with all the windows wide open, even in the middle of winter. This was all part of the mythology surrounding La Païva, which made her appear like some inhuman character who had swept in from the frozen wastelands of Siberia, cold-blooded, needing neither physical nor emotional warmth.

Unsurprisingly, the source for some of the exaggerated stories about Blanche can be traced to the Journal of the Goncourt brothers, whom Théophile Gautier introduced to the Hôtel Païva and its owners on Friday, 24 May 1867. As usual the brothers wrote up their experiences in misanthropic style, describing their hostess as resembling a provincial actress, with false hair and a false smile, and the dining room as being like a private room in an expensive restaurant. They claimed that all the guests were ill at ease, that Paul de Saint-Victor in particular sat twisting his hat out of discomfort at being unable to think of anything to say. They declared that they felt 'that horrible chill which characterizes the houses of tarts playing at being ladies'.[15] Nevertheless they returned for more of the same the following Friday, relating that on this occasion the table's centrepiece did not arrive until six o'clock when everyone was required to admire it and marvel at the cost. In their opinion, the only piece of art in the building worth admiring was Baudry's ceiling.

They also give an unflattering description of La Païva herself: her flesh white, her nose with its flattened end and pronounced nostrils, wrinkles which appeared black in the gaslight, her straight mouth a line of red lipstick in a face whitened by rice powder, with a horseshoe-shaped furrow on either side. They describe how, after coffee, they all went to sit in the small walled garden, from where they could hear the sounds of music drifting in from the nearby Bal Mabille, and where all the guests began to feel the cold – to which their hostess, with her bare shoulders, seemed quite impervious. There was nothing of conventional femininity about her, none of the usual softness – or consideration for her guests – which the brothers expected from a woman, but they could not help observing, despite themselves, that La Païva was far from stupid. She kept surprising them with reflections drawn from her life as a practical business-woman, by her ideas and axioms from her own experience and by a dry originality. They found the latter not to their taste (*antipathique*), and suspected that it came from her race and religion as well as from the prodigious heights and depths of her life to date.[16] She would on occasion appear to be absent in spirit from her guests, thinking about something to which they had no access, but when she was fully present she could always keep up with the conversation of her intellectual male companions. She read the most important news-papers in several languages, kept up to date with all the latest literature and music, and would astonish those around her by the depth and breadth of her knowledge.

The Goncourts returned on 3 January 1868, a snowy day. The celebrated historian, philosopher and critic Hippolyte Taine ('whom one runs into at all the great courtesans' houses'[17]) was dining there for the first time. The brothers stress again how cold seemed to be La

Païva's natural element – she was 'like a sort of monster from a Scandinavian myth' – and they also mention how she expounded on her theory of willpower. She believed, she said, that people can do anything if they seriously set their minds to it, and that the unfortunate only remain that way because at heart they have chosen so to remain. Taking herself as a case in point, she claimed at one time to have cut herself off from human society and even food for three years in order to concentrate on attaining her objective.[18] The Goncourts were there again on 14 February, as was Théophile Gautier, among others. Their comments on this occasion relate to the impossibility of pouring oneself a glass of water reddened with a little wine in La Païva's establishment, because all the jugs and carafes were so enormous ('crystal cathedrals') that they could only be lifted by a servant; they also say there was generally a commotion if one requested anything not on the 'programme'. They allege that Théo sat rather nervously next to his hostess, afraid of burning her robe with his cigar, but that he was nevertheless a wonderful talker and not at all verbally constrained in La Païva's presence.[19] They were there again a few weeks later, on Good Friday, when the conversation ranged from God to astronomy. In May they allude to those fascinating safes reputed to live on either side of her bed, in which she kept her silver, gold, diamonds, emeralds and pearls, and between which she dreamt – or had nightmares.[20]

Though much of what the Goncourts write is exaggerated and decidedly hostile, there is a vestige of truth behind some of their observations. That Blanche and Henckel enjoyed showing off their wealth is evident, and other guests besides the Goncourts have commented on how admiration of all the opulence was expected. This was the price to be paid for accepting Blanche's hospitality, but most of the guests do not seem to have found it too high a price to pay – they did, after all, keep coming back for more. And Blanche continued to expect high standards of conversation from her fellow diners, though a certain degree of post-prandial somnolence seems to have been accepted as well. But deferential charm was not part of her arsenal in her dealings with men, and she kept the assembled company on their toes. A letter from Théo, dated 14 January 1868, alludes to the need to be witty at her gatherings:

> He apologises for not having been able to attend the last two Fridays, but at this coming one he will resume, come hell or high water, his place on her right hand: 'If I am ill, you'll just have to let me lie down after dinner, as they did at Ida's [the wife of Alexandre Dumas *père*] to keep me fresh until the bourgeois people left. But at this banquet of Plato, I dare not say Aspasia, there are only clever people. One must be brilliant from the soup onwards. If I am dull, you will forgive me this once.'[21]

Arsène Houssaye found everything to his satisfaction: 'Never was talk more lively and unpredictable. I think this sumptuous table, supplied by the greenhouses of Pontchartrain, a royal castle, with grapes, cherries and peaches even when it was snowing, served just as well to stimulate the mind as did the frugal table of Mme de Maintenon.'[22] Not only could men of letters and the other arts eat and drink here to their hearts' content; they could also discuss their ideas and aspirations in a select company which – provided the Goncourt brothers were absent – was sympathetic and discreet.

Not content with owning a luxurious and well-appointed mansion in the centre of Paris, in the mid-1860s Guido had bought for Blanche the sixteenth-century château of Pontchartrain from Count Osmond for two million francs. This château, thirty-five kilometres to the west of Paris on the road to Rambouillet, had an eminent history. Louise de la Vallière, one of the *maîtresses en titre* of Louis XIV, had once lived there, and the park had been designed by Le Nôtre. The Osmond family, particularly Count Osmond's mother, had been revered by the local villagers, amongst whom there was some disquiet when the rumour got around that the Count had sold the castle and land – including the location of his mother's tomb – to a foreign woman of dubious reputation. The Count himself had not been concerned about the credentials of his purchasers. Having gambled away most of his fortune, all he had wanted was a quick sale for the best possible price. The proceeds did tide him over for a while, though he squandered some of them in 1866 by giving a famous ball at which all Paris danced until dawn. And so, for at least the second time in her life, Blanche de Païva profited from the fecklessness of a hopeless gambler and spendthrift.

On her arrival in Pontchartrain she had intended to follow the convention of paying introductory visits to neighbouring land-owners. She decided against continuing this practice, however, upon receiving an icy reception from Count Rougé, whose property bordered her own. The local workforce was eventually won round owing to La Païva's efficient management of the estate (though some of the villagers were scandalised by her masculine riding attire), but the aristocracy remained aloof and hospitality at Pontchartrain, as at the Hôtel Païva, was therefore restricted to her own circle of Parisian friends. The only exception to this was the local priest, a man named Got, who visited her frequently and esteemed her company.

Legends accrued around La Païva's life at Pontchartrain as around every other aspect of her life, often originating in gossip inspired by curiosity and a lack of concrete information. Some rumours were spread by disgruntled former staff, such as a certain Ballard who had been her steward until dismissed for insulting her. It was said that she was obsessive over the tidiness of the grounds, that she fined her staff if they allowed so much as a fallen leaf to remain on the ground when she made her daily inspection, and that she lurked in the alleyways to catch and fine anyone, including guests, caught walking on her private path. There was also the legend of the servant whose only task was to open and shut the château's one hundred and fifty windows. He began his work at six in the morning, carried on till midnight each night, and eventually dropped dead from exhaustion. Then there was the story that one day, having been thrown by her horse, La Païva took a pistol from her belt and shot the animal dead. This story was told to Frédéric Loliée[23] by the Count de Prémio-Real, who had it from his father Auguste Dreyfus-Gonzales, a later owner of Pontchartrain – and so on and so forth.

The greenhouses at Pontchartrain were a particular source of pride to Blanche; it was through these that she kept her Parisian table supplied with out-of-season fruits as alluded to by Houssaye, proving herself ahead of her time in doing what has since become commonplace. It has been said that she had the magic gift of always being a step ahead, of possessing and enjoying things before anyone else knew they existed.[24] She also had a special bath designed and made for her at Pontchartrain, commissioned from Pierre Manguin and sculpted by Donnadieu out of a single block of Algerian yellow onyx. Donnadieu received an award for this extraordinary item at the 1867 Universal Exposition.

---

1   Emile Bergerat, *Souvenirs d'un enfant de Paris*, Vol.2, Bibliothéque Charpentier, Paris, 1912, pp.300–1

2   Comte Horace de Viel Castel, *Mémoires sur le règne de Napoléon III (1851–1864)*, Vol.4, pp.41–2

3   A.J.B. Parent-Duchâtelet, *De la Prostitution dans la ville de Paris*, p.142

4   See, for example, Joanna Richardson, *The Courtesans*, p.82

5   See, for example, Janine Alexandre-Debray, *La Paiva, 1819–1884: ses amants, ses maris*, Librairie Académique Perrin, Paris, 1986, p.117

6   Comte Horace de Viel Castel, *Mémoires sur le règne de Napoléon III (1851–1864)*, Vol.4, p.68

7   See Charles A. Dolph, *The Real 'Lady of the Camellias' and Other Women of Quality*, p.79

8   Théophile Gautier, *Correspondance générale*, Vol.10, 1996, p.335

9   Arsène Houssaye, *Les Confessions. Souvenirs d'un demi-siècle 1830–1880*, 1885, p.95

10 Ibid.

11 Ibid., p.99

12 See Arsène Houssaye, 'L'Ancien Hôtel de la Marquise de Païva' in *Un Hôtel célèbre sous le Second Empire*, Paris, n.d., p.18

13 Princess Caroline Murat, *My Memoirs*, p.87

14 La Chroniqueuse, *Photographs of Paris Life*, p.231

15 Robert Baldick (ed. and tr.), *Pages from the Goncourt Journal*, p.128

16 Edmond et Jules de Goncourt, *Journal. Mémoires de la vie littéraire*, Vol.2: 1866–1886, Fasquelle & Flammarion, Paris, 1956, pp.87–8

17 Robert Baldick (ed and tr.), *Pages from the Goncourt Journal*, p.134

18 Ibid.

19 Edmond et Jules de Goncourt, *Journal. Mémoires de la vie littéraire*, Vol.2, p.134

20 Ibid., p.149

21 Theophile Gautier, *Correspondance générale*, Vol.10, 1996, p.24

22 Arsène Houssaye, *Les Confessions. Souvenirs d'un demi-siècle 1830–1880*, 1891, p.336

23 Frédéric Loliée, '*La Païva*', p.154

24 Frédéric Loliée, *Les Femmes du second empire. La Fête impériale*, Librairie Félix Juven, Paris, 1907, p.139

CHAPTER TEN

The English Beauty of the French Empire

P ART OF THE reason for the stir Blanche de Païva made in Paris, for the controversy she aroused and for the hostile opinions formed about her – particularly after the collapse of the Second Empire – was that she was foreign. She was seen as having come from abroad to lay siege to the rich young men of Paris, and as such she represented a danger to the whole of French society. Another woman viewed in the same light was 'The English Beauty of the French Empire',[1] the woman who called herself Cora Pearl.

She was born in Plymouth, probably in 1835, the second daughter of Frederick William Nicholls Crouch and his wife Lydia (née Pearson). The child was named Emma Elizabeth and years later people who claimed to know would variously give her original name as Emma Crutch,[2] Emma Cruch,[3] Emma Chruch[4] and even Emma Church.[5] Her father was a musician, and his chief claim to fame was that he composed the popular song 'Kathleen Mavourneen'; he styled himself 'Professor'. His wife also gave singing lessons, in between her numerous pregnancies and struggling to run the house-hold. The tumult of daily life can be imagined. As Emma herself put it: 'I was born to hear a great deal of noise, if not to make it; there was in my case a kind of predestination to clatter.'[6]

Her father was full of grandiose stories about his childhood successes: he had been playing in a theatre orchestra at the age of nine, he said, and was a choirboy at both St Paul's Cathedral and Westminster Abbey. The New Grove Dictionary of Music entry for Frederick Nicholls Crouch (born in London on 31 July 1808) describes him as a cellist, singer and composer. He studied music with his father Frederick William Crouch (who was the author of a *Complete Treatise on the Violoncello*, published in 1826) and his grand-father William Crouch, who was organist of Old Street church in London. At the age of nine he was indeed playing in the orchestra of the Royal Coburg Theatre (later the Old Vic). He entered the Royal Academy of Music in 1831 but left in June of the following year; during his time there he was also a cellist at the King's Theatre and in other orchestras, including Queen Adelaide's private band. He moved to Plymouth after 1832, working there both as a professional singer and as a travelling salesman. His famous song 'Kathleen Mavourneen' was composed between about 1835 and 1838. He gave occasional lectures on the songs and legends of Ireland, became a supervisor at the music publishers D'Almaine, and was thought to have contributed to advances in zincography, an engraving process.

In 1847 he left his first family and two years later, when Emma Elizabeth was about fourteen, he went to New York as a cellist, probably in order to escape creditors in the wake of a lawsuit (he had twice been declared bankrupt, and before leaving England had contracted the first of four bigamous marriages). Perhaps unsurpris-ingly in the circumstances, Lydia Crouch told her children that their father had died.

In the United States Crouch undertook several, mostly unsuccess-ful, musical enterprises, conducting, singing and teaching in Boston, Portland, Philadelphia, Washington and Richmond. He served as a trumpeter in the Confederate Army during the Civil War, and then settled in Baltimore as a singing teacher. In 1881 he was working as a varnisher in a factory; a testimonial concert was given for him in Baltimore in 1883.

An unattributed biographical notice of Crouch preserved in the Manuscripts Department of the British Library contains no mention of his first family. The impression conveyed is of a man unable to stick at any one thing, always chasing rainbows – including going off to El Dorado to prospect for gold – and having to support another (his fourth?) family of wife and five children. The notice concludes with the unlikely story of a devoted American disciple petitioning to change his surname from Marion to Crouch, in order to 'adopt' Crouch as his father and provide for him and his family. Thus, it is alleged, his days of penury were miraculously ended.

Not long after Crouch's flight to America, his wife Lydia took a lover. Her daughter Emma, now in her early teens, did not get on with him and it was decided to send her away to a convent school in Boulogne. She remained there for several years, returning to England in about 1854.

Much of what we know – or think we know – about Emma Crouch comes from her own memoirs, which were published in French shortly before her death and translated into English in the same year. We are thus presented with the picture of her which she wanted us to see, as well as with her view of her contemporaries – in particular, of her numerous lovers. At times, the memoirs are more obfuscating than enlightening. Details are given in non-chronological order and names are disguised – frequently, though not always, transparently. And, throughout, the author maintains the fiction that she was born in 1842, making herself about seven years younger than she actually was.

The French version of the *Mémoires* contains as its frontispiece a reproduction of a Certified Copy of Emma's supposed birth certificate, giving her date of birth as 23 February 1842. It is quite clearly a forgery (though it served her well in her life and even afterwards; her entry in the *Dictionary of National Biography*, for instance, gives this as her date of birth, and the year is also repeated in the *New Grove* entry about her father). What has been changed on this copy is the date (1841 has been changed to 1842) and the first name ('Emma' has been written over 'Louisa'). The original certificate, doctored in this way by Emma, records the birth of her youngest sister, Louisa Elizabeth, on 23 February 1841. The English version of the memoirs, which claims to be the 'Authentic and Authorised Translation from the Original', contains a printed version of the forged certificate. Not content with merely presenting this falsification, the author has the temerity to draw attention to it as a proof of her 'honesty': 'what I affirm is that I speak the truth, having no reason to hide it; the proof is that I begin by my date of birth, a thing that very few women would consent to reveal'.[7] From the start, Emma is poking fun both at her readers and at all those who were taken in by her – but also, and more engagingly, at herself.

But the author of her memoirs was not alone in treating her life story as a pretext for misinformation, embellishent and sheer invention. The English version is prefaced by a 'Press Notice', which is representative of the myth-making of much of what was written about this woman, using a skeleton of a few facts on which to hang a morality tale, demonstrating how the wicked invariably come to a bad end:

Twenty years ago, says a correspondent, the equipage of Cora Pearl was one of the sights of Hyde Park. The loungers by the rails threw a double intensity into their stare when her carriage passed with its perfect horses and irreproachable liveries. Great ladies were accused of dressing 'after' the celebrity. When she went to Paris and shortly after made her *début* at the Bouffes, the theatre was filled to overflowing with the ladies of the demi-monde and 'personages' titled and untitled. Never did a *première* excite so much curiosity. Certain of the boxes sold at 500f. each, and orchestra stalls fetched 150f. Before then Cora Pearl was well known to Parisians as an Amazon, a female Centaur . . . This is the woman who has just died in the most squalid poverty in a small room in the Rue de Bassano . . . When Madame Christine Nilsson was in America some years ago, on one occasion she sang 'Kathleen Mavourneen' as an encore. After the performance, a wretched-looking poverty-stricken man threw himself at her feet and thanked her with tears for singing so exquisitely his song, the child of his brain. This was Crouch, reduced to such straits that he was almost unable to command the price of a meal. Something was done for him in the way of getting up a subscription, and an American reporter, getting hold of the old man, elicited from him a story of almost life-long reverses, which went the rounds of the English press at the time. Among other things he stated that he was the father of Cora Pearl. During the last few years her poverty was as great as his. She was often seen in the Champs Elysées, gazing at the house where she once had lived, her dress faded and worn, but the red-dyed hair as conspicuously brilliant as of old; the rouged cheeks and artificially whitened brow giving her at a little distance a factitious air of youthfulness. The disdainful look had deserted her face, and wrinkles were seen, at a near approach, under the rouge. An air of fretful misery had replaced them. The ravages of a terrible disorder were reflected in her face. Her life was an antithesis, of which her death served to dot the i's and cross the t's . . .

A Paris correspondent telegraphs: About 20 persons only attended the funeral of the late Cora Pearl. Several of her former admirers joined in a subscription to pay the expenses of the burial, amounting to £32. Fifty francs was sent by the secretary of a very great personage to buy a five years' grave. A Protestant clergyman officiated out of charity. The deceased wished it to be known that she blamed nobody but herself for her final misery.[8]

The memoirs themselves begin with an explanation of the author's intent; she puts herself forward as a sort of social historian: 'I publish these memoirs because I think they will be interesting, and because they will put once more before the eyes of the world the society of the Second Empire.'[9] Emma is at her most attractive here, in her candour and in her refusal to indulge in self-pity: 'I have had a happy life; I have squandered money enormously. I am far from posing as a victim; it would be ungrateful of me to do so. I ought to have saved, but saving is not easy in such a whirl of excitement as that in which I have lived. Between what one ought to do and what one does there is always a difference.'[10] She makes no mention of her father having run off to America. She claims to have been close to him, that he died when she was only five years old and that she never came to know her mother well. (Quite apart from the fact that her father did not die, one has to remember to make an adjustment of several years every time she mentions her age; an added difficulty is that she is inconsistent in how many years she is subtracting.) She writes that she was sent to France for eight years, and that on her return she went to live with her grandmother (named as 'madame Waats' in the French version), 'and my remaining parent I only saw during an occasional visit, until considerations of delicacy forbade my being received in her house or that of any member of my family'.[11]

The memoirs turn next to one of the defining moments of Emma's life, as a result of which she lays claim to lasting psychological scars. 'Since the day of which I now write I have preserved an instinctive hatred against men. Among them I have reckoned many friends – too many, perhaps – and some sincere well-wishers for whom I had a frank and sincere affection. But the *instinctive* feeling of which I speak has never left me. The impression has remained ineffaceable.'[12] Emma recounts that she used to spend all week at her grandmother's, playing cards with her in the afternoons and reading to her in the evenings. It is thought[13] that she actually worked at this time as an apprentice milliner in Regent Street, but this is not the version of her life Emma chooses to give. On Sundays, she claims, she would visit her mother, accompanied by a maid. Her mother, who does not appear to have been desperate for Emma's company, would send her to church, where the servant would leave her to go for a walk. Dislike of her stepfather continues to be significant in determining her actions (though the following is not included in the English version):

I was not yet fourteen; I was still in a short dress and wore my hair in schoolgirl plaits. I was quite a good girl, and not overly shy. I had an extremely clear complexion. I usually went back to Mummy's after the service. Sometimes I went back to Mrs Waats'. It depended a bit on my stepfather's mood. When he was out, I stayed all day with my sisters.[14]

Then Emma tells the story of how one Sunday the maid does not arrive to collect her after church, so she sets out alone and is accosted by a man, whom she takes to be thirty-five to forty years old. He offers to treat her to cakes; she, totally innocent and unsuspecting, is proud to be out on her own. 'And I followed the gentleman. Why shouldn't I have followed him? I wasn't depraved – no, not at all – or even curious. And yet I did say to myself: "This is quite funny!" not out of defiance – I didn't know a thing – but with one of those little feelings of astonishment which make you smile – inside.'[15] The man takes Emma into some sort of drinking den, possibly near Covent Garden, and gives her gin. She awaits her cakes in vain, and finally falls asleep on her chair. 'The next morning I found myself by the side of the man in his bed. It was one more child ruined – wickedly, bestially. I have never pardoned men, neither this one nor the others who are not responsible for his act.'[16]

This route into prostitution was not, according to Dr Michael Ryan, uncommon in mid-nineteenth-century London. In fact he alludes to a case very similar to that described by Emma Elizabeth Crouch:

> A child, aged fourteen years, had lately applied to the [London] Society [for the Prevention of Juvenile Prostitution] . . . for protection. She was decoyed, at the age of twelve years, while passing to or from a Sunday school, into a brothel, and such was the influence gained over her, that, though she left not her home, she continued her visits to this abominable abode for about two years, unknown to her friends or relations.[17]

In the account Emma gives, however, there is no return to the family home. She claims that for her the experience felt like the end of the world and that she knew her old life was over. 'I didn't know what to think. It all felt like a dream. I was honestly expecting to wake up with a start. Yet I also felt that it was all up with me and that I would never again set foot in my grandmother's or Mummy's house.'[18] She refuses the offer her seducer makes for her to stay with him and go round London together, but accepts five pounds with which she decides to rent a room. She wastes no time worrying about the effect of her disappearance on her family. 'I would be telling a lie if I said that the pain of separation from my family made me cry. I had lived far away from them for too long and, on my return from Boulogne, couldn't help but see myself, through force of circumstance, like a child sent back from the wetnurse at the age of thirteen.'[19] Despite the trauma she has endured, Emma relishes her forced independence. 'I preferred the boarding-school to my family; but, even inexperienced as I was, I felt that independence was better than either. Moreover, was it not a real satisfaction to be able to say to myself "I am at home, in a home of my own"?'[20] The French version names the man (though the English does not): 'I never saw the wolf of my story again; it seems he was a diamond merchant by the name of Saunders.'[21]

Though much in Emma's attempt to portray herself as a Little Red Riding Hood figure, cruelly seduced in her innocence, has to be discounted – if it really happened after her return from Boulogne she would have been nearer twenty than fourteen, for instance, and probably nothing like as innocent as she makes out – there is some psychological truth here, at least, some trace of reality. Something happened to turn Emma from either her grandmother's companion or an apprentice milliner into a prostitute – for this is what 'renting a room' is a euphemism for here – and to explain why she never returned home. The fact that such things were known to happen, that other girls were decoyed into brothels or unwittingly raped, makes it neither more nor less likely that it actually happened to Emma. She could easily have heard or read about such an incident happening to someone else and decided to incorporate it into her own story. Nor was it uncommon for a family to reject a daughter who had 'fallen', even when the fall was not at all of her own making. Yet Emma's decision, as here recounted, to make an independent life for herself does seem precipitate. There is clearly much fictionalising going on here, and a condensing of the narrative. Yet there also lurks the shadowy figure of the distrusted, possibly abusive, stepfather. It is impossible to determine what part he may have played in the events which led to Emma's taking up a life of prostitution, but to a modern sensibility elements of this story – an adolescent girl sent away from home after her mother has acquired a new lover, that girl then proving unwilling to return home when he is around, her fanciful narrative of a rape scene by a man who might or might not have been called Saunders, and her total abandonment of and by her family – sound suspicious, to say the least. The words of Alexandre Dumas *fils* have a resonance in Emma's, as in Marie Duplessis's, life: 'The courtesan's excuses are ignorance, an absent or depraved family, bad examples, lack of education, religion and principles, and *always and above all a first error*, often involving a relative, sometimes the brother or father (see the statistics at the police headquarters), a mother who sold them, finally poverty and everything that goes with it.'[22]

The memoirs now turn to the first stage of the transformation of Emma Elizabeth Crouch into Cora Pearl:

> I was not long in making the acquaintance of a young man, Bill Blinkwell, proprietor of some Dance-Rooms. Well brought up, naturally sentimental, he conceived for me a very tender feeling. We spoke French together. He had a way of saying, 'Ma chère Cora!' which sometimes went to my heart. For I had taken the name of Cora Pearl from no particular reason, but purely from fancy.[23]

Emma makes it sound as though 'Cora Pearl' was the first name which came into her head, and maybe it was. Yet it is also a sign that she desired to escape her past, in particular her family, and choosing a name quite different from her birth name helped her to cover her traces effectively. She also enjoyed the play on words, making of herself a gem strung on a chain of lovers, though she affected to despise men who kept repeating the pun, especially when they accused the pearls around her neck of being as false as the Pearl who wore them. 'Bill Blinkwell' or, in the French version, 'William Bluckel', was actually Robert Bignell, proprietor of the Argyll Rooms, also known as the Argyll Theatre and the New Private

Saloon Theatre, just off Regent Street, and where Emma/Cora had been plying her trade. Still amending her age, she claims: 'He was twenty-five years old; I was fifteen. He loved me madly, and I was rather pleased with him.'[24] According to Cora, he even proposed, but 'I replied that I never wished to marry, for I detested men too much ever to obey one of them.'[25] Nevertheless, for the purpose of paying a visit to Paris together she allowed him to obtain a passport in which she was described as his wife.

In Paris Bignell introduced her to all the usual haunts of the tourist. 'We stayed at the York and Albion Hotel. The day after our arrival my "husband" took me upon the Arc de Triomphe, into the sewers, into the vaults of the Panthéon, to the fountains of the Tuileries, where we saw the gold fish.'[26] Cora may have been misremembering or embellishing here, as the sewers only really became a tourist attraction towards the end of the 1860s, whereas she arrived in Paris in the mid- to late 1850s. In any event, she enjoyed herself immensely. After a month, Robert told her it was time to return home; he had work to attend to. But Cora had other plans; she seized the joint passport and threw it on the fire. Robert realised he was defeated, paid the hotel bill and left. Cora knew whom to blame: 'What I had done was perhaps ill, but it was so spontaneous. It was his fault after all, poor boy! It is a mistake to bring your wife to Paris, when your property is London Dance-Rooms.'[27]

Cora Pearl's first Parisian lovers were undistinguished, as was the area of eastern Paris in which she lived, the Cité des Bluets. She subsequently lived in the place du Havre, followed by the rue Le Peletier and the rue Grange Batelière, all the while moving up the fashionable scale and closer to the area of operations of the highest class of courtesan. But, reading between the lines of her memoirs, she began as a common prostitute, most probably a *fille en carte* – that is, working independently rather than in a brothel. Cora records that the first 'acquaintance' she made in Paris was a sailor called d'Aménard. He had no money but was amusing and, when he set sail, promised to marry her on his return. She told him she would wait for him, but neither meant what she said nor expected to see him again, for 'a sailor is flotsam, an empty cask, a gangplank on which it would be reckless to count!'[28] Cora went on to use the services of a procuress: 'Then I was put in touch with Roubise, who was highly esteemed in her world and who procured many clients for me.'[29] One of these clients was a man Cora calls Delamarche; she claimed to be fond of him, but the relationship could not last as he had no money: 'But, in his case too, the heart was more wealthy than the wallet, and he spent both with the best will in the world. When the wallet is empty, the heart is full. What can you do then? Find shelter in the fields. That's what he did.'[30]

Before long Cora's career took off and she began to acquire the kind of lovers she wanted, men with sufficient wealth to make her wealthy too. She attracted them not only by her sexual prowess and striking appearance (her naturally red or dyed yellow hair and athletic physique seemed to fascinate the French, attracting and repelling in equal measure), but by her intelligence, her wit and her humour. As her 1930s' biographer, Baroness von Hutten, put it: 'She knew . . . how to make bored men laugh.'[31] She was also in the right place at the right time: 'However it came about, she appeared in Paris, at a time when the Second Empire was at its height of luxury, of pleasures and of power, and she knew how to please the men of leisure who follow women – if you will excuse this hunting term – like hounds track animals.'[32] Cora called the string of lovers she acquired her 'golden chain'. As in the case of Marie Duplessis, it is very difficult to work out exact dates for Cora's many affairs, both because various accounts conflict and because several of the liaisons were concurrent. Others were very short-lived.

Once she could afford it, she took a fine house at 61 rue Ponthieu (parallel with the avenue des Champs Elysées) which she shared with another courtesan, Caroline Hassé. The Count de Maugny, the man behind the pseudonym of 'Zed', recalled seeing Caroline at the establishment of Cellarius the dancing master, and described her as 'a splendid creature with thick golden hair and ample curves: a tall, beautiful person, cheerful and pleasant, glowing with freshness, youth and luxury'.[33] The relationship between the two women was not always harmonious – naturally enough, for they were in competition. 'Zed' also tells a particularly malicious story about Cora's attitude towards Caroline. One day, he relates, the house caught fire: 'By chance I was walking past at the moment of the fire. I went into the courtyard to see what was going on, and what did I find? Cora at the window, in her chemise, shouting at the top of her voice to her stable hands: "I'll sack the first person who takes a bucket of water to that cow upstairs!" '[34]

Cora had a long-term liaison with the man she calls 'Lassema' (a thin disguise for Victor Masséna); it lasted, according to her, for six years though was run concurrently with many others. Masséna, the third Duke of Rivoli and later the fifth Prince of Essling (and a grandson of Napoleon's great marshal), bought her dresses by Worth and Laferrière, and jewels from the rue de la Paix. He also maintained her servants, including her brilliant and profligate chef, Salé. 'He [Masséna] was unquestionably one of the first links in my chain of gold. Heir of a great name of the First Empire, rich, correct in his bearing, he was still most thoughtful, most anxious to please, most adorable, and, I should add, the man who received the least in return.'[35] Masséna was very jealous, Cora says, of 'Adrien Marut' – that is, Prince Achille Murat, another aristocratic lover and, at the time Cora met him, still only a teenager.

Achille was the youngest brother of Princess Caroline Murat. Both had been born, along with another brother and sister, in the United States during the time when everyone with Bonaparte connections was in exile. (Prince Joachim Murat, Caroline and Achille's grand-father, had been the brother-in-law of Napoleon I and became the King of Naples.) The Murats had arrived in Paris in October 1848 after the overthrow of Louis Philippe and some two months before the election of Louis Napoleon as President of the Republic. Prince Achille was the first man to make Cora the present of a horse. Unfortunately he had financial problems:

But he was as much in debt as in love, and that's saying a good deal. At the end of his resources, afraid of Papa who was also very fond of his little comforts, but who had a rather quick hand though an excellent heart, little Adrien ran to pour out his woes on the Emperor's breast. The latter forgave him, paid his debts and was so kind as to dispatch him to Africa.[36]

Some years later, in 1865, Prince Achille foolishly became embroiled in a dispute Cora had with a horse-dealer who had claimed that she owed him money. Prince Achille agreed to sign a certificate stating that she had already paid the money in question, which was untrue. The Republican journalist Henri Rochefort publicly criticised Prince Achille for this, who responded by challenging Rochefort to a duel. The latter suffered a slight wound in the thigh in the ensuing contest (which took place in the riding school at St Germain) and was most annoyed to find himself the subject of gossip, the popular rumour being that he had fought the duel over Cora herself. He was not at all averse, however, to having been seen in combat with a relative of the Emperor.

Next Cora tells us about 'le duc Citron', with whom, she says, she had another fairly long-lasting affair, punctuated by his absences from Paris. This is a transparent pseudonym for William, Prince of Orange, elder son and heir of the King of Holland. He was called Citron, a nickname he hated, by many of his friends. A weak and self-indulgent character, he was a great friend of the dissipated Duke de Gramont-Caderousse who died of consumption and exhaustion at the age of thirty in September 1865, a year in which, despite the improvements in public hygiene and sanitation, there was another cholera epidemic in Paris; at nearly four and a half thousand the fatalities were still high, but represented a marked improvement on previous figures. Cora may have had a very brief liaison with Gramont-Caderousse as well, but he was far more heavily involved with another courtesan, the actress Hortense Schneider, by whom he had a child. Whenever else Citron may have been in Paris, and thus renewing his acquaintance with Cora, he is recorded as visiting the court in January 1860 and he was one of the many foreign royal figures present during the

Universal Exposition of 1867. Cora makes it clear that her relationship with him was entirely mercenary:

> The last time that I saw him I was in a low-neck dress. He asked
> to come to my house. I refused, fearing I might have some
> reason to regret yielding too easily.
> He insisted.
> 'I offer you five blue bank-notes.'
> He came.[37]

Cora's name also came to be associated with two of the most
significant figures of the Second Empire. The first of these was the
Duke de Morny, already encountered as a business associate of Alfred
Mosselman and as the lover (in both cases until 1857) of his sister, the
Countess Le Hon. So central was Auguste de Morny to the history of
the Second Empire, so famed for having a finger in every pie, that
even the mention of his name could affect share prices:

> In the eyes of many people happy to depend for their informa-
> tion on the radical newspapers from the time of the Empire, M.
> de Morny spent his life in debauchery and speculation; the
> famous *Morny's mixed up in it* acquired currency everywhere,
> and so great is Parisian credulity that no small financial society or
> newspaper could be founded, no theatre or mildly significant
> shop could open without someone rushing to spread the
> rumour: *Morny's mixed up in it*, in an effort to entice share-
> holders.[38]

He was born Auguste Demorny in 1811, the illegitimate son of
Hortense Beauharnais, herself the daughter of the Empress Josephine
and the mother of the future Napoleon III (who was three years old
when Auguste was born). His real father was Joseph, Count de
Flahaut, and his official father a Prussian officer named Demorny. He
was brought up by Flahaut's mother, Madame de Souza, and watched
over by Flahaut from afar. His own mother never saw him after his

birth, and Louis Napoleon knew nothing of his half-brother's existence until after Hortense's death in 1837. Auguste began his career in the army, and was decorated for saving the life of a general. By 1835 he had resigned his commission and become a man-about-town, funding himself partly through his affair with Countess Le Hon. After appropriating the title 'Count' for himself and adjusting his name to de Morny he soon proved himself to be a skilled and unscrupulous businessman who knew how to make everything, including his own appearance and facial expression, work in his favour:

> A trim figure, very refined features, eyes with an expression subtle and diplomatic in its indecision, a pleasantly oval-shaped head, unmarred by its premature baldness, a posture dignified and reserved without being stiff, reminiscent of that of members of the English aristocracy: such was M. Morny.[39]

He first became involved in politics during the reign of Louis Philippe, but remained somewhat on the sidelines until the election of Louis Napoleon as President of the Second Republic in December 1848, at which point he arranged a meeting with his half-brother through a mutual friend, Count Bacciochi. From then on, he was never far from the centre of power.

Princess Caroline Murat was a great admirer of Morny's:

> In the early years of the Empire, the Duke de Morny was, without doubt, 'the king of fashion, of elegance, of refinement'. He looked a grand seigneur, his manners savoured of the old *régime*. . . . He acquired great influence with the Prince-President, with whom, by his position, he was a great favourite. He was also what people call lucky in all he undertook. Had it not been for his clever conception and manoeuvring, I doubt if the *Coup d'Etat* would ever have taken place . . .
>
> In politics he was clever, calmly resolute, inflexible, but with a certain charm of manner, a rare delicacy and *finesse*, which

served to gain his ends. He was the Emperor's most intimate adviser, and his friendship with the Empress guided her influence from the wrong direction as long as he lived.[40]

Though Morny was undoubtedly involved in the *coup d'état* on 2 December 1851, his fellow conspirator Emile de Maupas would not accord him quite the central position which Princess Murat (who had clearly fallen prey to Morny's charms) ascribed to him. According to Maupas, Louis Napoleon's feelings for his half-brother were never straightforward. Sometimes he appeared intimate towards him, sometimes markedly distant, but he was always somewhat distrustful. Consequently, though the Prince-President never concealed from Morny the fact that he was considering a *coup d'état*, he did not let him know the date and exact plans until just before the event, for fear that this arch-speculator might let the cat out of the bag.

Morny remained at the heart of Napoleon III's administration for the rest of his life. He was Minister of the Interior from 1851 to 1852, ambassador to Russia from 1856 to 1857, and President of the Corps Législatif from 1854. Whereas he had previously lived in a building adjoining the Countess Le Hon's *hôtel*, this latter post brought him, along with his salary of a hundred thousand francs, lodgings in the Palais Bourbon. Here he was able to live in the style to which he had always aspired, holding brilliant gatherings of the most distinguished members of Parisian society in the fields of politics, science and the arts. In 1857 he married his Russian princess, the delicately beautiful Sophia Troubetskaya, unceremoniously discarding Countess Le Hon, who had by this time been his mistress for some twenty years. Both the Emperor himself and the senator Eugène Rouher became involved in subsequent attempts to placate the Countess (who was also the mother of Morny's daughter, Louise), and an indemnity of three and a half million francs was paid to her out of the privy purse. It cannot be unconnected that it was during this same year that Morny ceased working alongside the Countess's brother, Alfred Mosselman, in the running of the Société de la Vieille-Montagne.

Morny fulfilled his duties as President of the Corps Législatif with aplomb, while still finding time to manage his many business affairs which included an involvement in the sugar beet industry, banking, the development of the railway system, the construction of the Suez Canal and the proprietorship of newspapers. He was also a developer and speculator – this was what really made him rich – and was the prime mover behind the creation of the resort town of Deauville. A member of the Jockey Club (founded by an uncle of Richard Wallace, Lord Henry Seymour), he played a major part in the establishment of horse racing in France at Longchamp and Deauville. In 1862 he was made a duke. He was an epicure and a gourmet, an amateur of painting and the theatre, and was said to have written the libretti for several operettas. The only one of these to have survived – *M. Champfleury restera chez lui*, written in 1860 and set to music by Offenbach – was in fact drafted by Halévy with a few interpolations from Morny.

Maxime Du Camp relates that, while Morny was one of the wittiest men he knew in private or in a small gathering, he was quite incapable of improvised public speaking, having to write down all his speeches to the Corps Législatif in advance and read them out, word for word.[41] Nevertheless, once installed in his official seat he exuded an absolute authority. His facial expression betrayed a constant lassitude, and he could rarely be bothered to finish his sentences – unless, exceptionally, he considered his interlocutor to be of equal intelligence to himself. He led an extremely well-ordered life, even allotting specified hours to relaxation. At whatever time he arrived home, he would get on with his work. People who had left him in the middle of the night would be amazed the next morning to find him well informed on subjects about which he had known little the previous evening. When he was dissatisfied with his health he would take a 'blue pill', a remedy which may have shortened his life by leading to the development of stomach ulcers. (Made of mercury with glycerin and honey of rose, 'blue pill' or 'blue mass' was widely used in the nineteenth century both as an anti-depressant and as a purgative; Abraham Lincoln was another user of it, until he realised it put him in a bad mood.) Maupas, who as Minister of Police must have worked closely with Morny, sums him up, somewhat dismissively, thus:

> To be precise, one could say of M. de Morny: he was a man of extreme elegance and rare *savoir-faire*; he was courageous always, skilful and strong when he felt like it; in business affairs he was adventurous and not entirely honest; but his name and his deeds made a great stir. That was his ambition, and he had the satisfaction of achieving it.[42]

Cora refers to Morny as 'Moray' in her memoirs and relates that she first met him while skating in the Bois one December. He subsequently invited her to his *résidence* and also bought her a white Arab pony, having admired her riding ability. Her description of him fits in well with those of other observers, and she esteemed him as much as she esteemed any man:

> My host embodied the type of the perfect gentleman. Sometimes he seemed to let himself go, but he always recovered himself. No one could turn a compliment better than he; yet his compliments were never bland: he hated banality. He even knew how to make a reproach sound obliging, so that there was pleasure in being scolded by him. He was one of those who do not grow old, and who always remain alive in one's memory. A passionate lover of the arts, he was particularly interested in the theatre. He worshipped Musset: and no one was surprised by that. Those who resemble one another esteem one another. He could have written a comedy between hosting a diplomatic reception and delivering an official speech. When he was at home, the most agreeable pastime, in those happy moments when I was able to see him, was to listen to him talk with his inexhaustible verve, his subtle jests, his expert and unpretentious criticism. He was charming, sitting at the piano in his purple velvet suit. He played with much feeling, and crooned with exquisite taste.[43]

Morny died on 10 March 1865, at the age of only fifty-four. His premature death has been attributed by some to his habit, common among fashionable Parisians, of taking not only blue pills but also arsenic, reputed to be a youth preserver. Cora was believed to indulge in the same remedy. In Princess Murat's opinion Morny's death was a disaster for the Empire:

> There is little doubt that the death blow to our prosperity was the passing away of the Duke de Morny in 1865. He was the heart and soul of the Empire. He alone held firm against the all-invading influence of the Empress; an influence always so sinister for France. His loss was irreparable. He died under the treatment of the English physician, his doctor and friend, and, I believe, medical man to the English Embassy, who administered very freely blue pill to an already weakened constitution.[44]

Maxime Du Camp relates how on his deathbed Morny instructed one of his secretaries (Montguyon, one of Marie Duplessis's former lovers) to burn all his private letters.[45] The process was begun, but then the chimney caught fire, so the letters had to be flushed down the water closet instead, with the aid of buckets of water and a broom handle – and so letters from actresses, duchesses, marchionesses, *grisettes*, ambassadresses and princesses all went floating off into the sewers of Paris. Another version is that all of his private papers were seized after his death, on the express orders of the Empress;[46] Morny may, of course, have anticipated this eventuality and so arranged for the really private documents to be disposed of before his death – which he insisted on referring to as his 'departure'. He left not only a grieving widow – for the Duchess de Morny had become very attached to him, despite her peculiarities and his affairs – but a two-year-old daughter who would one day attain notoriety in her own right as 'Missy', the lover of Colette. Morny's tomb dominates one of the crossroads in the cemetery of Père Lachaise, a miniature temple to the self-made man, ensuring that his ennobled name is as prominent in death as it was in life.

The other most noteworthy man to have been one of Cora's lovers was, as far as outward appearance was concerned, the antithesis of the suave and urbane Auguste de Morny. In intellect, however, he was more than Morny's equal and he too was central to the life of the Second Empire. This man was Prince Napoleon Joseph Charles Paul Bonaparte, cousin of the Emperor and brother of Princess Mathilde.

Contemporary memoirists rarely have a good thing to say about Prince Napoleon, particularly as regards his manners; Viel Castel, as usual, does not mince his words: 'The Prince is always, whatever he's doing, the same man, lifeless, coarse and badly brought up, detested by all who come near him.'[47] The Prince also offended the delicate sensibilities of La Chroniqueuse:

> The time was, and that not many years ago, when the name prince and gentleman were synonymous terms; now, *au contraire*. I don't think any *gentleman* would ride through the streets of Paris in an Imperial *calèche* with a cigar in his mouth and a straw hat stuck rakishly on the front of his head, his legs (don't be shocked, ladies, it is quite true) stretched out on the front seat, and his arm thrown over the back of the carriage![48]

Anna Bicknell, a English governess in the imperial household, was equally scathing:

> The physical likeness [to Napoleon I] was wonderful, but the expression was totally different. In the good portraits of Napoleon I, the clear eyes have a singularly piercing glance, at once conveying the idea of a commanding genius. With the same cast of features, there was something peculiarly low and thoroughly bad in the face of Prince Napoleon, which recalled in a striking manner the stamp of the worst Roman Caesars.[49]

She goes on: '. . . never were natural gifts so misapplied or so wasted. He could bear no restraint, no interruption in his life of sensual pleasures, and he never persevered in anything that he undertook, when any personal sacrifice was required to carry it out.'[50]

In her memoirs Cora refers to Prince Napoleon as 'Duke Jean', sometimes calling him 'Jean-Jean', a transparent disguise for the Prince's nickname of 'Plon-Plon'. She relates that during their first assignation he took her to drink milk at a farm near Meudon, ten miles from Paris, where the Prince had a château and where Cora had been hunting with Achille Murat. The visit to the farm lasted about an hour. 'An expert in agricultural matters, as in so much else, the Duke obligingly undertook my rural education.'[51] Cora was in no hurry to grant the Prince, or 'the Duke', sole rights over her, but the fact that he was able to pay far more than her other current conquests gave him a distinct advantage:

> At that time de Rouvray was my 'friend'. He cared about me perhaps more from tenderness of heart than from the desire to show off. On several occasions he encountered the Duke at my place and, unless I am much mistaken, benevolence was not really what they felt for one another. Godefroy, as Barberousse euphemistically called him, was another of my regulars. In this trio of performers or dilettantes, it was naturally the Duke who, destined by his high calling to produce the highest note, made it heard the most acutely.[52]

Even so, Cora insists that she remained in control: 'Far from feeling with him the least embarrassment, at the end I mastered him. He bent with good grace, and only revolted when spurred by pride and jealousy. With him, as with all the others, I took care to assert my independence.'[53] The Prince did hold a trump card, however, which even Cora admits threatened her much-vaunted independence, and that was the power to have her deported. And so, with this ultimate threat in mind, Cora, who had been pretending to have a twisted ankle in order to explain her avoidance of the Prince while she had been playing the field with other men, realised that it was to her advantage at least to appear to be faithful to him: 'For the time being, it was my interest to submit. I, therefore, got on my legs again, and went to sign peace.'[54]

Cora is one of the few people to say anything agreeable about the Prince: 'He was only rough externally. A very little knowledge of him revealed his real delicacy of manner.'[55] Astute and observant as ever, she realised that he could be a quite different person, depending on whom he was having dealings with: 'My first impression concerning the Duke has never been modified. This man was an angel to those who pleased him. His voice was agreeable, his laugh frank, his conversation witty, and at need playful; angel, I repeat, to those who pleased him; demon, roué, madman, unhesitating insulter towards others.'[56] Yet even Cora alludes to how difficult he could be and refers to habits which would certainly have been considered coarse and ill-mannered: 'He was in the habit of putting his feet upon a chair, and often complained of the tyranny of stiff waistcoats. Though of very moderate appetite at his meals, he sometimes had fits of hunger. On such occasions he would buy a roll at the first baker's shop he came to, put it in his pocket and munch pieces of it as he was walking along';[57] and 'It was an awful penance to him to go to the Tuileries on reception days. He never concealed what an annoyance to him were what he called the mummeries of etiquette.'[58]

In the real duties of public life, however, away from the 'mummeries of etiquette', the Prince could cut an impressive figure. His intelligence made a deep impression on the people around him, as did his oratorical skills:

When he was on the rostrum, as in his intimate surroundings, he demonstrated his powerful faculties. Almost without preparation, with the help only of his daily meditations, he would let no argument escape him which might serve his cause. Without concerning himself with method, he would throw himself into the discussion with the passion of his nature, and if he didn't succeed in convincing, because he too often made himself the defender of lost causes, he would succeed in obtaining applause for his talent, even from those who would condemn his principles.[59]

The Prince was a skilled administrator, as he had demonstrated in his role as president of the commission of the 1855 Universal Exposition. He also assimilated new ideas at speed and with enthusiasm so that scholars, inventors and exhibitors of all sorts could communicate with him easily. Despite the disparagement regularly meted out to Prince Napoleon in court circles the Emperor always stood by his cousin, tending to treat him as the child prodigy of the family. The Prince himself was very conscious not only of his imperial status, but also of the fact that he would always remain subservient to his cousin. There had been a time when he might have expected to succeed to the imperial throne, but such hopes were dashed when the Emperor married (it was noted that the Prince looked sulky at the wedding) and even more so when the Prince Imperial was born. Prince Napoleon never seemed to find quite the right outlet for his undoubted talents, which led to frustration and a degree of irascibility. He was known for flying into terrible rages when he was crossed, particularly if he felt he was being slighted in any way.

Cora gives an entertaining and enlightening picture both of Prince Napoleon's enthusiams and preoccupations and his tendency to get worked up about them, and of her own more prosaic concerns. One can almost hear the Prince pontificating while Cora waits impatiently for him to finish:

> Don't let him get started on America! It's there that the art of travel is practised with intelligence! Whereas our own railways are stagecoaches. Moreover, in France the real sovereign – the only authority in no danger of being assassinated – is routine. That's why the most intelligent nation remains backward, it's our lack of initiative, despite all attempts at improvement, and there's no willingness to profit from the progress which actually took place a long time ago.
>
> I would be saying to myself: 'If he carries on like this, we'll miss the Bouffes!'[60]

Cora sums up the Prince well, and not without a touch of humour:

> We never talked politics. It was evident, however, that the
> Duke had a perfect admiration for Napoleon I. For at heart he
> was very Bonapartist, but in a fashion of his own. He wrote
> concerning the First Empire, and gave himself up to patient
> literary researches. He was an excellent judge, a profound
> thinker, an indefatigable worker; and, at the same time, was
> good-natured, a friend to men and animals, much taken up with
> dogs and horses.[61]

On 30 January 1859, at the age of thirty-six, Prince Napoleon had
married the sixteen-year-old Princess Clotilde, daughter of King
Victor Emmanuel of Savoy. It was a match made for political reasons,
this being a period of constantly shifting allegiances among the
various European powers over the future of Italy, and it was clear
from the outset that the couple were unsuited. Clotilde was a very
devout and serious young woman, said to speak five languages
fluently as well as knowing Greek and Latin, and was completely
out of sympathy with the party-going and frivolity of the Second
Empire. La Chroniqueuse described her appearance, after having
encountered her at an exhibition of Ary Scheffer's paintings in May:
'To those who may feel interested I will state that she is not pretty,
and not excessively *distinguée*; in figure she is *petite*, her hair is auburn,
and her nose decidedly *retroussé*; still she seems very modest, even
retiring, and in this forms a striking contrast to her ladies of honour,
who, from their supercilious airs, might by the inexperienced be
taken for the Princess herself.'[62]

At the beginning of that month war had been declared on Austria,
which had attacked Piedmont a few days previously. Shortly after the
victory of the French and Sardinians at the battle of Solférino towards
the end of June, and partly through shock at the enormous bloodshed
resulting from this battle, the Emperor Napoleon suddenly deserted
his Sardinian ally and made a separate peace with Austria at Villa-
franca. La Chroniqueuse, however, considering that her readers were

more likely to be interested in a princess's personal appearance than in international politics, continued her scrutiny at the Opéra in September when she wrote of Clotilde: 'She has, what is very rare among French ladies, a beautiful complexion, and I honestly believe does not make any use of any of the preparations for the skin with which Paris is filled. Her hair is light, rather inclined to be red; but her shoulders and neck are superb, and can vie successfully with those of the Empress. She is decidedly not pretty, having an over-hanging brow, which makes her look ill-tempered.'[63] The imperial governess Anna Bicknell pitied the Princess for having to put up with her awful husband, but even she had to admit that the marriage was not easy for either party. She also calls into question Clotilde's reputation as a scholar:

[Princess Clotilde] was, and is still, a princess of medieval times, a Saint Elizabeth of Hungary, neither very highly educated nor very clever, caring only for her religious practices and her works of charity. She soon ceased to pay much attention to her toilet, reaching even the point of carelessness, which greatly annoyed her husband. It must be acknowledged that the devotion of the Princess Clotilde went perhaps beyond what was quite judicious, but no one had any influence over her, and what she considered her duty was performed with a sort of gentle, placid stubbornness which allowed of no expostulation . . . During the Empire, even in her early youth, no one dared to show the least familiarity in her presence; but the stiff decorum of her circle did not make home life particularly agreeable. During the day, her ladies accompanied her to the churches, where they unwillingly awaited her pleasure for hours; in the evening they were seated round a table with their work, while the Princess herself diligently plied her needle, speaking very little and not encouraging any one else to do so.[64]

There was no attempt made to disguise the nature of the relationship between Prince Napoleon and Cora (and neither did she by any means represent his only extra-marital adventure). She was given free access to the Palais Royal, the official residence of the Prince and Princess and their children, where, if Cora is to be believed, the affair was conducted in close proximity to the family:

> I had a key which gave me access from a side street. I sometimes slept in a room next to the apartments of Madame X, a companion of the Duchess. The return of the latter presented no obstacle to our meetings. I would dine immediately after her, in the same room, and served by the same butler. While taking my meal, I would hear the Duchess talking and the children playing in the next room.[65]

Cora's next sentence, however, has been far less frequently quoted, and is not even included in the authorised English version: 'I was always aware of that and it embarrassed me.'[66] Princess Clotilde had presumably come to some sort of accommodation over her husband's infidelities, though in the first months of the marriage she had protested at his behaviour and attempted to change it. La Chroniqueuse had reported the following event on 28 September 1859:

> A very unpleasant, but not wholly unexpected, affair has occurred in high quarters. The Prince N. left Paris about ten days ago to travel in Switzerland. His Royal and Imperial spouse, hearing that the suite of her husband comprised other persons than those strictly necessary to keep up the state of a prince, resolved to join him without further delay. Her unexpected arrival at Geneva angered her lord and master beyond control, and he asked the lady by whose authorisation, and by what right she dared follow him. 'The right that every wife has to join her husband,' she replied; 'but since my presence is so obnoxious to you, I will return to my father, whose love for me will prevent his considering State interests before the happiness of his child.' So saying, the young Princess C. left the Prince.[67]

Yet the marriage survived, and Clotilde attracted much sympathy:

> She was almost a saint, and bore her domestic trials with so
> much dignity and quiet superiority that she compelled the
> respect of her husband and his associates, and the admiration
> of the rest of the world . . . She moved, grave and irreproach-
> able, amidst the levity and frivolity of the second Empire; it was
> a piteous sight to see her at the theatre, her head slightly
> drooping, her eyes vaguely fixed on the stage, her thoughts
> evidently far away, always silent, always solitary.[68]

At one time Cora appears to have been conducting simultaneous
affairs with Prince Napoleon (while attempting to convince him that
she was faithful to him), Paul Demidov (the nephew of Princess
Mathilde's estranged husband Anatole) and Demidov's compatriot
Narischkin. She was expert at playing them off one against the other,
ratcheting up the value of the presents that each would give her. She
also had a liaison with Khalil Bey, an imposing blue-spectacled Turkish
gentleman, the former Ottoman ambassador in St Petersburg. He was
one of the wealthiest and most lavish of her lovers; arriving in Paris in
the late 1860s, he startled even the jaundiced Parisians with his oriental
magnificence and enormous expenditure. Cora writes approvingly of
him – particularly as, according to her, he knew how to treat a *demi-
mondaine* with respect; she changes his name by only one letter in her
memoirs (he becomes Khadil rather than Khalil):

> One of the most extraordinary men in my opinion was old
> Khadil-bey. He appeared to me like a character out of the
> *Thousand and One Nights*. His *hôtel* was splendid. All the marvels
> of the Orient came together there. A magical conservatory,
> enchanted apartments. In spring he received in his salon; during
> winter in his garden . . .
>   The master was the most striking aspect of the whole *hôtel*, a
> charming and lovable curiosity. Majestic in his whole person, his
> majesty excluded neither grace nor playfulness. He loved like an
> artist and entertained in grand style. He cultivated beauty in all

its forms, and was himself a type of beauty, and even more of bounty . . .

He was one of those men – and they are rare – who would think themselves dishonoured if they had, I don't say shown, but even conceived the slightest contempt for a woman they had received in their house, and whose smile they had tenderly and magnificently rewarded.[69]

Cora enjoyed luxuriating in this Moorish-style mansion in the avenue Montaigne, rented fully furnished to Khalil Bey by Jules de Lesseps: 'I bathed in the pink marble basin, I slept long hours on the couches, breathing the scent of flowers, and dreaming of enchanted places; and when I awoke, the reality appeared more beautiful than the dream.'[70] There were games to play at Khalil Bey's too, and one afternoon the high-spirited Cora indulged herself. There is a sense in her narrative of a harem-like atmosphere; a number of 'ladies' were present during the following scene:

One evening before tea, the maid requested the ladies to wait a few moments. Khadil-bey was having a nap. I noticed a box of toys on the table. I could see no reason for not opening it, and I have always loved poking around in things: this curiosity has often got me into trouble. The box contained all sorts of games. Skittles, shuttlecocks, dominos, rackets. I had had, since time immemorial, a huge desire to play skittles. Without more ado, I got down on the floor and started playing. I had been abandoning myself to this exercise for some minutes, fairly energetically, I must admit, when in came Khadil, and the ball, vigorously thrown by me, hit him right in the legs. Highly embarrassed by my clumsiness, I made haste to pick up the skittles and put them back where they belonged.

'Take this box away,' he instructed a maid. That was all his revenge.

We had tea, we chatted.

On getting home, the first thing I saw was the box. Sculpted

all over in ivory. Valued at 4,800 francs. Khadil had had it taken
to my house during the evening.[71]

This rather suggests that the unsentimental Cora had the gift valued
on receipt.

If Cora managed her multiple lovers with comparative ease, she
showed far less skill in the management of her finances. In fact she did
not attempt to manage them at all, constantly spending far more than
the considerable sums she was given by Prince Napoleon and others
(the Prince bought her two *hôtels* – one at 101 rue de Chaillot and
another in the rue des Bassins – as well as providing her with an
allowance of twelve thousand francs a month), a prey to unscrupulous
servants and 'friends of friends' more than happy to indulge themselves at her expense. She admits that she ran out of money on more
than one occasion: 'How many times I've ended up without a
farthing! I remember being in this fortunate position in Baden. I
was due to rejoin Lassema, who had set off a few days before me for
Paris. I had to pawn my diamonds in order to make the journey.
Money slipped through one's fingers with a speed you can't imagine.'[72] She was consistently extravagant and realised, at least in
retrospect, that she was as consistently cheated: 'In order to know the
price of goods, one must know the value of money; I have not the
least idea what a louis [the equivalent of twenty francs] is worth.
Tradesmen, nay, even financiers had charge of my education in such
matters, and the information they impart is one-sided.'[73]

Cora's costliest servant was her chef, Salé, who ran up an enormous
bill during one of her stays in Baden and was clearly running a part-
time business from her kitchen, charging the bills to her and taking
the profits himself. Cora describes the situation vividly:

In addition to his important role in the kitchen, Salé did the
shopping himself and handed in his accounts, which he sim-
plified as much as possible into round figures.

The long addition of his culinary contrivances was hypnotic:
one didn't wake up until the total.

Lassema and I were about to leave. We went down into the kitchen.

The first thing to strike us was a row of five beautiful chickens, plus some enormous quarters of cooked beef – a whole display of cold meats. A real roast meat shop. And I don't just mean that's what it resembled.

'So who is all this for?' I asked Salé.

He replied imperturbably: 'For the Duke.'[74]

In 1864 Cora rented the château de Beauséjour on the banks of the Loiret, a few miles from Orléans. Here she imported a large bronze bath, made specially by Chevalier of Paris, and engraved with her monogram of three intertwined Cs. She spent an enormous amount of money entertaining, inviting groups of people to stay, in a semi-deliberate parody of the imperial *séries* at Compiègne. Cora was always an extravagant hostess: 'In the winter at my suppers I used to have the fruit brought on table embedded, instead of in moss, in Parma violets which had cost me fifteen hundred francs. I believe no guest of mine can reproach me with my lack of attention. I always made it a point of honour to faithfully fulfil my duties as mistress of the house.'[75] In Vichy, where she stayed with Masséna for two weeks, she entertained day and night, to the extent that she likened her villa to a hotel: 'My *White Horse* hotel was always open to friends, and to friends of friends. It was this entirely friendly addition which put a deplorable strain on my budget. There was dancing in the morning, and dancing in the evening! Everything skipped about at my place: both people and money.'[76] Cora's, or rather Masséna's, hospitality was abused by people she hardly knew: 'There are some hungers which are never satisfied. I'm far from complaining about it, but I would have preferred to restrict myself to feeding my friends. I didn't even know the names of most of my guests; and it was these anonymous appetites which afforded me a very expensive satisfaction.'[77] Cora justly remarks on her value to the local economy:

My presence at Vichy was an era of blessedness for the suppliers. One day, at ten o'clock, I met my faithful Salé carrying half a sheep on his shoulder.

'What have you got there?'

'You can see very well, Madame, it is half a sheep.'

'Why half a sheep?'

'Madame, they don't sell it in smaller quantities.'

It must be a joy for an artist to cook in a country where life is interpreted generously: 30,000 francs-worth of food in a fort-night.[78]

The guests at Vichy played at *tableaux vivants* and charades; two of them, according to Cora, vented their spleen at having come off badly in a game of charades by spreading the rumour that their hostess had made an unsuccessful play for the Emperor who happened to be staying in Vichy at the same time. Cora herself denied having made any attempt to seduce him. There was the occasional mishap as a result of the high spirits of her guests, as in the case of one 'Castelnar', a short-sighted elderly gentleman who tried to climb in through a window and got stuck: 'His rather voluminous stomach bounced against the window jamb, he lost his footing and found himself suspended from the hook, from just below the waist.'[79] This was not the only example of tomfoolery among Cora's guests, much of it being orchestrated by Achille Murat: 'My worthy chef was not the only one to play tricks. There was a spirit of all sorts of eccentricities in the air. You would have taken them for a group of schoolboys on holiday. The ones who looked the most serious were the craziest. They would go running through the streets in the evenings, changing the shop signs and smashing the streetlamps.'[80]

Cora also lost money through gambling, particularly in Monte Carlo, where her most disastrous gambling exploit took place and where she seems to have resorted to petty burglary in order to get home:

In short, I lost seventy thousand francs in eight months. A nice way of discharging my obligations towards my suppliers – so polite and deferential as long as they knew or believed me to be rich, so hard and merciless, so insolent afterwards! Nevertheless they were paid; just a little late, that's all. But for the moment I had absolutely nothing. I owed the hotel seven hundred francs. They kept my luggage.

All the same I returned to Paris. I had to. But how? Here's the best, the glorious part of the story. I took five hundred francs from the cashdesk, for the journey. Being poor, I travelled like the poor. There was no reason to blush about that. And yet I visited this same year, during my stay, some very great ladies who have since . . . But then it was all part of the game.[81]

---

1 Emma Elizabeth Crouch, *The Memoirs of Cora Pearl*, George Vickers, London, 1886, title page

2 In *The Pretty Women of Paris*, 1883, in Captain Bingham's *Recollections of Paris*, 1896, and in Henry Vizetelly's *Glances Back through Seventy Years*, 1893

3 In Philibert Audebrand's *Petits Mémoires d'une stalle d'orchestre*, 1885, in Henri Rochefort's *The Adventures of My Life*, 1896, in S. Kracauer's *Jacques Offenbach ou le secret du Second Empire*, 1937, and in Henri d'Alméras' *La Vie parisienne sous le Second Empire*, 1933

4 In Pierre de Lano's *L'Amour à Paris sous le Second Empire*, 1896, and in Zed's *Le Demi-monde sous le Second Empire*, 1892

5 In Maurice Allem's *La Vie quotidienne sous le Second Empire*, 1948

6 Emma Elizabeth Crouch, *The Memoirs of Cora Pearl*, p.5

7 Ibid.

8 Ibid., frontispiece

9 Ibid., p.1

10 Ibid., p.2

11 Ibid., p.5

12 Ibid., pp.6–7

13 See Polly Binder, *The Truth about Cora Pearl*, Weidenfeld & Nicolson, London, 1986, p.20

14 Emma Elizabeth Crouch, *Mémoires de Cora Pearl*, Jules Lévy, Paris, 1886, p.16

15 Ibid., p.18

16 Emma Elizabeth Crouch, *The Memoirs of Cora Pearl*, p.10

17 Michael Ryan, *Prostitution in London*, p.167

18 Emma Elizabeth Crouch, *Mémoirs de Cora Pearl*, p.20

19 Ibid., p.26

20 Emma Elizabeth Crouch, *The Memoirs of Cora Pearl*, p.13

21 Emma Elizabeth Crouch, *Mémoires de Cora Pearl*, p.26

22 Alexandre Dumas *fils, Théâtre complet*, Vol.1, p.33

23 Emma Elizabeth Crouch, *The Memoirs of Cora Pearl*, pp.13–14

24 Ibid., p.14

25 Ibid., p.15

26 Ibid., p.16

27 Ibid., pp.17–18

28 Emma Elizabeth Crouch, *Mémoires de Cora Pearl*, pp.37–8

29 Ibid., p.38

30 Ibid.

31 Baroness von Hutten, *The Courtesan. The life of Cora Pearl*, Peter Davies, London, 1933, p.20

32 Pierre de Lano, *L'Amour à Paris sous le Second Empire*, p.105

33 Zed, *Le Demi-monde sous le Second Empire. Souvenirs d'un sybarite*, Ernest Kolb, Paris, 1892, p.63

34 Ibid., p.64

35 Emma Elizabeth Crouch, *The Memoirs of Cora Pearl*, p.19

36 Emma Elizabeth Crouch, *Mémoires de Cora Pearl*, p.39

37 Emma Elizabeth Crouch, *The Memoirs of Cora Pearl*, pp.25–6

38 Hippolyte de Villemessant, *Mémoires d'un Journaliste, Vol.3: A Travers Le Figaro*, E. Dentu, Paris, 1873, p.341

39 Vicomte E. de Beaumont-Vassy, *Les Salons de Paris et la société parisienne sous Napoléon III*, Ferdinand Sartorius, Paris, 1868, pp.200–1

40 Princess Caroline Murat, *My Memoirs*, pp.179–80

41 Maxime Du Camp, *Souvenirs d'un demi-siècle*, p.227

42 C.E. de Maupas, *Mémoires sur le Second Empire*, Vol.1, E. Dentu, Paris, 1884, pp.294–5

43 Emma Elizabeth Crouch, *Mémoires de Cora Pearl*, pp.51–2

44 Princess Caroline Murat, *My Memoirs*, p.179

45 Maxime Du Camp, *Souvenirs d'un demi-siècle*, p.235

46 W.H. Holden, *The Pearl from Plymouth*, British Technical and General Press, London, 1950, p.56

47 Comte Horace de Viel Castel, *Mémoires sur le regne de Napoléon III (1851–1864)*, Vol.3, 1885, p.180

48 La Chroniqueuse, *Photographs of Paris Life*, pp.100–1

49 Anna Bicknell, *Life in the Tuileries under the Second Empire*, T. Fisher Unwin, London, 1895, p.64

50 Ibid., p.65

51 Emma Elizabeth Crouch, *Mémoires de Cora Pearl*, p.113

52 Ibid., p.121

53 Emma Elizabeth Crouch, *The Memoirs of Cora Pearl*, p.59

54 Ibid., p.69

55 Ibid., p.80

56 Ibid., p.59

57 Ibid., pp.76–7

58 Ibid., p.77

59 C.E. Maupas, *Mémoires sur le Second Empire*, Vol.2, p.122

60 Emma Elizabeth Crouch, *Mémoires de Cora Pearl*, pp.124–5

61 Emma Elizabeth Crouch, *The Memoirs of Cora Pearl*, p.60

62 La Chroniqueuse, *Photographs of Paris Life*, p.31

63 Ibid., p.113

64 Anna Bicknell, *Life in the Tuileries under the Second Empire*, pp.78–80

65 Emma Elizabeth Crouch, *Mémoires de Cora Pearl*, p.129

66 Ibid., p.130

67 La Chroniqueuse, *Photographs of Paris Life*, pp.129–30

68 A Cosmopolitan, *Random Recollections of Court and Society*, Ward & Downey, London, 1888, pp.148–9

69 Emma Elizabeth Crouch, *Mémoires de Cora Pearl*, pp.189–90

70 Ibid., p.191

71 Ibid., pp.191–2

72 Ibid., pp.67–8

73 Emma Elizabeth Crouch, *The Memoirs of Cora Pearl*, p.34

74 Emma Elizabeth Crouch, *Mémoires de Cora Pearl*, pp.65–6

75 Emma Elizabeth Crouch, *The Memoirs of Cora Pearl*, p.51

76 Emma Elizabeth Crouch, *Mémoires de Cora Pearl*, pp.73–4

77 Ibid., p.75

78 Ibid., p.79

79 Ibid., p.77

80 Ibid., p.79

81 Ibid., p.69

CHAPTER ELEVEN

Putting on a Show

T HE AMBITION ATTRIBUTED to the Duke de Morny by Emile
de Maupas to 'make a great stir' could equally be seen as the
ambition of the great courtesans, and certainly of both Cora Pearl and
La Païva. Quite apart from their natural propensity to be noticed,
they used several methods to achieve that ambition; both methods
and ambition were in tune with the spirit of the age, for the ethos of
the Second Empire was itself grounded in the importance of display,
of showing its grandeurs to the world, of achieving those 'pyrotechnical victories'[1] which the *Illustrated London News* had predicted for it
at the outset. Certain words occur again and again in descriptions of
the Second Empire, nouns such as *fanfreluches* (trimmings, frills and so
on), *frivolité, luxe, réclame* (fame, or publicity) and *l'effet*, adjectives
such as *fastueux* (lavish, sumptuous) and *tapageur* (loud, flashy or
blatant), and the verb *paraître* (to appear – with its double meaning of
being visible and things not being quite what they seem). The overall
impression conveyed is of froth and frivolity, of the world as a stage-
set, of the supreme importance of the show.

One of the first things an individual needs to do when setting out
to make a stir and to put on a show is – as we have seen in the case of
each of these *demi-mondaines*, as indeed of that of Auguste Demorny
in his detaching of the 'de' – to choose an appropriate name. The
importance attached to names was not a phenomenon peculiar to the
Second Empire, though that era was permeated by the resonance of
the name 'Napoleon'. (An element which adds to the confusion in
sorting out Bonaparte family history was Napoleon I's insistence that

all his male descendants should have 'Napoleon' included in their names; there was also a preponderance of the names Louis, Jerome and Charles in various combinations. Louis Napoleon's elder brother, for instance, who died in 1831, was called Napoleon Louis, while Prince Napoleon, or to give him his full name Prince Napoleon Joseph Charles Paul, who was the son of Prince Jerome, was himself also known as Jerome by the family.)

For the woman desiring to be noticed her physical appearance is even more important than her name, and Second Empire fashions in dress provided ample opportunities for display. This was an age of ostentation, when the urge to compete for attention could on occasion take on ridiculous proportions. Ostentation in female attire attained its apogee in the crinoline which, despite its impracticality, enjoyed a long dominance. Originally a sort of horse-hair stuffing which enlarged the hips, it became refined over time into a metal cage over which the skirts were spread. Above this a woman would typically wear a corset which squeezed the waist and emphasised the bust. Under the cage, which could sway unpredictably to reveal the legs, pantaloons were worn. The crinoline posed problems in the areas of transport (there was no room for men in carriages alongside the voluminous skirts of their female companions), safety (the flaring skirt was particularly susceptible to fire), and accommodation. The theatre at Compiègne, which comfortably held eight hundred in Louis Philippe's day, was crowded with five hundred during the Second Empire. The proportion of women to seats in churches altered too, causing church authorities to worry about decreased revenue.

Maxime Du Camp tells how in October 1856 the Gymnase put on a play entitled *Les Toilettes tapageuses* and how the lead actress, according to the satiric intent of the piece, wore a ludicrously large crinoline. The morning after the first night, however, various society ladies were making enquiries about copying it, and within a few days the crinoline worn in the fashionable world was twice as large as before.[2] The Paris correspondent of the *Illustrated London News* lamented in January 1860: 'The prediction of the decrease in the amplitude of ladies' dresses in 1860 still remains unrealised, and the generally-condemned crinoline has not yet been compelled to hide its diminished head. We cannot tell to what we ought to attribute this persistence in enormous proportion, unless it be the ordinary diffi- culty of suppressing a bad custom.'[3] Princess Pauline Metternich, wife of the Austrian ambassador and a friend of the Empress's, is credited with having brought about the crinoline's gradual demise; in 1861 she gave a ball for which the invitations specified that ladies were not to wear them. The Empress, however, continued to wear hers until the last years of the Empire.

When women finally gave up their crinolines and became 'de- flated', they did not necessarily abandon wearing yards and yards of material. La Chroniqueuse writes of the fashion for trailing dresses, which sound nearly as impractical as the crinoline (and these fashions certainly provided a boost to the textile industry): 'It appears that the Imperial fiat has gone forth as regards crinoline, as I observe some of our *élégantes* already walking up and down the Champs Elysées, like Dorothy Draggletail, performing the ignominious office of street- sweeper, with silks at twelve shillings a yard. Rather an expensive broom, you will say, but "*que voulez vous*," these ladies must be in the fashion.'[4]

Male fashions were less capricious. Particularly in vogue during the Second Empire were knee breeches which showed off a man's calves, and cylindrical top hats, known vulgarly as stove pipes (*tuyaus de poêle*). Gloves were less to be worn than to be carried.

The most famous *couturier* of the Second Empire, the founder of modern Parisian *haute-couture*, who dressed both society women and *demi-mondaines*, was an Englishman, Charles Frederick Worth (the French, according to La Chroniqueuse, pronounced his name 'Mon- sieur Voss').[5] Born in Lincolnshire, he was apprenticed at thirteen to Swan and Edgar in Piccadilly. Fascinated by the Paris fashions which he had studied in magazines, he set off for the French capital in 1846, at the age of twenty-one, with no knowledge of the language and a hundred and seventeen francs in his pocket. He found a job at Gagelin and Opigez, a fashionable fabric retailer in the rue de

Richelieu, married a former Gagelin *demoiselle de magasin*, was soon creating costumes for her to model and was allowed to establish a dressmaking department. In 1858 he accepted the offer of a wealthy Swedish friend to set him up in business at 7 rue de la Paix. To begin with, he catered to a moderately well-off middle class clientèle, but his great opportunity came in 1860 when he persuaded Princess Metternich to buy one of his gowns. The Princess proceeded to recommend Worth to the Empress, and his career became meteoric. After 1864 he made all of the Empress's evening dresses, and by 1867 he had a workforce of twelve thousand and was dressing the nobility and royalty of France, Russia, Austria, Spain and Italy. Even Queen Victoria bought several gowns from him, as did the wives of American millionaires.

Apollonie Sabatier was fascinated by clothes but held herself rather aloof from conventional fashion, preferring to create her own style. She enjoyed wearing original outfits, which were sometimes designed especially for her by artist friends. Her dress sense was not infallible, however, as is clear from a letter Théophile Gautier wrote to Ernesta Grisi on 8 November 1856:

> . . . on the subject of the Présidente, she outdid herself at the first performance of the Bouilhet. She was wearing a ridiculous headdress – one of those frightful basin-shaped caps, the colour of chocolate, with feathers, ribbons and other extravagant trimmings. I think she managed to make herself look ugly, something very difficult to achieve . . .[6]

Ernesta replied: 'as for Mme Sabatier I think she's going crazy at the idea that she's getting older, she shouldn't worry, no one will copy her weird outfits.'[7]

If Apollonie was known for her 'weird outfits', Cora Pearl and La Païva were both renowned for their extravagant, not to say excessive, use of make-up. Jean Philippe Worth, son of the couturier, describes Cora's appearance succinctly: 'Her teeth were incomparable, but her make-up was shockingly overdone, and she looked much better at a distance.'[8] She was nevertheless credited with a degree of originality and an occasionally successful audacity in her self-ornamentation: 'She was the first person to colour her hair yellow and to think of making her eyelashes iridescent, of illuminating her eyes, making her forehead shimmer and powdering her flesh with silver, frost, snow, milk, stars and pearls.'[9] Powder, made of various starches and mixed with other substances such as talc, magnesia and oxide of zinc, and applied with a hare's foot or a puff made of swan's down, was a compulsory element in the arsenal of any lady of fashion. Cora's originality seems to have lain in what she added to the powder to create her special effects.

The habit of dyeing her hair seems to have provoked particular fascination and spawned much imitation: 'And then, oh unsurpassed glory! Cora Pearl introduced to the world the tincture, thanks to which a brunette can give herself the pleasure of hearing a poet compare her hair, dyed red or pink, to a Bengal rose or to a crimson veil.'[10] The turning of her hair yellow may conceivably have been a mistake, or at least achieved by accident rather than design. A known recipe for dyeing the hair black involved the use of nitrate of silver, water and sulphuret of potassium, but if the sulphuret was not fresh it would have the effect of turning the hair yellow rather than black. (It was not only women who practised the art of hair-dyeing; it was noticed that, when the Italian patriot Orsini was guillotined in March 1858, his hair, which had been raven-black at the time of his arrest two months previously, was now iron-grey. His supporters claimed that he had gone grey as a result of the treatment meted out to him in prison, but G.W. Septimus Piesse, the author of *The Art of Perfumery & the Methods of obtaining the Odours of Plants, with instructions for the manufacture of perfumes for the handkerchief, scented powders, odorous vinegars, dentifrices, pomatums, cosmetics, perfumed soap etc.*, published in 1862, is convinced that the real reason was that during his incarceration he was deprived of his habitual hair-dye.) A less drastic method of achieving a golden glow was to sprinkle the hair with *poudre d'or* or golden powder. The Empress Eugénie was the first woman to appear thus glittering, at a festival in 1860. The best (and most expensive) sort of *poudre d'or* consisted of crushed gold leaf, though a similar effect could be created using powdered bronze.

Cora was also very fond of jewellery, nearly always wearing broad gold bracelets on her arms and wrists, a necklace, flowers in her hair, and jewellery or flowers in her corsage. Usually she wore a broad belt, pulled as tight as possible, to emphasise her waist. She also often wore a ring on the third finger of her right hand, attached by a slim chain to a bangle on her wrist. She was exceedingly proud of her elegant hands, and had models or casts of them spread around as ornaments in her drawing room.

Though Cora could undoubtedly overdo the make-up and overall presentation, she had the natural performer's ability to amuse, and her exaggerated self-display served as an effective ploy to get herself noticed in her chosen milieu. She is even reputed to have dyed her dog blue to match her outfit – or, according to Mrs Burton Harrison, a young American woman visiting Paris from Virginia in 1867 – yellow to match her hair.[11] The element of humour was missing from La Païva's ostentation, however, and her abundant use of make-up was never admired but only derided. Never considering her face to be her best feature (she avoided having portraits painted of herself for this reason), she mistakenly believed that heavy make-up would improve her appearance and, as she grew older, wore more and more of it. Jean Philippe Worth commented on her overuse of kohl, made at the time from Indian ink dissolved in rosewater and applied with a fine camels' hair brush: 'I did not see her until she was no longer young and her beauty was already on the wane. And I am afraid that I did not appreciate it. Her eyelids were shockingly blackened, and this, combined with the prominence of her eyes, made her look fierce and hawklike.'[12]

Both Cora Pearl and La Païva may have been over-lavish in their personal adornment, but then not much store was set by subtlety in the society in which they flourished. In this era of conspicuous consumption, women paraded their finery and men paraded their women. As Alexandre Dumas *fils* put it:

Women were luxuries for public consumption, like hounds, horses and carriages. There was fun to be had in taking a girl who, eight days earlier, had been selling fish in the market or pouring drinks for early morning bricklayers, and covering her with velvet and rattling her about in a carriage; one no longer set any store by wit, gaiety, or spelling; rich today, you could be ruined tomorrow, so in the meantime you'd better have supper with this or that famous woman . . .[13]

Part of the transaction between a courtesan and her rich protector was that she was to act as a status symbol, to declare to the world that he could afford to keep an expensive mistress and that he knew how to do so in style. And in the case of those who consorted with the highest class of courtesans, there was the *cachet* to be obtained in showing off that one had been chosen out of an array of suitors for the privilege of being allowed to pay for the favours of a particular woman. And, as Dumas *fils* pointed out, in this era of speculation, of opportunities for investment in roads, railways, property development and the new telegraph system, when fortunes could be made and lost within the space of a few weeks, it was considered better to spend the money one had while one still had it, and to enjoy being seen to be rich, at least for a while.

If men used courtesans as status symbols, the courtesan could always respond in kind. The rank a courtesan had reached could be measured by the social standing of her clients and Cora, for instance, is careful whom she selects out of her many clients to include in her memoirs. She mentions the odd sailor or impoverished young man in her early days, partly for comic effect, but the bulk of her narrative is concerned with the Massénas, the Mornys, the dukes and the princes, to convey the impression of her own significance through her contact with these significant men.

Cora, happy to play along with contemporary society's preconceptions about women, to be paraded as an expensive status symbol and to be amply financially rewarded for being a 'sex object', would spend much of her day on an elaborate beauty routine. 'From the moment of getting up it would be, first, a manicure, intimate attentions with all their arsenal, then the arrival of the linen-keeper

or outfitter and a natter with her, a visit from the jeweller, billets-
doux to be dispatched in all directions, and serious matters. All that
would take until about four o'clock or half-past four.'[14] Then she
would go out, probably for a drive down the Champs Elysées or in
the Bois de Boulogne (the Emperor and Empress being in the habit of
taking their drive around the lake earlier in the afternoon, the *demi-
mondaines* generally saved their display until later). She might also visit
an establishment such as Worth's in the afternoon, or receive a client,
perhaps even several.

The evenings could include visits to the theatre and to a fashionable
restaurant, particularly to one of the private rooms in an establishment
such as the Café Anglais. Another, more select, restaurant frequented
by Cora was the Petit Moulin Rouge (no relation to the Montmartre
cabaret) which was located off the Champs Elysées and boasted, in
addition to its main entrance, a secret door in a side street for the use of
diners requiring the strictest privacy. There were large dining rooms on
the ground floor, while the usual *cabinets particuliers* were located on the
two upper floors. The renowned chef Escoffier began working at the
Petit Moulin Rouge on Easter Monday 1865 and in his memoirs recalls
the use Cora made of the establishment, likening her ability to fleece
young men to the art of pigeon plucking:

> The same evening, in a private dining room close to the one
> reserved by the Count de Paris, Cora Pearl could be found
> dining with a young lord, or perhaps I should say a young
> pigeon. This beautiful woman, who is far from forgotten, was
> particularly talented in the art of plucking these little birds so
> beloved by sensitive women. She took care to find them just as
> they left the nest, ready to fly alone, and then lavished her charm
> upon them until they were completely picked clean. Then,
> considering the deal closed, she turned to someone else.[15]

Escoffier invented a dish named after her: Noisettes d'Agneau Cora.[16]
The noisettes of lamb were to be sautéd and then placed inside freshly
cooked artichoke hearts, intended as a pun on '*cœur d'artichaut*', a term

used to designate the kind of man who falls in love with every girl he meets (and thus likely to fall prey to Cora's pigeon-plucking charms). It has frequently been asserted[17] that on one occasion Cora had herself served up naked on a huge silver platter in the room known as the Grand Seize at the Café Anglais, where she is also said to have exposed her breasts at a women's dinner party – which suggests that she enjoyed display for the sake of it, and not just to attract a potential client. Another courtesan, Marie Colombier, refers to this event, and to Cora's inventive use of make-up, in her memoirs:

> At a dinner party of women, in the Grand Seize of the Café Anglais, it was only possible to find one criticism which could be made of these goddess-like breasts: it was claimed that she must have put make-up on them, because the pale pink which coloured her nipples looked as though it had been stolen from wild rose petals.[18]

Cora's aptitude as a horsewoman was another important aspect of her self-display; horse-riding had long been considered a particular strength (or foible) of the English, though the women of Paris had been becoming increasingly fond of it since the early 1830s. It is not without a touch of professional jealousy that Marie Colombier alludes to Cora's talents in this direction, and to the supposed effect such a sport had on her physique:

> Cora Pearl personified what can be termed the English style of courtesan. She was above all a sportswoman, riding a horse like a jockey, wielding her crop with a swagger; she had bandy legs, which gave her, when she walked, the rolling gait of a stable lad; and, to complete the resemblance, she drank a lot and often; but her bust was beyond reproach, her bosom marvellous and worthy of being moulded by some illustrious artist of antiquity.[19]

Cora was renowned not only for riding on horseback but also for running a splendid carriage, and she was determined to outclass any rivals in the drives or rides around the Bois. Her competitors in the aristocratic world included the *équipages* of Princess Metternich (an imitation of whose famous bright yellow livery was worn by Cora's jockeys, while her *calèche* was upholstered in sky-blue), Madame Musard (an American), the Countess de Pourtalès, the Marchioness de Gallifet (the wife of one of Cora's conquests), Madame de Contades and the Duchess de Persigny, while in the *demi-monde* her chief rivals included Blanche d'Antigny (who had at one time been a rider in the circus), Giulia Barucci (reputed never to have refused herself to a member of a fashionable club) and La Païva, who was herself an able horsewoman. Nestor Roqueplan wrote admiringly of both Cora's horsemanship and her management skills in this area. He is influenced by ideas about racial stereotypes, ascribing the small stature and gravity of her grooms to their Englishness:

All Paris knew Cora Pearl. She was a centauress; she created the amazon.

She was the first to appear in our elegant promenades on a real horse which she rode with unequalled distinction and skill, or in carriages which the most refined people considered models in terms of their design and colour, just as they admired her so well-matching pair, the style and standard of her harness, her livery and her servants, whose smallness and good manners contrasted with their gravity.

No one who knew about horses could ever have confused Cora Pearl with the awkward centauresses who sometimes tried to compete with her. Clumsy efforts, soon abandoned! Poor stables, bad drivers; cardboard horses, arrangements just for show; incomplete and fleeting chic.

Cora Pearl's stables generally consisted of a dozen horses groomed and looked after by English servants, who do not laugh, a favour never obtained by the spendthrift and disorganised tarts who aspire to be amazons, who pay their people badly and let them play cards in their apartment.

For Cora Pearl, the horse is not only a luxury, it is an art; it is not only an art, it is an enterprise. A visit to her stables makes one realise how ridiculous sums can be spent in all seriousness under this one item of a fantastic budget. It is a form of rational insanity.[20]

Between 1863 and 1868 Cora bought more than sixty horses; in the space of three years she spent ninety thousand francs with one horse-dealer alone. This scale of expenditure was all part of the show.

Though Julian Osgood Field's *Uncensored Recollections* could equally be called 'Unreliable Recollections' and contain more than an element of anti-semitism, they do capture something of Cora's spirit, the liveliness of her presence and her delight in display (as well as presenting an amusing picture of the dumbstruck reactions of a couple of adolescent English public schoolboys when confronted with her):

I knew Cora Pearl very well, although, of course, not in her zenith . . . She was an amiable, but very stupid woman, and very fond of playing coarse, silly monkey tricks. I remember lunching at her house once in the Rue des Bassins when she put her hand into a dish of cutlets or something and put a large dripping piece of whatever it was on the head of Ferdinand Bischoffscheim. He took it very meekly and smiled a weak semitic smile through the veil of thick sauce that covered his face. But the Duke of Hamilton, who was there, seeing her put her hand into the dish again, cried: 'Damn you, Cora, if you put that on my head, I'll strangle you.' Cora shrieked with laughter – that was her idea of fun. Speaking of her and the Duke of Hamilton (who, although almost old enough to be my father, was my bosom chum), I saw a very funny thing years before that at Baden Baden. Cora was gracefully sailing into the Kursaal, all dressed in white satin and white lace, covered with diamonds and pearls, on the arm of Salamanca, the Jew banker of Madrid . . . when they were very politely and firmly stopped by an official with a big gold chain round his neck, and Cora was told her presence would cause a scandal and she must retire. I, with two other English boys from my school, was standing by, and I remember remarking that the train of Cora's dress was so extravagantly long that it had not yet entirely got into the room when she was forced so to speak to double back and retire. We callow chickos, of course, thought all was now over, and the eclipse final. But not a bit of it; lo and behold! within half-an-hour Cora and her red hair and white jewels and her interminable white dress, again appeared in the doorway triumphant, for this time being on the arm of the Duke of Hamilton (whose hair, by the way, almost matched hers in colour), whose mother was a Princess of Baden, her progress was unimpeded; in fact, all the Casino officials bowed to the ground as she advanced. I very distinctly remember how I (little beast) swelled with pride as I went forward and was warmly greeted by the duke and Cora, and how I was envied by my companions. Cora delighted – positively revelled in the most wild and reckless extravagance, and no doubt she was quite right, for in her special profession it is more than half the battle to keep in the limelight and have all the drums incessantly beating. Prince Napoleon sent her once a huge vanload of the most expensive orchids. She gave a supper party, strewed the orchids over the floor and dressed as a sailor, danced the hornpipe, followed by the Can-can over them.[21]

Cora's extraordinary reputation was summed up by Zed in his book about the *demi-mondaines* of the Second Empire. Some of what he says is hearsay, or memory mixed with a good dose of invention and exaggerated by repetition – if the infamous book in which she was supposed to have recorded the performance of her clients ever existed, for instance, it has never been discovered. But his sense of bewilderment – precisely what was it about this woman which ensnared so many rich and powerful men? – was shared by many, particularly among the French, whose bewilderment included the fact that Cora was an Englishwoman and hence, almost by definition to a fashionable Parisian, deficient in matters of style and taste:

I humbly admit that hers was a success I never understood, that it must be noted, as it did exist, but there is no justification for it. To me, she represents a stain on what was, taken all in all, a scintillating group, refined and aristocratic, of the gallant women of her epoque and from whom she differed absolutely in every respect. She was a personality apart, a specimen of another race, a bizarre and astonishing phenomenon. And perhaps this is what explains her notoriety and was the cause of her prestige.

English by birth, character and appearance, she had the head of a City worker, neither good nor bad, fiery blonde, almost red, hair, a vulgar and unbearable accent, a raucous voice, exceedingly common manners and the tone of a stable boy.

But she rode extremely well and her admirers assured us that she was perfectly shaped, that her body was a marvel. I acknowledge that there was some truth in this opinion, for I was allowed to see her, as were my comrades, in the costume of Eve before the fall, a costume of which she was particularly fond and which was often her version of a dressing gown in which to receive visitors.

Cora led her lovers by the nose and was not at all hesitant to address the most violent and offensive words to them in public. She spared them in nothing and for nothing and made their lives very hard . . . None of which prevented her from dragging behind her chariot princes of the blood, one of whom – a future king, if you please – made her a present of a pearl necklace of phenomenal value, as well as noblemen of the highest rank, very popular young men, and very estimable men of all sorts. What hidden lure, what secret potion did she have that she was able to live it up, for twenty years, to the tune of fifty thousand francs a month, to have jewels, outfits and carriages like no other, to stun and astound Paris?

She swallowed up money and, moreover, like the far-sighted daughter of Albion that she was, she was systematic, very systematic. One day we discovered at her house an amazing register, divided into three columns. In one column were

inscribed the names of her clients, most of whom were our
friends or known to us; in the second, alongside each name, the
date of their visit; in the third . . . the price the pilgrim had paid
for the hospitality received . . .

· There was even, God forgive me, a comment column in the
fatal register. Not too pleasant for some, the comments![22]

Cora's most blatant moment of self-display, of literally putting on a
show, came on 26 January 1867 when she made her début as Cupid in
Offenbach's operetta *Orphée aux enfers* at the Théâtre des Bouffes
Parisiens. According to her own account she was approached by the
producer and asked if she could sing, as he was lacking someone to
play Cupid and time was getting short. She claimed to know the part
off by heart, though admitted to having had no formal singing lessons.
These were arranged for her, and she was coached for the part by
'Collinvert, the teacher and husband of the great singer Urbine' who,
as Cora puts it, 'drummed my role into me at speed, singing with me,
miming with me, helping me with the pauses, and finally initiating
me into all the little tricks which served me so well during the
flaunting of my perhaps rather unorthodox Cupid'.[23] This was no
mean undertaking, for though the part of Cupid is short, it is virtuosic
and most untrained singers would have had no hope at all of
mastering it. Cora had inherited some musical ability from her
parents, she had a quick wit which would undoubtedly have helped,
she had a sense of adventure which made the opportunity hard to
refuse, and she knew that her appearance could probably carry the
day even if her singing and acting skills lacked finesse. The men in the
audience on the first night included a selection of Cora's past and
present lovers: Prince Napoleon was there, as were the Princes
Achille Murat, Narischkin and Troubetskoy, Khalil Bey, the Duke
de Rivoli, Mustapha Pasha and the Prince de Sagan. The *demi-monde*
was also there in force. Cora had considered that a normal dressing
room was insufficient for her needs, and Prince Napoleon had had an
adjoining apartment adapted for her use. Access from it to the theatre
was via a door inserted for the occasion, and the exit was by way of a

private staircase. This also made the apartment a very convenient trysting place for the Prince during the weeks devoted to rehearsal and performance.

As the curtain went up for the second act there was Cora, asleep on Mount Olympus. The critics are united that, as an actress and singer, she was not a resounding success. But they were all struck, as she (and the producer) had known they would be, by what she was wearing: very little, apart from a mass of jewels. Philibert Audebrand recalls: 'Cora Pearl appeared on the stage half-naked, singing quite brightly with a funny little Anglo-Saxon accent the couplets which begin: *I am Love*. That evening the Jockey Club filled the house in force. All the armigerous names to be found in the Golden Book of the French nobility were there, in white gloves and holding ivory lorgnettes . . . It was a success of sorts.'[24] Marie Colombier fulminated about 'those circumflex legs' and laughed at Cora's pronunciation: '*Je souis Kioupidone*',[25] while Paul Foucher wrote of the 'profound mockery' contained in the enthusiasm of the audience and complained about Cora's 'hip-swaying sincerity'.[26] The *Illustrated London News* managed a more measured response:

> Mdlle. Cora Pearl, the dashing *Amazone* of the Bois de Bou-logne, made her début the other evening at the Bouffes Parisiennes, in the part of Cupid in 'Orphée aux Enfers'. She was one blaze of diamonds – diamonds in her hair, round her neck, on her tiny cloak, round her arms, round her waist, and round her ankles. She displayed great nervousness, and sang much of her part with her eyes closed. The reception she met with, however, was most enthusiastic.[27]

Foucher too noted that Cora kept her eyes closed for much of her performance – either she was indeed nervous or this was her interpretation of Cupid's blindness. One of the other singers taking part in this performance was Madame Ugalde, who twenty years previously had performed at a charity concert with the other Madame Sabatier. Her professionalism, her 'voice changed by the rigours of a hectic career, but in accents inspired by genius',[28] could not help but emphasise the amateur nature of Cora's efforts. Nevertheless Cora made her exit in style, kicking up her heels to display her diamond-studded soles (and much besides). Captain the Hon. D. Bingham spoke for many of the men present when he wrote: 'I remember little of the performance, except that Cupid played with great self-possession, that she was not much encumbered with garments, and that the buttons of her boots were large diamonds of the purest water.'[29]

Cora managed a dozen performances before a group of students decided to disrupt the event in protest at the role being given to a foreign courtesan with no professional acting or singing experience; their hissing and whistling became too loud for her to continue. Cora's own comment on her theatrical adventure is succinct:

> I played twelve times in a row. My band of friends brought the house down. At the end I was hissed. I left the boards without regret, and with no desire to tread them again.
>   Such is glory.[30]

Later that year Paris put on its own show: the Universal Exposition of 1867 was opened on 1 April by the Emperor's small son, the Prince Imperial, who was then eleven years old. After weeks of rain, the day was crisp and clear. Planning had begun four years earlier, again under the aegis of Prince Napoleon, and the aim was to demonstrate to the world (in the wake of the London Exhibition of 1862) that the quality of French industry was in no way inferior to that of Great Britain and that Paris could justly be viewed as a universal model.

The Exposition occupied the entire site of the Champ de Mars on the left bank of the Seine, opposite the Butte de Chaillot which was levelled in preparation. The main exhibition building, of whom the chief engineers were Gustave Eiffel and Jean Krantz, covered almost forty acres; it was a vast structure of oval design, with concentric rings of galleries surrounding a central garden. Hydraulic lifts carried visitors from the ground floor to the roof, where there were walk-

Apollonie Sabatier. This engraving by Mathey is based on an
1854 oil painting by Apollonie's friend and mentor Ernest Meissonier.

Portrait of Apollonie Sabatier by Gustave Ricard: *La Dame au petit chien* ('The Lady with the Little Dog'). This was one of Apollonie's favourite portraits of herself, and it helped establish Ricard's reputation when it was exhibited at the Paris Salon of 1850.

Photograph of the prolific journalist, critic and poet Théophile Gautier by Nadar. Gautier, known as Théo to his friends, was an indispensable member of the entourages of both La Païva and La Présidente, and the most accomplished practictioner of the 'dirty talk' for which Apollonie's soirées were famed.

Photo RMN: P. Schmidt

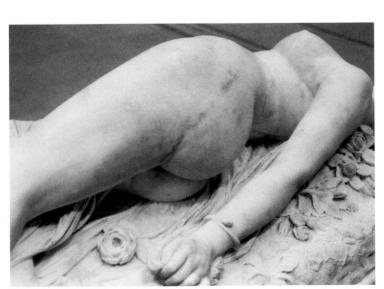

Photo: Martin Dudley

La Femme piquée par un serpent (The Woman Bitten by a Snake) by Auguste Clésinger, exhibited at the Paris Salon of 1847, and for which Apollonie was the model. The realism of this scuplted woman, clearly in the throes of orgasm, provoked a scandal and had a lasting effect on the way men related to Apollonie.

Blanche de Païva consistently refused to have her portrait painted, and this engraving (above left) is one of the very few, possibly the only, extant image of her face. Aware that she was not a conventional beauty, Blanche preferred to exhibit her power and wealth through the opulence and magnificence of the mansion she had built for herself, the Hôtel Païva. Prouder of her body than she was of her face, she did nothing to counteract the rumours that she was herself the model for some of the figures on display in the Hôtel, such as this one (above right) on one of the mantelpieces.

La Païva's bath (left) and the onyx staircase (right) at the Hôtel Païva.

The ceiling of the salon of the Hôtel Païva, painted by Paul Baudry, was considered
by the Goncourt brothers to be the only work of real artistic merit in the Hôtel.
The model for the figure of 'Night' was reputed to be La Païva herself.

Above: An engraving after Henri Grevedon of the celebrated
pianist Henri Herz. As Herz's 'wife', the future Blanche de Païva
became a well-known figure in Parisian artistic circles and
succeeded in depleting Herz's wealth until she was thrown out
of the house by his brother.

Right: Caricature of Count Guido Henckel von Donnersmarck by
Sem. Henckel von Donnersmarck, La Païva's third husband and
an assured source of wealth for her, was viewed by many Parisians
as the archetypal dour and bearded Prussian – particularly
in the aftermath of the Franco-Prussian War.

Cora Pearl, 'the English
Beauty of the French Empire',
adorned with her favourite
bracelet which was attached
by a chain to her finger. She
was particularly proud of her
beautiful hands.

Cora wearing a crinoline, that most voluminous and ostentatious of Second Empire fashions.
Though it could look elegant in a pose such as Cora's, it presented problems
in the fields of locomotion, seating capacity and fire prevention.

An image of Cora Pearl that belies the description given of her by 'Zed':
'English by birth, character and appearance, she had the head of a City worker,
neither good nor bad, fiery blonde, almost red, hair, a vulgar and unbearable accent,
a raucous voice, exceedingly common manners and the tone of a stable boy.'

ways offering splendid views. The oval galleries represented themes, while the transverse avenues divided the building into national sections.

The central theme was 'The history of labour and its fruits'; the Exposition was also intended to symbolise the prosperity and material achievements of the Second Empire, to show off the new Paris and to state the case for economic liberalism. The arts as well as industry were represented, the fine art exhibits including paintings and sculptures from fifteen countries, executed between 1855 and 1867 and representing the largest collection of contemporary art ever assembled. Unfortunately, the process of selection ensured the imposition of official taste and avant garde painters, including Camille Pissarro and Paul Cézanne, were therefore rejected. Edouard Manet's submissions were not even sent on to the jury; he responded by organising his own exhibition, as did Gustave Courbet, just outside the Exposition grounds.

This was the first Exposition both to have national pavilions and to offer a carnival atmosphere. Every French wine district had its own exhibits and cellar, while cafés and restaurants offering a variety of international cuisines encircled the main building and opened on to the outer gardens. The French pavilion, a miniature palace, was used as a lounge for the imperial family and their guests, who included the brother of the Emperor of Japan, the Kings of Belgium, Greece, Portugal and Sweden, Tsar Alexander II of Russia (the target of an assassination attempt at Longchamp on 6 June), King William I of Prussia, the Khedive of Egypt, the Sultan of Turkey, the Queen of Württemberg and the Emperor of Austria. Prince Napoleon also made use of a room for himself, as alluded to by Cora Pearl:

When we wanted to meet at the Universal Exhibition, we always went there separately. The Duke had there a room fitted in the Turkish fashion, where I found him every day at the same hour. He often brought papers there so as to waste as little of his working time as possible. He examined with extreme pleasure the smallest details relating to foreign manufactures, particularly machines which had to do with new applications of electricity.

Many times I have seen him draw portions of machinery, and note upon his drawings any novel points, concerning which he would afterwards have prolonged interviews with the exhibitors. The subject of aërial navigation interested him equally. He had a large collection of engravings representing balloons of all kinds.[31]

At the heart of the Exposition was the machinery gallery, which included a display of Prussian military might which the French would have done well to take note of – a gigantic fifty-ton Krupp cannon made of steel which could fire shells weighing a thousand pounds.

By May the Exposition was in full swing and people began to flock to Paris from all over Europe. Maxime Du Camp, writing from a rather jaundiced post-Empire perspective, noted that Paris was also subject to a vast influx of prostitutes at this time, that the Exposition 'drew from the four corners of the world all the fallen women, or those who wanted nothing more than to fall'.[32] He even appears to suggest that the authorities deliberately brought in such women, to encourage the visitors to have a good time and lavish their money on the entertainments of all varieties which Paris had to offer. There were more and more shops to enjoy, new department stores opening in the second half of the 1860s including the Printemps near the Gare Saint-Lazare, La Samaritaine between the Pont Neuf and the rue de Rivoli, and the Grand Bazar de l'Hôtel de Ville. In 1863 Aristide Boucicaut had bought his partner's interest in the Bon Marché and four years later issued the first French mail order catalogue for the benefit of provincial customers. Then in September 1869 the foundation stone of a new and magnificent building for the Bon Marché was laid; the architects were L.A. Boileau and Gustave Eiffel, both pioneers in the use of iron and glass in functional architecture. The fashionable restaurants were also continuing to flourish: the owner of the Café Anglais, for instance, was able to afford the life of a country gentleman and to pay his celebrated chef, Adolphe Dugléré (whom Rossini named 'the Mozart of French cooking'), twenty-five thousand francs a year.

The great ceremony for the distribution of prizes by the Emperor was held on 1 July in the Palais de l'Industrie before twenty thousand invited guests. The Exposition was closed after seven months on 3 November; more than eleven million visits had been recorded. The buildings were immediately demolished and the Champ de Mars returned to its former state.

The aim of Parisians and visitors alike was summed up by the courtesan Marguerite Bellanger in her *Confessions*: 'To have fun, fun and more fun was everyone's preoccupation.'[33] There is a sense of glitter – of *poudre d'or* – about Second Empire Paris at its zenith, accompanied by an underlying disquiet that all that glitters may not really be gold. 'Celebrities sprang up like mushrooms and shrivelled even before the sun went down. One lived fast, feverishly. What did tomorrow matter so long as today was exhilarating?'[34] As the English governess Anna Bicknell put it: 'Paris was a sort of fairyland, where every one lived only for amusement, and where every one seemed rich and happy. What lay underneath all this, would not bear close examination – the dishonorable acts of all kinds, which too often were needed to produce the glamour deceiving superficial observers.'[35] Not all non-Parisians were so judgmental; Dr Thomas W. Evans, for example, Napoleon III's American dentist and a man highly valued in court circles throughout Europe for his anaesthetic skills, clearly liked what he saw and enjoyed the emphasis on the outward show:

It was a society full of movement and originality, of unconventionality, and gaiety, and charm. The admirable taste, the artistic sentiment and distinction shown by those who best represented it, especially in everything relating to manners, and dress, and the outward appearance of the person, found expression in a word which was then frequently used to symbolise the sum of all these mundane elegancies. The women of those days were not more beautiful than are the women of the Republic; but the women of the Empire had *chic*.[36]

Arsène Houssaye wrote of the self-confidence of the best years of the Empire: 'no black specks on the horizon; the peacefulness of luxury and of money: one lived just for the sake of living – from day to day. One spoke in the Chamber merely to demonstrate one's eloquence. We were afraid of nothing, we thought we dominated the world, never had Paris been so widely acknowledged as the universal capital.'[37] Count Horace de Viel Castel, however, could be predicted to see the dark side and to see it before most other people; his final diary entry, dated 27 August 1864, three months before his death, was doom-laden: 'We are in decline, and what was young in the Emperor's entourage is growing old, and what was not yet corrupted four years ago is now corrupted absolutely.'[38]

The Second Empire saw the beginning not only of modern French industry, finance and social reform, but also of modern poetry, painting and fiction. Official recognition of some of these developments had to wait for a later period, however; Maxime Du Camp noted in his *Souvenirs d'un demi-siècle* that this was a time when literature and art were scorned, when only what was practically and immediately useful was valued, that taste was debased and fashions ridiculous.[39] Light opera drew the crowds more than any other form of entertainment and Offenbach triumphed with a string of operettas, most notably *Orphée aux enfers* at the Bouffes in October 1858, *La Belle Hélène* at the Variétés in December 1864, and *La Vie parisienne* at the Théâtre du Palais Royal in October 1866. This last work particularly captured the spirit of Paris during the heady days leading up to the Exposition of 1867, the chorus expressing the delight with which visitors flocked to the city to experience all the pleasures it had to offer:

> We come running, we hurry
> To know, oh Paris,
> To know the intoxication
> Of your days and of your nights.
> All the enraptured foreigners
> Rush towards you, oh Paris![40]

During the Exposition itself another Offenbach operetta, *La Grande Duchesse de Gérolstein*, was playing at the Variétés, and visitors from all parts of Europe were amused by this satire about an absurd German principality.

And more than the art and literature, the plays, operas and fireworks, more even than the monumental building works and the Expositions, it was the women, and particularly the women of the *demi-monde*, who were the main source of fascination for visitors to the city, and who gave Second Empire Paris its lasting reputation:

> As I have already observed, the things as well as the people of the Second Empire provoke an extreme curiosity in the public, and the political or historical facts which marked this epoch are by no means the only reason for this curiosity. It is aroused quite as much, if not above all, by the gossip of the period, and one can hardly mention the reign of Napoleon III without mouths puckering in malicious smiles and eyes winking mischievously. By gossip, one means primarily, in effect, the question of love – which was, it must be admitted, under the Second Empire, one of the most important questions on the agenda, not only of the Tuileries, but also of the salons and the elegant boudoirs.[41]

The final great official spectacle of the Second Empire was the opening of the Suez Canal on 16 November 1869, the celebration of one of the greatest engineering achievements of the nineteenth century. Constructed over the course of ten years, the Canal provided the first direct maritime route between the Mediterranean and the Red Sea and was largely the result of the combined efforts of Ferdinand de Lesseps and Napoleon III. It was opened by the Empress Eugénie and de Lesseps on board *L'Aigle*, leading a flotilla of sixty-seven ships carrying representatives of the European powers on a voyage from Port Said to Suez. Amidst the celebrations, both here and back in Paris where Verdi's *Le Bal masqué* was opening at the Théâtre Lyrique, there was no presentiment of how near the end was:

Ask all these society women whom they envy. There will be only one reply: Cora Pearl. In frivolous society, which is not – let this be understood – synonymous with French society, but which cuts across it like a cotillion, with its flashiness and smiles, the women's coquetry, the men's intoxication, they are all so blind that no one sees silhouetted on the walls of the room the shadow of Bismarck . . .[42]

1 *Illustrated London News*, No. 575 Vol.XXI, Supplement, Saturday, 21 August 1852

2 Maxime Du Camp, *Paris: ses organes, ses functions et sa vie jusqu 'en 1870*, p.680

3 *Illustrated London News*, No.1014 Vol.XXXVI, Saturday, 28 January 1860

4 La Chroniqueuse, *Photographs of Paris Life*, p.189

5 Ibid., p.156

6 Théophile Gautier, *Correspondance générale*, Vol.6, 1991, p.247

7 Ibid., p.252

8 Jean Philippe Worth, *A Century of Fashion*, tr. Ruth Scott Miller, Little, Brown & Co., Boston, 1928, p.103

9 Gustave Claudin, *Mes Souvenirs*, p.248

10 Théodore de Banville, *La Lanterne magique*, p.272

11 Mrs Burton Harrison, *Recollections Grave and Gay* (electronic edition), Charles Scribner's Sons, New York, 1911, p.253

12 Jean Philippe Worth, *A Century of Fashion*, p.110

13 Alexandre Dumas *fils*, *Théâtre complet*, Vol.1, pp.23–4

14 Zed, *Le Demi-monde sous le Second Empire*, p.30

15 Auguste Escoffier, *Memories of My Life*, tr. Laurence Escoffier, Van Nostrand Reinhold, New York, 1997, p.13

16 Ibid., p.14

17 See, e.g., Claude Blanchard, *Dames de cœur*, Editions du Pré aux Clercs, Paris, 1946, p.26

18 Marie Colombier, *Mémoires. Fin d'Empire*, Flammarion, Paris, 1898, p.306

19 Ibid.

20 Nestor Roqueplan, *Parisine*, pp.60–1

21 Julian Osgood Field, *Uncensored Recollections*, Eveleigh Nash & Grayson, London, 1924, pp.55–8

22 Zed, *Le Demi-monde sous le Second Empire*, pp.52–5

23 Emma Elizabeth Crouch, *Mémoires de Cora Pearl*, pp.294–5

24 Philibert Audebrand, *Petits Mémoires d'une stalle d'orchestre*, Jules Lévy, Paris, 1885, p.222

25 Marie Colombier, *Mémoires*, p.307

26 Paul Foucher, *Entre Cour et jardin. Etudes et souvenirs du théâtre*, Amyot, Paris, 1867, pp.432–3

27 *Illustrated London News*, No.1411 Vol.L, Saturday, 2 February 1867, p.102

28 Paul Foucher, *Entre cour et jardin*, p.433

29 Captain The Hon. D. Bingham, *Recollections of Paris*, Vol.1, Chapman & Hall, London, 1896, p.61

30 Emma Elizabeth Crouch, *Mémoires de Cora Pearl*, p.295

31 Emma Elizabeth Crouch, *The Memoirs of Cora Pearl*, p.75

32 Maxime Du Camp, *Paris: ses organes, ses fonctions et sa vie jusqu 'en 1870*, p.351

33 Marguérite Bellanger, *Confessions*, Librairie Populaire, Paris, 1882, p.11

34 C. Simond (ed.), *Paris de 1800 à 1900, Vol.II, 1830–1870*, Librairie Plon, Paris, 1900, p.431

35 Anna Bicknell, *Life in the Tuileries under the Second Empire*, p.118

36 E.A. Crane (ed.), *The Memoirs of Dr Thomas W. Evans. Recollections of the Second French Empire*, Vol.1, T. Fisher Unwin, London, 1905, p.139

37 Arsène Houssaye, *Les Confessions. Souvenirs d'un demi-siècle 1830–1880*, Vol.1, 1885, p.6

38 Comte Horace de Viel Castel, *Mémoires sur le règne de Napoléon III (1851–1864)*, Vol.6, 1884, p.331

39 Maxime Du Camp, *Souvenirs d'un demi-siècle*, p.136

40 Meilhac and Halévy, *Théâtre*, Vol.4, Calmann Lévy, Paris, c.1904, p.385

41 Pierre de Lano, *L'Amour à Paris sous le Second Empire*, p.3

42 C. Simond (ed.), *Paris de 1800 à 1900, Vol.II, 1830–1870*, p.432

CHAPTER TWELVE

The Collapse of Empire

O N NEW YEAR'S DAY 1870, all the usual festivities took place at the court of the Tuileries. At eleven o'clock in the morning the imperial family luncheon was attended by Prince Napoleon and Princess Clotilde, Prince and Princess Murat, Princess Mathilde and other relatives. The guests also included the Emperor's old friend and physician Dr Conneau (who had helped him escape from the fortress of Ham in 1846), members of the palace staff such as the Chamberlain, the Master of Ceremonies and the Prince Imperial's tutor, General Bourbaki of the Maison Militaire and Marshal MacMahon. During the course of the day a number of visitors came to pay their respects, including Baron Haussmann, the Count de Nieuwerkerke and the President of the Corps Législatif, Monsieur Schneider. The favourite ladies of the court were also very much in evidence, including the Princess Metternich and the Marchioness de Gallifet. The *Illustrated London News'* report of the day read as follows:

> Shortly after the conclusion of mass in the chapel of the Tuileries the Emperor, proceeding to the throne-room, received the congratulations of the Corps Diplomatique, to whose address he replied in the ordinary conventional terms, professing to see in it 'a new proof of the good relations existing between France and foreign Powers,' and expressing a hope that the new year would tend to increase concord and the advancement of civilisation.[1]

The immediate event which triggered the Franco-Prussian War later that same year is known to posterity as the Hohenzollern candidacy. Prince Leopold of Hohenzollern-Sigmaringen, the nephew of the Prussian King William and a brother of King Ferdinand of Romania, agreed in the spring of 1870 to a request by the Spanish government to pose his candidacy for the Spanish throne, vacant since the overthrow of Queen Isabella in September 1868. Although Prince Leopold was initially reluctant to become a candidate and the Prussian king viewed the Hohenzollern candidacy with misgivings, his Chancellor, Otto von Bismarck, was taking an active interest in the matter – hoping, in fact, to provoke a war with France as part of his plan to bring about a unified German empire by rallying the south German states to Prussia's cause against the French. The intention was for the Cortes, Spain's lower house of legislature, to hold a secret election to ratify the candidacy, but there were delays, and in the process France got wind of what was going on. (It so happened that at the time of the Hohenzollern candidacy the French Foreign Minister was Agénor, Duke de Gramont – formerly Duke de Guiche – the erstwhile lover of Marie Duplessis and probably of Blanche de Païva, and once characterised by Bismarck as the 'stupidest man in Europe'.)

On 6 July the French Foreign Minister declared to the Corps Législatif that France would not tolerate a Prussian prince on the Spanish throne, and France's minister in Berlin, Count Vincent Benedetti, was instructed by Agénor de Gramont to go to Bad Ems to try to persuade King William to advise Leopold to withdraw his candidacy. The King, however, was reluctant to take the initiative in a matter that constituted a personal decision by Leopold and supposedly did not concern the Prussian government. In the event it was the Prince's father who decided to withdraw the candidacy. The French were further incensed, however, when King William refused to give a guarantee that he would not authorise such a candidacy in the future.

Bismarck then stepped into the picture, by editing King William's account to him of the discussions at Bad Ems (known to history as the Ems telegram) and publishing it on the evening of 13 July in a way calculated to ignite both French and German chauvinism and to precipitate a war he was confident of winning. France fell into the trap and on 19 July declared war on Prussia. The French Minister of War, Marshal Edmond Lebœuf, exuded confidence, and both French hopes and the calculations of Europe's military experts held that the Napoleonic professionalism of the French army would prove irresistible, this despite the facts that the French standing army had remained at its pre-1866 strength of under four hundred thousand men and that France continued to lack an effective system of mobilisation and trained reserves.

On 21 July the Corps Législatif adjourned, on the 23 July the Empress was appointed Regent, and on the 28th July the Emperor, in great pain from a gallstone which had been plaguing him for years (he often used to wear make-up on public occasions, to disguise how ill he felt), left for the front from his private railway station at Saint-Cloud and the next day assumed control of the French forces at the garrison town of Metz. The French mobilisation was chaotic: complacency led them to make far less effective use than the Germans of such relatively new technical developments as the railway and the telegraph system. (Though there may have been disarray in matters of strategic military importance, other priorities were not overlooked. On 25 July Escoffier, the chef at the Petit Moulin Rouge, accompanied by his assistant Bouniol, was drafted to Metz to serve as *chef de cuisine* to the second section of the General Staff.)

Unrealistic French joy and over-confidence at going to war soon vanished, although censorship prevented the French people knowing the true course of events until early September. On 4 August the Germans had crossed the border into Alsace. They defeated the French at Wissembourg, pushing back the troops under Marshal MacMahon's command to Châlons-en-Champagne and forcing a wedge between these troops and those of General Bazaine, centred on Metz. The Germans then began to advance towards Paris, while the attempt by Napoleon III and MacMahon to rescue Bazaine led to an encounter between the French and the Germans at Sedan.

The battle of Sedan began on 30 August. On the afternoon of 1

September, recognising the impossibility either of defending the besieged city or of escaping from it with his army, Napoleon III ordered the raising of the white flag – a task undertaken by a former lover of Cora Pearl, Prince Achille Murat. On the following day the Emperor met with the Prussian King and his chief minister, Bismarck, to sign the instrument of surrender.

First word of the disaster reached Paris by telegraph at about six o'clock on the evening of 2 September, and was conveyed to the Empress. The Corps Législatif met on the following afternoon, the Chief Minister admitting the defeat but concealing its full extent. Shortly after they had adjourned a telegram was received from Napoleon III, confirming the events at Sedan. The Council of Ministers was unable to agree on a course of action, beyond informing Paris of the situation and calling the Corps Législatif to convene at noon on 4 September.

Crowds were now gathering in various parts of the city, and the collapse of Empire followed swiftly. A mob had invaded the Palais Bourbon, preventing the Corps Législatif from resuming its sitting. Léon Gambetta and Jules Favre, republican lawyers and statesmen who had long been known for their opposition to the imperial regime, then led most of the mob and part of the Corps Législatif across Paris to the Hôtel de Ville, where at about four o'clock in the afternoon a republic was proclaimed. Meanwhile the Senate had been meeting under the presidency of Eugène Rouher and had voted unanimous support for the Bonaparte dynasty. During the course of the afternoon a huge crowd assembled around the Tuileries palace. Inside, the Empress Eugénie was being advised to leave by her friends the Austrian and Italian ambassadors, and by the Prefect of Police. Accompanied by a maidservant, she succeeded in slipping away from the palace unobserved and took refuge in the home of the imperial family's dentist, Dr Thomas W. Evans, where she spent the night. On 5 September, while Eugénie quietly left Paris in Evans' carriage and Napoleon III arrived at Wilhelmshöhe to begin his captivity, the Corps Législatif was dissolved and the Senate abolished.

Blanche de Païva had left for Silesia some weeks previously. Her position was not an easy one, for the man with whom she shared her life was not only a prominent Prussian industrialist but had close links with Bismarck's administration. Despite rumours of impending war, life had continued as usual in Paris until the summer of 1870: La Païva was still giving her usual Sunday dinner parties for twenty guests at the end of June. Then in early July Guido Henckel von Donnersmarck, who was well apprised of the situation between France and Prussia, impressed the urgency of departure on his mistress. Blanche did not wish to leave Paris but bowed to Guido's insistence. Accompanied by him, she travelled by train to Silesia and arrived at the old castle of Neudeck, where she had never enjoyed staying.

Blanche had visited Guido's property in Silesia several times during the course of her relationship with him. On the first occasion that he had taken her to Tarnowitz she had immediately appreciated the importance of this enormous property and of its industrial and mining concerns, and had understood the actual and potential power of her lover. She had been less impressed, however, by its lack of material comforts and by heavily Germanic interior decoration. Before long she had persuaded Guido to have the whole place rebuilt, and this time she chose as her architect a man with close imperial connections – Lefuel, who had worked on the completion of the Louvre for Napoleon III. Furthermore, she insisted that the plans be closely based on those of the Tuileries. As with the Hôtel Païva, she wanted the edifice to reflect her self-image, to speak loud and clear of the importance she attached to herself and to demonstrate her power to have whatever she chose. Work began on the building of the new castle in 1870 and was not completed until 1874.

Having safely deposited Blanche at Neudeck, Donnersmarck set off for Berlin whither he had been summoned by Bismarck. (He did not expect hostilities to last long, having laid a wager with Emile de Girardin that the victorious Prussians would be marching past Girardin's mansion near the Arc de Triomphe a month after the declaration of war.) He enlisted with the army, and proceeded to play a prominent role on the Prussian side throughout the war, being appointed temporary Prefect of Lorraine on 23 August.

During the war Blanche did not forget her tenants at Pontchar-train, arranging for the provision of a monthly pension and foodstuffs for all the women whose husbands had been conscripted to fight for the French. After the war and during the period of Prussian occupa-tion, Guido invited General von Thann to establish his residence there. Blanche persuaded Guido to ensure that the local villagers were exempted from paying war taxes; on her eventual return the response towards her was far more positive than it had been previously.

Cora Pearl kept herself busy during the war in her usual fashion, enjoying a liaison with Baron Abel Rogniat. After her extravagance had succeeded in ruining him, he retired to Civitavecchia in Italy where he founded a soap factory. She also corresponded with Prince Napoleon, reproducing in her memoirs various letters which she claims to have received from him. In a letter of 15 September he seems to be expressing the hope that all is not yet over for France and the Empire:

Dear P.,

I have just received your letter of the 7th. I do not know how it came to me from Florence. I have arrived here with much difficulty, passing again through France. I have been with my family for some days. The disasters have been great, but they do not astonish me. I have no plans yet, and it will be impossible to make any for some days; it will be necessary to await the result of the Attack on Paris. For two days we have had no commu-nications. I do not even know whether this letter will reach you. My head is well, but I suffer much from my legs. What events during the last few weeks! Come what may, we must hope. I have known so many misfortunes of late that I have become very calm. Your letter gave me great pleasure, my poor P.

They have even detained my shirts at Paris, where everything has been sequestrated. That, however, does not affect me much.

I want you to go to England and live in some quiet nook for a few weeks, while the present storm blows over. We must have calm and patience, and wait. *It cannot be for long*. Write to me often, and give me your exact address.

I am very poor, very disgusted, but not cast down. I feel for the country much more than for myself. What does oneself matter after all – life is short; but we must struggle as much as possible. Let us hope always for better times. Write to me. I embrace you.[2]

The Prince's optimism was misplaced, though his resilient attitude served him well in the years of exile which followed. The siege of Paris by the Prussians began on 19 September. On that day Cora succeeded in getting eight of her horses out of Paris, pretending that they were being taken out for exercise. Later on she, like many other women of both the *haut* and the *demi-mondes*, played an active part in nursing the wounded, turning her *hôtel* in the rue de Chaillot into a field-hospital. (The Baroness de Ladoucette did the same thing with her house in the same street as Cora's, as did the Baroness de Rothschild in the rue Lafitte and the Duchess de Galliéna in the rue de Varennes.) Everything, Cora writes, was done at her expense. 'The doctor of the committee had only to give orders and his time. I even paid the funeral expenses. My fine linen sheets were turned into shrouds. Eight beds constantly occupied. Well dressed, more than decently fed, I do not think that my guests had any reason to complain of me. All this cost me twenty-five thousand francs.'[3]

Apollonie Sabatier's fortunes now took a distinct turn for the better, despite all the political and military turbulence going on around her: two days before the siege commenced, Richard Wallace arranged for her to receive an annual income of twenty-five thousand francs. On the death of the fourth Marquess of Hertford on 25 August he had inherited an immense fortune, along with the château of Bagatelle and the art collections housed in the *hôtel* at 29 boulevard des Italiens, and, despite the ending of their amorous relationship, Richard had not forgotten Apollonie. That she did not refuse this gift, as she had refused money from Alfred Mosselman after their break-up, suggests that either the years of relative poverty had weakened her resolve to fend for herself, or that there had been anger and resentment in her refusal of Alfred's offer which were absent from her relations with Richard.

It was prudent for Apollonie to accept the offer of a reliable income in 1870. She was by this time forty-eight years old, and knew that the likelihood of finding any other way to make sufficient money to live on comfortably was remote. (It would certainly have been unwise to hope for any financial assistance from her other lover of the 1860s, the eccentric Delaborde; he was currently giving a series of concerts in London, accompanied by a retinue of a hundred and twenty-one parrots and cockatoos.) Wallace's action was in keeping with his habitual generosity – during the siege he had also donated money for an ambulance service, opened a hospital in his own house, distributed food and firewood, and was the first to subscribe to a fund for the relief of families who had lost their houses through shelling. It also shows him as a man who believed in honouring his promises; according to Flaubert, he had promised Apollonie at the time of their affair that he would provide for her should he ever become rich. He must also have retained respect and affection for her, despite the breaking off of their liaison, and wanted her to be able to live the rest of her life in security and in the style she liked.

On 29 October Count Henckel von Donnersmarck was appointed Prefect of Metz. This was the same day on which Prussian troops entered the garrison town, which had been holding out under General Bazaine since the fall of Sedan. (After the fall of Metz, Marshal MacMahon was also taken prisoner and transferred to a villa in Wiesbaden; his staff officers were lodged nearby. Once again Escoffier was commandeered to cater for them.)

By the third month of the siege, near-starvation conditions were existing in Paris. According to Edmond de Goncourt, whose younger brother Jules had died of syphilis on 20 June, meat and even vegetables cost more than anyone could afford, and half a pound of horsemeat represented two people's rations for three days. The staples of cheese and potatoes were nowhere to be found, and most people subsisted on a diet of coffee, wine and bread.[4] At the end of December and beginning of January three elephants from the zoo were slaughtered for food. Charles Garnier's new opera house, still unfinished at the fall of the Empire, was being used as a munitions store. Throughout all the disturbances the theatres did not go dark, but opened or closed from day to day, depending on outside events. The cold was so intense in the dimly lit auditoria that actors and spectators could hardly see one another through the condensation of breath.

On 18 January 1871 William I, King of Prussia, was crowned Emperor of Germany in the Hall of Mirrors at Versailles. On the same day Edmond de Goncourt recorded in his diary:

> It is no longer a case of a stray shell now and then as it has been these last few days, but a deluge of cast iron gradually closing in on me and hemming me in. All around me there are explosions fifty yards away, twenty yards away, at the railway station, in the Rue Poussin, where a woman has just had a foot blown off, and next door, where a shell had already fallen the day before yesterday. And while, standing at the window, I try to make out the Meudon batteries with the aid of a telescope, a shell-splinter flies past me and sends mud splashing against my front door.[5]

The siege ended with an armistice and the capitulation of Paris on 28 January. On the following day Count Henckel von Donnersmarck travelled from Metz to Versailles to see Bismarck, who invited him to stay to lunch.

A note dated 3 February 1871 from Prince Napoleon tells Cora: 'The other day my poor servants and whippers-in from Meudon, where they had been taken prisoner, were sent back here to Mayence! It reminded me of our lovely hunts. I thought about you a lot.'[6] As for Cora herself, she professed to be annoyed that her efforts on behalf of the wounded during the siege had done nothing to rehabilitate her in the eyes of society or the authorities. The gulf between the world of respectability and the *demi-monde* could not be bridged by mere acts of charity on the part of the *demi-mondaines*, or by anything else. In Cora's indignant words, 'I did not even receive a diploma.'[7] She demanded an indemnity of fifteen hundred francs because of the trouble and expense she had gone to and, after appealing to the courts, was awarded it. In later life, she seemed to regret having let her pique at being treated differently from society ladies propel her into taking this action: 'Were it to be done again, I should not appeal to the law. It was troubling it about a very trifling matter. Very polite, the law, all the same. I would rather have taken the slight with a cheerful heart. There are some things about which one is sorry to have been annoyed; this is one of them. A certificate – a mighty fine thing. The best diploma is the gratitude of the people.'[8] Richard Wallace, on the other hand, received more than a diploma; he was honoured in both France and Britain, being made a commander of the Legion of Honour in the former and awarded a baronetcy by the latter.

On 12 February the National Assembly convened in Bordeaux and Adolphe Thiers became premier five days later. (And on 15 February Richard Wallace married his long-term mistress, Amélie Castelnau, the mother of his son Edmond, who had served in the cuirassiers during the war.) Preliminary peace talks were held on 26 February. Three days earlier, when the preliminaries to peace were being discussed, the men deputed by Bismarck to examine the financial clauses of the treaty with Thiers were the Berlin banker Bleichroeder and Henckel von Donnersmarck. The latter had become very useful to Bismarck, because of his knowledge both of international affairs and the French way of life, with footholds in the intellectual and social life of Paris as well as in the world of high finance. Bleichroeder put forward the figure of three thousand million francs as the war indemnities which France should pay. Henckel, better informed about French resources and how much the country could afford, suggested that a figure of not less than six thousand million would be more appropriate. No decision was taken immediately but, in order to continue the discussion, Bismarck asked Henckel to stay with him. Then on 6 March they took the express train together to Metz, where Bismarck stayed with Henckel at the Prefecture. The war indemnity was eventually fixed at five thousand million francs.

Meanwhile Blanche de Païva was continuing to supervise the building work at Neudeck, staying informed about what Guido was doing from a distance. She kept a low profile at this time, aware of the precariousness of her position. France was the country she had chosen to live in and to which she wanted to return as soon as possible, and yet her partner was heavily involved, in his role as a loyal Prussian and adviser to Bismarck, in bringing about the humiliation of that country. By this time Guido was forty years old: no longer the tall, slim young man of the 1850s, he had put on weight, grown his beard and acquired a rather ponderous manner. He had an aura of calm self-assurance, the result of wealth and success. Blanche herself was now fifty-one, though continued to present herself to the world – including Guido – as only forty-four. But documents are easier to forge than faces and by 1870 she was losing such beauty as she had previously enjoyed, though she went on trying to reproduce it by an abundant use of make-up. She had also grown fat, and wore a variety of different-coloured wigs. Yet there is no trace of Guido ever having been interested in another woman during his relationship with Blanche. During the 1860s Bismarck had even offered to find a wife for him, saying he was prepared to introduce him to a charming young relative of his. But Guido was interested only in Blanche.

On 1 March the Prussians rode in triumph into Paris, as part of the arrangement made between Bismarck and Thiers (who had resolved to endure the triumphal entry in exchange for not having to cede additional territory to Prussia). Despite it being a beautiful sunny day, there was hardly anyone out on the streets to greet them or watch them ride by, and the statues representing the cities of France in the place de la Concorde were draped in black. No newspapers were published that day and no public transport was running. The shops were closed, as were the shutters of nearly all the houses. Only one café was open, the café Dupont at the Rond Point of the Champs Elysées, and it paid for its temerity when it was ransacked later during the Commune.

Later in the day the Kaiser reviewed his troops at Longchamp and then they marched down the Champs Elysées, preceded by fifes and drums. The Kaiser had returned immediately to Versailles, while Bismarck accompanied the troops only as far as the Arc de Triomphe. Legend has it that the only building in the Champs Elysées to be open and illuminated was the Hôtel Païva, and that Count Henckel von Donnersmarck was standing in full dress uniform on the steps to salute his comrades as they rode by, thereby giving a slap in the face to France and to French public opinion.[9] The more prosaic truth is that some time between 1 and 3 March Henckel, who was staying with Bismarck at Versailles, rode to Paris and, while he was there, visited the Hôtel Païva to check that it had survived the war and the siege intact. It is likely that he put on some lights inside the house, which thus provided a contrast with other buildings in the street. It was perhaps not the most tactful thing to do, nor the most sensible time to choose to visit Paris, but the fact that no reprisals were ever taken against the Hôtel Païva suggests that the Parisians did not view this act as the great affront which it became in some later embellished accounts.

As part of the peace terms provisionally accepted by the French the Prussians withdrew from Paris two days after entering it, and so on 3 March they retreated back up the Champs Elysées. Again, hardly anyone came out to watch. On 7 March Bismarck stopped on his way back to Germany at the Prefecture in Metz, to have dinner and a long conversation with Henckel von Donnersmarck.

On 18 March there was a revolt in Paris, when the National Guard of the city refused to disarm and submit to the Thiers regime. Thiers fled to Versailles and on 26 March the Parisians elected a municipal council; two days later the Commune was officially installed. While the victorious Prussian troops affected neutrality outside the city, the Versailles troops loyal to Thiers began their own siege of Paris on 11 April. Fighting intensified over the course of the next five weeks.

France had no choice but to sign Bismarck's harsh peace terms of the Treaty of Frankfurt, which included the loss of Alsace and part of Lorraine, on 18 May. The defeat of the Commune, in what came to be known as the 'bloody week' (*La Semaine sanglante*), began on 21 May. The Versailles troops entered the city, despite the desperate defence put up by the Communards, who erected barricades, shot hostages (including the Archbishop of Paris and the *curé* of the Madeleine) and set fire to the Tuileries palace, the Hôtel de Ville and the Palais de Justice. The severe reprisals that followed the final defeat on 28 May resulted in more than eighteen thousand Parisians dead and almost seven thousand deported. Count Henckel von Donnersmarck, despite the offer from Bismarck of a post in his cabinet, elected to return to his business affairs and to his life with Blanche in Paris.

The humiliating defeat of the Franco-Prussian War, the subsequent Prussian occupation of parts of French territory and the annexation of Alsace-Lorraine had noticeable effects on the French psyche. There was a desire to find someone and something to blame. An obvious target was Napoleon III and his Empire, and writers in the 1870s indulged in much moralising about the most noticeable manifestation of that Empire which had been so easily shattered by Bismarck: the showy, shallow and extravagant *vie Parisienne*, epitomised by the opulent, brash lifestyles of the most famous courtesans who now found themselves the scapegoats for all the ills of France. J. de l'Estoile, writing in 1871, epitomises this form of post-Empire paranoia:

> When, after the fall of Bonaparte, public feeling was troubled by the disastrous state of our finances, the first thought to enter everyone's head was to wonder where all the missing gold had gone . . .
>
> . . . you naive people, your gold promenaded under your noses for twenty years, around the lake of the Bois de Boulogne, the spoils of the Imperialists, feasting to the music of Offenbach! The garnish of decadence, familiar to Parisians, had ruined the country, and blind Paris took a malicious pleasure in seeing [*sic*] the daily parade of the bitches who were consuming France.[10]

This moralising reactionary goes on to spell out his agenda clearly: 'To make woman moral is to create society; for to make woman moral is to make the mother, and good mothers make real men, patriots, citizens of strong nations, members of well ordered societies, which nothing can cause to disappear, of which nothing can jeopardise the fate.'[11]

It is an indication both of how deeply affected the French were by the events of the war and its aftermath, and of how different Apollonie Sabatier was seen to be from the typical *demi-mondaine*, to find her good friend (and womaniser) Maxime Du Camp also infected with post-Empire paranoia. In his monumental work, first published between 1869 and 1875, *Paris: ses organes, ses fonctions et sa vie jusqu'en 1870*, he attributes many of the ills of contemporary society to prostitution, professing to see it as a gangrene arising from the lower depths of society, invading the entire social body during the Second Empire. This desire of both the conservative and liberal bourgeoisie to repress sexual activity, seen as a flood about to engulf society, resulted in intense repression of prostitutes between 1872 and 1877, and the introduction of new by-laws in October 1878. The exaggerations in Emile Zola's portrayal of Nana (a composite figure and type of the courtesan, in the creation of whom Zola drew on stories of Cora Pearl, La Païva and others) reflect the extent to which he too was influenced by this anxiety. In one of his harshest diatribes, he likens a woman such as Nana to a disease-carrying fly:

> Muffat was reading slowly Fauchery's article entitled 'The Golden Fly', describing the life of a harlot, descended from four or five generations of drunkards, and tainted in her blood by a cumulative inheritance of misery and drink, which in her case has taken the form of a nervous exaggeration of the sexual instinct. She has shot up to womanhood in the slums and on the pavements of Paris and tall, handsome, and as superbly grown as a dung-hill plant, she avenges the beggars and outcasts of whom she is the ultimate product. With her the rottenness that is allowed to ferment among the populace is carried upwards and rots the aristocracy. She becomes a blind power of nature, a leaven of destruction, and unwittingly she corrupts and dis-

organises all Paris, churning it between her snow-white thighs as milk is monthly churned by housewives. And it was at the end of this article that the comparison with a fly occurred, a fly of sunny hue, which has flown up out of the dung, a fly which sucks in death on the carrion tolerated by the roadside, and then buzzing, dancing, and glittering like a precious stone, enters the windows of palaces and poisons the men within by merely settling on them in her flight.[12]

Zola also, in common with many other post-Empire writers, continued to reiterate the stereotypes catalogued by Parent-Duch-âtelet nearly half a century earlier, dwelling on the prostitute's instability and talkativeness, her taste for alcohol, her love of food and passion for gambling, her propensity towards laziness, lying and anger. On the positive side, the emphasis remained on her sense of solidarity, her love of children, animals and flowers, her modesty when confronted with the medical profession and, above all, her religiosity.

Despite the depressing forecasts of the moralisers, in many respects life did carry on as before after the Empire, yet a certain spontaneity and unselfconscious enjoyment had departed and there was less money to throw around. As Marie Colombier put it in her memoirs: 'We still love, but we no longer have fun. We still get drunk, but the cocktail has replaced the champagne.'[13]

1 *Illustrated London News*, No.1575 Vol.LVI, Saturday, 8 January 1870

2 Emma Elizabeth Crouch, *The Memoirs of Cora Pearl*, pp.81–2

3 Ibid., pp.169–70

4 Robert Baldick (ed. and tr.), *Pages from the Goncourt Journal*, p.181

5 Ibid., p.182

6 Emma Elizabeth Crouch, *Mémoires de Cora Pearl*, p.158

7 Emma Elizabeth Crouch, *The Memoirs of Cora Pearl*, p.170

8 Ibid., pp.170–1

9 See, e.g., Marcel Boulanger, *La Païva*, p.72 and Joanna Richardson, *The Courtesans*, p.63

10 J. de l'Estoile, *Les Courtisanes du Second Empire*, Office de Publicité, Brussel, 1871
11 Ibid., p.27
12 Emile Zola, *Nana*, p.246
13 Marie Colombier, *Mémoires*, pp.314–15

CHAPTER THIRTEEN

La Femme de Claude

O N TUESDAY, 28 October 1871 Count Guido Henckel von
Donnersmarck married Blanche de Païva at the Eglise Evan-
gélique de la Rédemption, the Lutheran church in the rue Chauchat.
He had been pressing Blanche to marry him since 1863. The problem
had been that she was still married to the Marquess de Païva. Divorce,
which had been possible in France from 1792 to 1816, was not
permitted again until 1884, and so the only possible way out was to
obtain an annulment, a long and complicated process. Neither
Blanche nor Guido ever made any allusion to their friends about
the negotiations which went on over several years with the Papal
nuncio; it was important not to allow gossip to compromise their
chances of success. Guido, who had contacts everywhere including in
Rome, first broached the matter of an annulment of the marriage
between Francesco de Païva and the widow Villoing in 1865. In 1871
his lawyers finally managed to persuade the Sacred Congregation of
the validity of the case, and the marriage was annulled, as far as the
Church was concerned, on 16 August.

A further complication was that the burning of the Hôtel de Ville
by the Communards had destroyed the records of the civil marriage
between Blanche and Païva, and Guido therefore had to approach
the Portuguese consulate to get the necessary documents drawn up to
effect the annulment of the civil marriage. These formalities were
duly completed on 26 September, and Blanche returned to Paris and
her beloved *hôtel* to make the preparations for the wedding ceremony. She first had to abjure Roman Catholicism (as she had

previously abjured both Judaism and Russian Orthodoxy) and promise her allegiance to the Lutheran Church, and then the German ambassador had to be petitioned to authorise the marriage.

Blanche was fifty-two years old, though the wedding certificate gives her year of birth as 1826 (and her place of birth as Moscow). Her father's occupation is recorded as 'capitalist' and Villoing's as 'banker'. The witnesses to the marriage were Count Léon Henckel von Donnersmarck from Nassenheld in Prussia, Blanche's architect Hector-Martin Lefuel, and two old friends – Julien Turgan and the 'taster' Dumont de Montcel. As a wedding present Guido gave Blanche the three-row diamond necklace which had previously belonged to the Empress Eugénie and which she had been forced to sell. This was Blanche's apotheosis.

Despite this marriage and the publicity attendant upon it, the new Countess von Donnersmarck never escaped her sobriquet of 'La Païva'. It had taken on a life of its own, becoming a defining aspect of the woman who had chosen it, the axis of legend, the encapsulation of the image of the *grande horizontale*. The story of this name, of its refusal to detach itself from the woman who had adopted it, clinging to her long after she had renounced all legal claim to it, illustrates how those who dedicate their lives to the presentation of a particular image, who use their freedom to create that image, may ultimately find that they lose their freedom through it too, that the image takes over and offers no escape.

Once reinstalled in Paris and with the wedding festivities completed, the woman who was always to be known as La Païva proceeded to resurrect her salon, which would in future include a sprinkling of political men such as the German ambassador, the Prince of Hohenlohe. The presence of such guests could not help but add fuel to the fire of innuendo which would surround La Païva and her husband to the end of her life and beyond.

To the moralising which went on in France after the collapse of the Second Empire was added the fear of espionage, the reason again being the attempt to find some explanation for the rapid and total defeat of France and its subsequent fall into chaos. The popular imagination saw spies round every corner, and what better place to find them than the Hôtel Païva whose foreign occupants – one a fiendish Jewess who thrived on cold and the other a bearded Prussian closely allied with Bismarck – still showed off their opulence in a most unrepublican manner? Allegations that Blanche and Guido were spies, or at least that they were suspected as such and therefore asked to leave France, have been repeated so often[1] that they have acquired the patina of truth, though no real evidence supporting these allegations has ever existed – and the couple were not in fact asked to leave France. Guido's very taciturnity has told against him, as guests remembered him – or those who were never invited imagined him – sitting there week by week listening to the conversations of the men surrounding his mistress. 'The presence of the coldly formal Silesian who covered the expenses of these showgrounds did nothing to dissipate the sense of unease hovering in the room, no matter how courteous his welcome, how engaging his diplomat's smile tried to be.'[2]

But what can these writers and artists have been discussing that was of any substantive interest to the Prussians, since the conversations generally revolved around art, artists, women and digestion? Marcel Boulanger has suggested that La Païva would pass on information from Arsène Houssaye or Emile de Girardin on the state of mind of the Parisians and on opinions at court, gossip which would be backed up with facts from Guido.[3] He also alleges that she simultaneously urged the Prussians on to war whilst reassuring the French that war would never come.[4]

Such assertions accord her far more power than she ever had, and also ignore the professionalism of the Prussian spy network which did undoubtedly contribute towards the rapidity with which the French were defeated. Amateurs like La Païva would hardly be necessary to the Prussians. Neither is there any evidence that Blanche ever betrayed negative feelings about France, the country in which she had chosen to live and make her name. Moreover, there is nothing in French police files to implicate either Blanche or Guido in spying activities, despite the fact that a Prussian of Guido's importance would have been under close surveillance.

In 1872 Blanche's former husband, the Marquess de Païva, shot himself. The years since he had returned to his mother's estate in Portugal had not been happy. He had left Porto in 1860 and moved to Braga, where he had earned some money teaching French at the college of Madre de Deus and to a foreign family. This work had enabled him to save enough money to return to Paris, which he finally did in 1872, harbouring the illusion that all his old friends would be both pleased to see him and prepared to lend him the funds he considered necessary to re-establish himself through gambling. In other words, his experiences of the last few years had not changed him. He did succeed in borrowing money for a few weeks, until his friends grew tired of funding him, for what he won one day he would lose the next. In early November Païva wrote to a former friend, requesting a final loan of two thousand francs. He then sat in his hotel at 114 rue Neuve-des-Mathurins, awaiting a response. It came after two days, and was negative.

This was the end for Païva, who went upstairs and shot himself in the chest. Even in suicide he was unsuccessful: he lingered on for several hours, dying at the Beaujon hospital at nine o'clock on the evening of 8 November. His death certificate read: 'Death certificate of Aubin-François de Païva-Araujo, of no profession, aged forty-five years, married to (no information available), said deceased born in Lisbon (Portugal).'[5] The minister for Portugal paid the expenses of his burial at Père Lachaise; no one attended the funeral.

Païva's mother was still alive and, when she was informed of her son's death, was also told of the extent of his most recent debts. She was forced to sell her property in order to pay them off, and thereafter retired to a small house on the outskirts of Porto, supported by a small allowance paid to her by her sister.

In addition to running her salon in Paris and to spending time managing her investments, Blanche Henckel von Donnersmarck also made frequent visits to Neudeck to supervise the continuing building works. The Countess's own apartments were to be sumptuously decorated, and a whole wing was to be devoted to guest rooms as the Henckels anticipated entertaining on a grand scale. They continued to hold receptions and to make public appearances in Paris, though from time to time they were forcibly reminded of their unpopularity. There was a story put around by Xavier Feuillant and repeated by Frédéric Loliée, among others, that La Païva was hissed by the audience when she appeared at a performance of Offenbach's *La Périchole* in May 1872 and that Thiers, the President of the Republic, then had to make reparations by inviting her to dinner.[6] In fact *La Périchole* was not performed after the war until 25 April 1874, when a new version was staged. Xavier Feuillant had himself, however, hit Count Henckel in the face with his riding crop in the Champs Elysées, and it was as a result of this incident that Thiers had asked the Prefect of Police, Léon Renault, to visit the Count and Countess to apologise and smooth things over. The Henckels had already indicated that they did not want this unpleasantness to be blown up into the status of a diplomatic incident.

Thiers had begun to give large dinners, followed by soirées, first at Versailles and then at the Elysée Palace, and he decided it would be politic to invite the Henckels to one of these, both to keep the German ambassador happy and to soothe the Henckels for the affronts that a section of Parisian society was determined to mete out to them. Emile Bergerat, who married Théophile Gautier's younger daughter in 1872, claimed to have first encountered La Païva around this time, at a Wagnerian concert held in the photographer Nadar's salons. In one of the most extreme descriptions of her ever produced, he writes that she resembled both an automaton and a vampire, who had spent her life sucking the blood of various men and now, at the age of sixty-five – an exaggeration of at least ten years – had the Siegfried-like Henckel in tow. He adduces the fact that her origins were obscure as further evidence of her evil, other-worldly nature, mentioning the hypotheses that she may have been Circassian or Irish, and the conclusion of Adolphe Gaiffe that she was the progeny of a witch and a broomstick. He declares that she was only ever in love with her money, and that she hated dogs, cats, birds and children.[7]

Alexandre Dumas *fils* would seem inclined to agree with Bergerat.

The former's youthful experiences appear to have left him with a bitter and puritanical attitude towards women, particularly courtesans, and he was also seriously affected by post-Empire paranoia. He launched an implicit attack on La Païva and her husband in his strange play *La Femme de Claude*, which opened at the Gymnase on 16 January 1873. Claude, a virtuous Frenchman and cuckolded husband, has invented a cannon whose deterrent effect will be the salvation of France and may even put an end to war altogether. He is assisted in his work by his adopted son, Antonin; these two alone know the secret formulae of Claude's invention. When the play opens Claude's wicked wife, Césarine, has just returned to his house three months after having run away with her lover. The lover has abandoned her, and she has had an abortion. It is made clear that she had previously already committed the 'unforgivable' sin of not having loved her illegitimate child (she had originally tricked Claude into marrying her in an attempt to cover up this particular lapse). Claude describes his wife thus: 'She is always in need of new sensations to make herself believe that she is alive, for she is more dead than those whose death she has already caused.'[8]

A man called Cantagnac arrives on the scene. He speaks with a Marseillais accent, but is really a foreign spy (Prussian, as is made clear in the preface). He is ostensibly there to discuss the sale of Claude's property (for his patriotic inventions are on the point of bankrupting him), but his real intention is to steal the secret of Claude's cannon. He means to do this by blackmailing Césarine, the assumption being that if Claude were to find out about the abortion he would hand her over to the courts. Césarine's way of getting at the secret will be to seduce Antonin who, foolish youth, is in love with her. The other characters in the play include Rebecca and her father Daniel, who are about to leave to go searching for the lost tribes of Israel. Rebecca is in love with Claude, but hers is a 'pure' love, which is why she is leaving with her father, never to return. Claude himself has been too damaged by his former love for Césarine to love anyone or anything except his cannon and his country. Finally there is Edmée the servant girl, given to listening at keyholes. She it is who eventually reveals the fiendish plot to Claude.

Césarine's first thought had been to pretend repentance and get Claude to agree to forgive her again (in advance of knowing all she has done), a promise which, if once made, she believes he would stand by even when informed of the 'crime' of her abortion. Claude, however, does not believe in Césarine's repentance and is immovable. He utters what is intended to be the real indictment of Césarine:

> No! this woman does not love me, neither me, nor anyone else. Did she not leave behind for ever not only love, but humanity, when she could not love her child? Do I owe anything to such a mother other than indifference and her daily bread, and is not such a woman no more than the form of a human being, more alien to me than the least of the dumb animals, who are hardworking and useful?[9]

In the face of Claude's upright self-righteousness and hostility, Césarine determines to exact revenge. She is trying to wrest the secret manuscript from Antonin when Claude appears and shoots her dead. The play ends with Claude telling Antonin (who drops to his knees in gratitude) to get back to work.

Dumas *fils* attempted to explain his intentions in writing this play and to justify its ending in his preface, in which he ostensibly addresses a critic who has taken him to task for apparently suggesting that a husband has the right to murder his unfaithful wife. The playwright has clearly fallen prey to an overwhelming fear of the fallen woman. He relates a vision he had while contemplating the state of the nation, during which he 'saw a huge bubbling welling up in the crucible; and . . . out came a colossal Beast with seven heads and ten horns, and on its horns ten diadems . . . and above each of the seven [*sic*] diadems, in the middle of all sorts of blasphemous words, there blazed this word, bigger than all the others: Prostitution.'[10] Dumas goes on to explain that this 'Beast' was 'none other than a new incarnation of woman', who, after thousands of years of slavery, had decided to revolt and finally get the better of man. An imaginary

speech she makes to mankind, and which Dumas 'overhears', shows
how she intends to go about this:

> You will no longer have a mother, you will no longer have a
> wife, you will no longer have a daughter, you will no longer
> even have a mistress; you will no longer have anything except
> the incessant and implacable sensation which will slacken your
> muscles, discolour your blood, poison your bones, cloud your
> reason, annihilate your will and extinguish your soul; for I will
> no longer resist you, and that will be my revenge; but you will
> possess no more of me than my rouge, my white and my black,
> my false hair, my rice powder and my perfumes, my surfaces in
> fact, which I will make you adorn and adore, which you will
> show in public and brag about in a loud voice. My inner being
> will remain obscure and closed to you; you will never penetrate
> it . . .[11]

Dumas then writes that, having heard what the Beast was saying to
herself, he made a point of following her around and of identifying
her beneath her disguises of 'the great lady, the wife, the mother, and
the girl, whose functions she does not accept, but whose clothes and
bearing she borrows'.[12] And in identifying the Beast, Dumas asserts,
he also became aware of the mortal danger France was in by 1870:
'She it was who showed me, before anyone else had seen them, the
barbarians marching towards Paris, the triumph of the populace, and
the ruins in the midst of which we have been stumbling for two
years.'[13] Ultimately, of course, it is all the Beast's fault: '. . . it is to the
Beast that we owe [the harsh lesson], for it was she who began to
dissolve our vital elements, by undermining little by little morality,
faith, family, work . . .'[14] Having dealt with the evils of this new
incarnation of woman, Dumas turns his attention to the dangers
inherent in the Prussian who still lurks in the midst of French society:

> Look at this man who prowls around your father's house, your
> dear home, breached, dilapidated and mortgaged, the remains of

which you are forced to sacrifice to your work and your mission. This man gets right inside; he has an open expression and an outstretched hand; he understands you, he loves you, he offers you his friendship and his wallet; he shares your hopes, he wants to be associated with your work and your retaliation . . . It is the neighbour, it is the false friend, it is the stranger, it is the hater, it is the spy who has slipped, over the years, into your family, and who, while all the time playing with your children, being saucy with the maid, talking to you of his blonde fiancée waiting at home, has been copying your locks, your accounts and the plan of your house . . .[15]

Dumas *fils*, in building himself up to his final peroration, is at pains to stress the dire consequences of the Prussian spy joining force with the wicked woman, and he becomes frenzied as he seeks to justify his hero's action:

Claude does not kill his wife, the author does not kill a woman, they both kill the Beast, the vile, adulterous, prostituted, infanticide Beast, who undermines society, dissolves the family, soils love, dismembers the fatherland, enervates man, dishonours woman, whose face and appearance she takes, and who kills those who do not kill her.[16]

He concludes by uttering a clarion call to patriotic Frenchmen: '. . . it is no longer appropriate to be clever, light, libertine, mocking, sceptical and playful; enough of that . . . God, fatherland, work, marriage, love, woman, child, all that is serious, very serious, and rises up before you. Either all that must live or you must die!'[17]

La Païva ensured the failure of *La Femme de Claude* by recruiting a cabal from among her supporters. The effort was probably unnecessary, as the public did not like the play anyway. The press was also negative about it, hardly surprising given both the quality of the play and the number of journalists who were good friends of Blanche's. The ravings of Dumas *fils* may be the most extreme example of post-

Empire paranoia, but they do serve to point up the underlying reasons behind the hostility felt towards Blanche by so many contemporary and later commentators. These include her foreignness, her alliance with an influential Prussian and the suspicion that she was a traitor to France, her history as a promiscuous woman who knew how to take advantage of weak men and, in particular, her 'unnaturalness', her lack of conventional femininity and her rejection of the 'redemptive' gift of motherhood. Despite her best efforts at concealment, the fact that she had given birth to two children whom she had ostensibly abandoned was known and held against her.

Count Henckel von Donnersmarck, still apparently unaware of the extent to which he was viewed as the hated Prussian, now made a significant error of judgment. Bismarck had decided that on 1 February 1874 the new subjects of the German Empire would be called to elect to the Reichstag in Berlin fifteen deputies, of whom four would be for Lorraine and four for Alsace. This gave the election great importance and people throughout Europe, particularly in France and Germany, would await the result with heightened emotions. The annexed populations resolved that, in order to make their protests as vehement as possible, they would shelve their normal differences, conservatives and democrats working side by side on this occasion. Nowhere was this determination stronger than in Metz where the diocesan bishop, Mgr Dupont des Loges, was chosen as the candidate. He was accepted with enthusiasm by the public as champion of the French cause. Despite this obvious popular support, however, the committee of the German colony of Metz decided to field a candidate against the bishop.

The committee may have felt they had to do this, or there may have been pressure on them to do so. What is less explicable is Count Henckel von Donnersmarck's decision to agree to be the candidate. He seems to have imagined that the economic power and influence which he wielded in the locality, where he had invested heavily, would guarantee him the popular vote. And so he set about campaigning, offering the voters various benefits should he win.

The result of the election on 18 February was embarrassing for

Guido, who polled only 2,346 votes, all these coming from civil servants and German immigrants. Even his own workers at Ars sur Moselle had refused to vote for him. Mgr Dupont des Loges was duly elected deputy for Metz, with 13,054 votes. This seems to have been one occasion on which the astute Blanche either failed to offer sensible advice to her husband, or he refused to take it. In any event, in both Alsace and Lorraine the successful candidates were only protestors. After the first session of the Reichstag, during which the deputy for Saverne made a solemn protest against the enforced annexation of Alsace-Lorraine, the eight deputies for the region left the building and never returned.

This unfortunate incident did not dampen the Henckels' taste for politics, and throughout the 1870s they tried to assist in bringing about a Franco-Prussian rapprochement. Their efforts were tinged with a degree of naivety, as neither of them ever seemed to grasp the extent of French mistrust and dislike of Prussians in general and of themselves in particular. Nevertheless Blanche did have some success in entering the political arena, if only by securing from 1876 Léon Gambetta, the French Minister of the Interior, as one of her regular Friday evening guests. Whenever a large number of guests was present, Gambetta would restrict himself to discussions of literature; once most had departed, and only a few diplomats and the Henckels remained, the talk would become political. Emile de Girardin, one of the first literary men to return regularly to the Hôtel Païva after the war, was also interested in bringing about closer links between France and Germany, arguing for this in the daily paper *La France*, the editorship of which he had resumed in 1874. The idea behind this hoped-for rapprochement seems to have been that, if France allowed Bismarck to make other territorial conquests, he might agree to return Alsace-Lorraine. It also seems, however, that this was largely wishful thinking. In the spring of 1878 the Henckels were plotting to contrive a secret meeting between Bismarck and Gambetta to negotiate about Lorraine, but it never happened. Either Count Henckel von Donnersmarck was not as important as he liked to think he was and Bismarck only took notice of him when it suited his own interests, or Gambetta realised Bismarck was only toying with him and decided it would be unwise to proceed. There is no trace after the summer of 1878 of relations of any sort between Bismarck and Gambetta. The latter continued to dine frequently at the Hôtel Païva, however, and to charm the other guests, who would generally include representatives of all the French political parties.

The last years of La Païva's life were difficult. On 12 January 1880 she made her will, leaving everything to her husband. If he were to predecease her, then half of her fortune was to go to help the arts and artists in Paris. That year her health began to deteriorate rapidly, but she kept believing that she would recover, trusting to the attentions of the French and German doctors Count Henckel urged her to consult. The Count also suggested that she should try a change of air, and so she visited Baden and Berlin as well as continuing to make trips to Silesia. But she was unhappy away from Paris, for she missed her old friends as well as her *hôtel*. Then, as more of them began to die – both Paul de Saint-Victor and Emile de Girardin died in 1881 – even Paris became less of a solace. At least there were still plays, concerts and operas to sustain her interest (though the last performance at the Théâtre Italien had taken place on 15 December 1878, after which the theatre was turned into a bank). But then the doctors counselled, and Guido agreed, that the excitement of life in Paris only worsened her state of health, and Blanche was persuaded to retire to Neudeck until she recovered. Guido assured her that the Hôtel Païva would be ready and waiting to welcome her again as soon as she was better. In late autumn 1882 Blanche set off, accompanied by the still adoring Guido, for Neudeck.

For a while she did feel better in her luxurious new castle, glad to rest after the strain of life in Paris. Soon, however, she began to feel bored. She had Guido for company, but longed for the stimulating conversation with which she had taken care to surround herself for most of her life. There was no one to talk to at Neudeck, only nurses and doctors who told Guido that guests would be injurious to his wife's health. So the sumptuous guest wing remained uninhabited. For exercise Blanche was allowed to go for drives in the area around the castle and to take very slow walks in the lanes around Tarnowitz. She had had to abandon horse-riding while still in Paris, when her obesity – the heart disease she was suffering from caused her body to swell – had prevented her from mounting even the most docile of horses.

She had four personal maids whose job it was to try to cover up the ravages of old age and sickness. Each day she took a series of baths to try to counteract the acidity of her blood. She tried everything in the attempt to regain her lost attractions, but nothing prevailed – not the daily walks, nor the careful diet, nor the attentions of her doctors. She also began to suffer from a constant fear of robbery or assassination. Her cardiac trouble confined her more and more to her bedroom and finally to her bed. Then she had a stroke. Suddenly she seemed to have become a very old woman.

Blanche died at Neudeck on 21 January 1884, at four o'clock in the afternoon. She was buried in the Henckel von Donnersmarck family vault. Guido, overcome by grief, declared at the funeral that he would never remarry. Her death merited only a brief mention in the Paris press.

Even after her death La Païva continued to be the stuff of legend, the most detailed account of the following story being given by Emile Bergerat.[18] Despite his declaration at the funeral, a little over three years later Guido did remarry. Bergerat reports that Guido told his new wife, in true Gothic horror fashion, that she was free to go wherever she pleased in his castle, with the exception of one room which he kept locked and which he forbade her to enter. At certain times he would lock himself into this room and stay there for hours; he never told anyone what he was doing there and would emerge in a very strange mood to go galloping off through the woods. But one day, when he was out on one of these mysterious gallops, his wife happened to notice that he had left the key in the lock of the forbidden room. Curiosity overcame her; she turned the key, opened the door – and screamed. Hours later she was found by the servants in a dead faint on the floor – while dancing up and down like a life-sized puppet in a huge jar of embalming fluid was the body of La Païva, from whom the poor widower could not bear to be parted, even by death.

In June 1888 Count Henckel von Donnersmarck sold the château of Pontchartrain to the financier Auguste Dreyfus-Gonzales. More attached to the Hôtel Païva, he had briefly thought, shortly after Blanche's death, of transporting it stone by stone to Germany. He had asked the architect Rossigneux to look into the possibility of this project, but it ultimately proved too difficult to undertake. In December 1891 Guido took his wife Catherina to Paris for the first time, where he was amazed to find she hated the *hôtel*, which she declared was too small and completely uninhabitable. What she did not say, but which was more to the point, was that it was completely impregnated with the character of Guido's first wife; no successor to La Païva could possibly be happy there. And so Guido sought a purchaser, finding one in 1893 in a Berlin banker and racehorse owner. During the Exposition of 1900 an erstwhile chef from the imperial court of Russia, Monsieur Cubat, became the tenant and installed a restaurant there but, despite the sumptuous décor extolled in the promotional book *Un Hôtel célèbre sous le Second Empire*, the restaurant did not succeed. Monsieur Cubat also took insufficient care with various alterations he made, bequeathing major problems to the subsequent owners a few decades later. In 1904 the building was acquired by the Travellers' Club.

The Hôtel Païva not only still stands at 25 avenue des Champs Elysées, the sole surviving example of a private Second Empire mansion, but has now been listed as an historic monument and, as such, is in receipt of state funding to ensure it can be maintained in good repair. Major work had to be carried out during the 1970s and 1980s as one of the ceilings was in danger of collapsing entirely after damp had got into the supporting beams. It now belongs to the Travellers' Club in perpetuity. It has thus retained something of the exclusive *cachet* its founder intended; (male) members from around the world can stay there, while it is open to the public for guided tours only on certain Sunday mornings. The booklet for sale in the foyer describes Blanche's beloved *hôtel* as 'one of the most magnificent examples of French 19th-century architecture',[19] and a comment made by a tourist – 'It's just like Napoleon III's apartments in the Louvre' – would undoubtedly have delighted her.

Blanche's building project in Silesia did not fare so well. In 1922, when the province of Silesia was attached to Poland, Neudeck changed its name to Swerklianec. Twenty-three years later the great castle of Swerklianec was entirely destroyed by fire. All that remained were the ruins of the chapel and part of the park.

---

1 See, e.g., Marcel Boulanger, *La Païva*, p.68

2 Frédéric Loliée, *La Païva*, p.192

3 Marcel Boulanger, *La Païva*, p.68

4 Ibid., p.70

5 Quoted in Janine Alexandre-Debray, *La Païva, 1819–1884*, p.76

6 See Frédéric Loliée, *La Païva*, pp.242–3 and Marcel Boulanger, *La Païva*, pp.82–3

7 Emile Bergerat, *Souvenirs d'un enfant de Paris*, Vol.2, pp.295–302

8 Alexandre Dumas *fils, La Femme de Claude*, Michel Lévy Frères, Paris, 1873, p.19

9 Ibid., p.75

10 Ibid., pp.xli–xliii

11 Ibid., p.xliv

12 Ibid., p.xlv

13 Ibid., p.xlvi

14 Ibid., pp.xlix–l

15 Ibid., pp.liv–lvi

16 Ibid., pp.lxxv–lxxvi

17 Ibid., p.lxxviii

18 Emile Bergerat, *Souvenirs d'un enfant de Paris*, Vol.2, pp.302–3

19 D.S. Neave in P. Fleetwood-Hesketh, *Hôtel Païva*, Editions Champflour, Marly-le-Roi, 1994, p.23

CHAPTER FOURTEEN

Last Years

T HE RELATIONSHIP BETWEEN Cora Pearl and Prince Napoleon continued for some time after the Franco-Prussian War,
though their meetings were of necessity infrequent and rarely took
place in Paris. In his letters, wrote Cora, 'he . . . gave me the most
loving advice and, although very dejected himself, he raised my
spirits'.[1] A note from him when he was in Paris for several days,
having received permission for a short visit, gives a flavour of what life
was like for a Bonaparte in post-Empire France:

> It would make me very happy to see you, but where? *that is the*
> *question*? [original in English] Impossible at my place. As for yours, I
> find it rather repellent, that *hôtel* . . . Do you understand? In
> addition I am watched a lot, although I'm a simple bourgeois, and
> the press are very irritatingly interested in my doings. I would hate
> to cause you any embarrassment with those you're seeing or in
> your affairs. The best thing would be to go this evening to the Bois
> de Boulogne. The weather's so warm. If a walk suits you, I can be
> in front of the Jardin d'Acclimatation at half past eight when I can
> kiss you and we can talk while we walk. Let me know.[2]

Other letters make it clear that the Prince's relations towards Cora
had now taken on an almost avuncular tone:

> Look, don't give up: you must be brave and sensible. I can
> assure you that I'm in just as much difficulty myself, but

one must struggle on. Lessen your expenses as much as you
can . . .

Tell me what you're doing and how you are. What are
these pains you've got? Your pretty face swollen – the
thought of that upsets me. I keep busy enough, despite being
alone and sad, as you can imagine. I would like to see you
again as well; when? where? Recent events force me to take a
rather prudent course as I am horribly *spied on*. But I'm still
stubborn and determined.[3]

The Prince spent much of the rest of his life wandering around
Europe. During 1871 he visited London several times, living for a
while at 108 Lancaster Gate and at other times staying incognito, as
the Count de Moncalieri, at Claridge's. The following episode,
which Cora does not date specifically but which probably occurred
after the siege of Paris and before the Commune (this being the most
likely time for Cora to have left Paris for a while), has been much
quoted:

After 1870 I went to London, where the Duke was to join me
incognito, and engaged a grand suite of rooms at the Grosvenor
Hotel, where, by the way, I returned after my expulsion.
    One morning the manager came up and said to me: 'You are
Mdlle Cora Pearl?'
    To which I replied: 'What is that to you?'
    'I cannot allow you to remain here,' he retorted.
    'But I have paid a month in advance for the rooms on the first
floor.'
    'That will be for the expense you put the hotel to.'
    That is the way in England.
    I was compelled to seek another hotel, only I did not pay in
advance. The Duke arrived a week afterwards, but this time he
objected to stay in the hotel; there were some Germans on the
ground floor. He rented a house for five weeks for £1,000.[4]

After their stay in London they went together, according to Cora, to Switzerland. She relates an incident which occurred there, involving some young men only too ready to rejoice at the misfortunes of a Bonaparte. Cora's response suggests that she was as fond of the Prince as she was of any man, and that she appreciated him for his dignity almost as much as for his money:

He suggested boating one day. We had rowed a few yards out when a boat with some young men in it passed ours.

'Halloa!' said one, pointing out the Duke to his comrades, 'look at him, that's he!'

'He has forgotten his big sword!' said another.

Coarse and pointed rudeness like this is very painful. Had one of the blackguards been within reach of my hand, I would have slapped his face with pleasure.

The Duke said nothing. It was on that beautiful lake that, perhaps for the first time, I felt happy in being his friend.

When we landed, after our excursion, the same individuals once more began insulting him, but from a distance. The weather was fine, the lake limpid, and the Duke very calm; and I took his arm.[5]

Cora and the Prince are also reported to have toured the west of England together, where she was sometimes mistaken for Princess Clotilde and fêted accordingly. There is even a story that they visited Dublin, where the Lord Mayor mistook her identity and asked to call and pay his respects. (The trustworthiness of Pierre de Lano's account of this alleged incident is somewhat called into question, however, by his locating Dublin in Scotland.)[6]

In 1872 when Cora was about thirty-seven, though still maintaining the pretence of being only thirty, a young man in his mid-twenties called Alexandre Duval fell in love with her. Alexandre's father Louis, originally a Paris butcher, had built up a chain of restaurants known as the Bouillons Duval. An early version of the fast food outlet, there were a dozen such establishments in Paris by the time of Louis' death in 1870. The restaurants were characterised by clean marble tables, attended by neat and efficient waitresses, and clients could choose from a printed fixed-price menu. A complete meal, with wine, would cost less than two francs. Alexandre had inherited this business along with a large personal income, which he began rapidly to deplete through his infatuation with Cora. In addition to giving her such extravagant gifts as a book whose leaves consisted of a hundred banknotes of a thousand francs each, he had been paying for the upkeep of 101 rue de Chaillot and of a country house at Maisons Lafitte. He had also given Cora several carriages and horses, including some which had been purchased from the former imperial stables. Before long he ran out of money; his family prudently refused to give him any more, and Cora – now that he was no longer useful to her – refused to see him, giving orders to her servants that he was no longer to be admitted. The desperate Alexandre kept begging to be let in and then, during the afternoon of Thursday, 19 December, having spent most of the morning wandering the streets in the rain, turned up with a gun, forced his way past the servants and shot himself in front of Cora. The wound was severe but not fatal – the bullet entered below his lung, just missing his stomach and lodging in his back. There were those who said Cora's only concern was the mess his blood was making of her carpets.

Alexandre was eventually nursed back to health by his family, but the post-Empire authorities were not prepared to turn a blind eye towards the ruin and near-death of a young Frenchman through the agency of a foreign courtesan, and Cora received a visit from the Prefect of Police who gave her to understand that she was to leave France immediately. Cora herself was astute about the reaction of high society to her expulsion, and implies that some of those who most applauded it were her erstwhile clients who felt they could not now be seen to support her:

Those whom it is the done thing to call honest people could not but applaud the expulsion of 'a person of my sort'. For them the trial was judged in advance. The majority of those who approved of the punishment inflicted on me were themselves 'honest people': they held tightly to this designation, which they would not however have been afraid to lose in deigning to pay me a visit or two. But they would have been afraid to show a little sympathy for a woman who had fallen on hard times. I went down in their estimation precisely because of my disgrace. Other times, other rules![7]

On 14 January 1873, a week after the death of the ex-Emperor Napoleon III in exile in England, *Le Figaro* published a list of Cora's creditors. Her debts included the sums of four thousand five hundred francs owed to a building contractor, three hundred francs to a publisher, six thousand six hundred and twenty-five to a dressmaker, five thousand four hundred and forty to a linen draper and over two thousand five hundred to a firm of cutlers. These creditors attempted to take advantage of Cora's enforced absence by seizing the contents of 101 rue de Chaillot under a law applicable to alien debtors. She successfully resisted this seizure of her goods, through her lawyer Monsieur Lefoullon, on the grounds that she was still a property-owner in Maisons Lafitte and Paris, which was her normal place of residence despite the temporary banishment. In February 1873 she sold 101 rue de Chaillot to another courtesan and took refuge for a while in Monte Carlo with her friend Caroline Letessier, who was being kept at the time by the son of the Prince of Monaco. From there Cora moved on to stay at Caroline's villa in Nice, and then travelled on to Milan where she succeeded in finding Prince Napoleon.

The Prince went on sending money to Cora whenever he could, for as long as he could. As he explained, however, 'If I do not write you oftener, it is because I should like to send you the wherewithal to make you happy; and it is not always possible.'[8] He had long ago given up any exclusive claim on her, and sometimes wished her well in making money from other men.[9] In 1874 he reached a decision that a definitive change in his relations with Cora was necessary. From what she quotes as his final letter it is clear that this change included the cessation of financial aid and probably the end of any sexual relationship (the two, of course, always going together as far as Cora was concerned):

> In the face of duty, no hesitation is possible! I make up my mind against you, and against myself for what is necessary. You understand my motives. I have a life of labour which must not be frittered away in dissipation, nor be under the sway of pleasure. You have always been charming, and you please me much; but with time, you will feel I could not act otherwise. I send you a last present which may be useful to you. I shall not see you for a few days: but later I shall shake you by the hand, and kiss you with great joy if you like, my dear Cora.[10]

Prince Napoleon lived on for another seventeen years, dying in exile in Rome in 1891.

As women like Cora became unable, both because of the inevitable ageing process and the changes in the social climate, to command the high prices they had previously charged and thus to enjoy a luxurious lifestyle, their lives began to be rewritten as morality tales, the wicked supposedly coming to a satisfyingly bad end. Zola provided the pattern in his novel *Nana*, first published in 1880, portraying in the death of Nana from smallpox just as the Franco-Prussian War breaks out the only fitting conclusion, according to the moralisers, for women of her type:

> Nana was left alone, her face upturned in the light from the candle. What lay on the pillow was a charnel-house, a heap of pus and blood, a shovelful of putrid flesh. The pustules had invaded the whole face, so that one pock touched the next. Withered and sunken, they had taken on the greyish colour of mud, and on that shapeless pulp, in which the features had ceased to be discernible, they already looked like mould from the grave. One eye, the left eye, had completely foundered in the bubbling purulence, and the other, which remained half

open, looked like a dark, decaying hole. The nose was still suppurating. A large reddish crust starting on one of the cheeks was invading the mouth, twisting it into a terrible grin. And around this grotesque and horrible mask of death, the hair, the beautiful hair, still blazed like sunlight and flowed in a stream of gold. Venus was decomposing. It was as if the poison she had picked up in the gutters, from the carcases left there by the roadside, that ferment with which she had poisoned a whole people, had now risen to her face and rotted it.

The room was empty. A great breath of despair came up from the boulevard and filled out the curtains.

'To Berlin! To Berlin! To Berlin!'[11]

Though he did not have the satisfaction of seeing her rotting in death, Henri Rochefort makes the ageing Cora sound as disgusting as possible, with 'her negress lips, her little grey eyes, and her dripping nose'.[12] He also attributes the following sentiments to an older and, it is implied, wiser Alexandre Duval:

. . . one night while we were at the theatre together, we saw the ugly profile of the old wreck peering out of a box, and my friend whispered to me furiously –

'When one thinks that I lay for three months between life and death on account of that disgusting harridan, whom I wouldn't touch today with a pair of tongs, well – well, I wonder where my head was!'[13]

Pierre de Lano was another commentator who relished the chance to describe a Cora gone to seed: 'After having fled [Paris], she returned there, but she became sinisterly isolated, poor, stripped of almost everything, a lugubrious shadow, badly dressed, atrociously painted, left with only the memory of her splendour of yesteryear.'[14] 'Zed' also paints an exaggeratedly gloomy portrait of Cora's life after the Duval affair; he goes so far as to trace the start of her decline to January 1867 and her appearance on stage as Cupid:

This was her Waterloo. From this moment, despite new and scandalous amorous exploits, despite the mad passion she inspired in a nice young chap who tried to kill himself for her, despite the expulsion which ensued, despite the publicity, she steadily declined and ended by falling into disrepute and ridicule. One saw her only from time to time, caked in make-up and poorly rigged out, looking like something from an old puppet show. This brought down on her one day, in the guise of a funeral oration, this cruel epigram on the part of her former friend Emilie Williams, with whom she had fallen out: 'Get lost, you old clown!'

Shortly afterwards, she disappeared from circulation altogether.[15]

The reality was not quite so gruesome. Cora had indeed succeeded in returning to Paris after her banishment in 1872 and she did lead a precarious existence, returning to the ups and downs of her early life as a prostitute. That Cora was, at least during certain phases of her life, officially registered as a *fille soumise* is attested to by the fact that she, unlike either La Païva or La Présidente or indeed most of the grand courtesans, merits an entry in *The Pretty Women of Paris* which is subtitled 'a complete Directory or Guide to Pleasure For Visitors to the Gay City' and was privately printed in 1883 at the Press of the Prefecture of Police 'by subscription of the members of the principal Parisian clubs'. One of its sources is clearly the register of prostitutes compiled by the police and kept at the Prefecture. The entry for Cora includes the standard observations about her and is written in a generally approving tone:

Pearl, Cora
    6, rue Christophe Colomb
    One of the most celebrated whores of her time. She has charmed a generation of votaries to Venus, and still goes on undaunted. Her real name is simply Emma Crutch, and she hails from Portsmouth in Great Britain. No supper party was com-

plete without her society, and she was once served up naked, with a sprinkling of parsley, upon an enormous dish, borne by four men . . . An accomplished horsewoman, her stables were as handsome as her apartments. She never thought of counting her money, and gold ran through her fingers like water . . . Now she is poor, almost friendless, and up to her neck in debt, but she has not lost her merry disposition. No woman was ever so really good-hearted and generous when she had money, and none of her old lovers speak of her except in terms of praise. Her features are not pleasing; her hair is dyed fair, but her teeth are magnificent and healthy; and her skin is of dazzling milky whiteness. When undressed, she is a picture, and her flesh is yet hard and cool, although she is quite forty now. She has never omitted using cold water, and is continually drenching her frame with an enormous sponge. To these ablutions and healthy exercise on horseback, we may ascribe the marvellous preservation of her bodily beauty. Every man of any note for the last fifteen years has passed a few hours with Cora, and time flies quickly in her company . . . There is a great lack of all ceremony about her, and she never took a penny from any man unless he cared to offer it. She is a jolly good fellow, and consequently will die in poverty and misery, as all unselfish people do, whether respectable men and women, or only simple-minded whores, like poor old Emma Crutch, who after sleeping in black satin sheets, embroidered with the arms of the Empire, now sheds tears of joy when an amateur slips a bank-note in her hand.[16]

One thing Cora did not lose was her sense of humour, her ability to laugh both at the men she encountered and at the scrapes she got herself into. A liaison she contracted late in her life was with a doubtful character from the Balkans, a former Serbian soldier, whom she calls 'the Prince of Hersant'. He sounds rather strange, to say the least:

He professed a great admiration for the plays of Dumas *fils*.

He said to me after a performance of *La Dame aux camelias* which we had attended together. 'That story is my own, provided you make Marguerite Gautier into a man, and old man Duval into a mother-in-law.'

I could never imagine what his story might be. Sometimes it occurred to me that the worthy man was completely off his head. At other times I had suspicions about his princely status. I wondered – afterwards I repented, but one spends one's life repenting, only to fall back into the old error – I wondered whether I might be dealing with a crook.[17]

The dénouement was predictable:

He spent a fortnight with me, without giving me anything. Finally, at the beginning of the third week, he did it . . . or rather he did me, for he never came back. His disappearance coincided with that of a very valuable brooch, given to me by Duke Jean [Prince Napoleon].

I didn't go to the prefecture to lodge a request for restitution. I didn't want to be thought too friendly with M. de Hersant.

He was a bargain-basement prince, and a chevalier . . . of ingenuity![18]

On 24 and 25 May 1877 Cora sold her silver and other items at Drouot's, the auction house. The catalogue listed two hundred and thirty-two pieces, mostly from the eighteenth century. Quite a large sum was raised, most of which went to pay creditors. She continued to receive clients in the apartment she had moved to at 23 avenue des Champs Elysées, over the premises of Georges Pilon the coachbuilder and next door to the Hôtel Païva. There is no record of the two women having anything to do with one another. It was while she was living here that Cora claimed to have received the attentions of a lovelorn poet – only one among many, according to her.

I cannot pass over in silence the more or less platonic loves, the troubadours who came to scratch at the guitar below my windows.

The most sentimental was quite a young man: blond beard with black eyes, a type of beauty which I must say I don't admire that much in a man. He wore a round and remarkably tall hat, and a tailcoat with completely unbelievable tails: over this outfit, an overcoat which hardly reached his calves. I was living in the avenue des Champs Elysées. It was three o'clock, and it was pouring with rain.

My poet – he couldn't have been anything other than a poet – walked up and down a couple of times, crossed the road, and went straight to a bench, situated just opposite my window; he then opened his umbrella, spread it out upside down, took out his pencil and sharpened it, his eye trained on my window, behind which I was standing in my dressing gown, watching his carryings-on. Without doubt, he was dreaming up poetry, and preparing to write me an ardent ode. I didn't miss one of his gestures, and I felt sorry for him. His hand moved feverishly. Three times the pencil broke under the strain of his vigorous scribbling, three times he sharpened it again. The song was ended and the poet soaked, thanks to his umbrella which was still open but had not for an instant covered his head. He stood up, blew me a languorous kiss, stowed away his billet-doux, and finally went away, though not without turning round more than ten times. Was it a dream? I was for a while tempted to believe so, as I received no verse of any kind in the post. Perhaps the poor devil didn't have enough left in his wallet for a stamp. Perhaps, and this must have been the case, he did indeed deliver his poem into my newspaper box, where it got mixed up with all the others which I received every day.[19]

In 1881 Cora visited Monte Carlo, the setting for a pathetic story related by Julian B. Arnold in his memoir *Giants in Dressing Gowns*. Arnold claims that he encountered Cora in a destitute state one night and took her back to his villa, where two bachelor friends – 'a tall Scotchman and a short-statured Irishman'[20] – were staying with him. There they gave Cora a good dinner and a bed for the night. Mr Arnold continues the tale:

> That night I was reading alone in the library of the villa. The armchair in which I was seated had its back to the door, so that when later it was opened softly I supposed that one of my friends had entered, and I did not look up from my book but continued reading. Presently I heard the voice of Cora Pearl, 'Forgive my disturbing you.'
>
> Glancing up from my book, I discovered that the lady of the voice was standing directly in front of me. She was wearing a man's dressing-gown much too long for her and obviously appropriated from the wardrobe of the tall Scotchman. Hastening to rise from my chair, I found my embarrassment not lessened when she incontinently let fall to her feet the dressing-gown, which fell in crumpled folds around her ankles, leaving her as unencumbered as Venus arisen from the foam![21]

This display was intended, says the author, to demonstrate that, whatever else Cora might have lost, she still had a beautiful body.

In 1883 Cora was involved in litigation (which she lost) with a Madame Perron, a dealer in lingerie and clothes with a shop at 46 rue de Provence, over a bill for thirty-two thousand francs, and with a Monsieur Denugent over a bracelet. Captain Bingham asserts in his *Recollections* that Cora was robbed of over twenty thousand pounds towards the end of her life, forcing her into abject poverty.[22]

One of the ways in which Cora kept herself entertained during her last years was by the study of Volapük, an artificial language and the precursor of Esperanto invented in 1879 by a German priest called Johann Martin Schleyer. It spread first to Austria, where it awakened considerable interest, the first society for its propagation being formed in Vienna in 1882. Until 1884 its adherents outside the German-speaking countries were very few and far between. In 1885 Dr

Auguste Kerckhoffs, a professor at the School of Higher Commercial Studies in Paris, published several articles, lectures and treatises on Volapük. This caused a great sensation in France, and it must have been at this stage that Cora took up the study of the language, demonstrating that she still had a keen interest in life and a certain irrepressibility, no matter what her personal circumstances. In 1884 she had sold her *Mémoires* to the publisher Jules Lévy as a way of raising some much-needed cash. In his book published a year before Cora's death, Philibert Audebrand writes as though she were already dead. Perhaps he thought she was:

> Although everything passes as quickly as a lightning flash, Paris has not forgotten this Englishwoman with the red chignon who came to us from London at the same time as Louis Bonaparte. It is not without serious motives that I link these two names. The britannic Phryne was one of the brightest stars in the firmament of the Second Empire. It is unanimously acknowledged that she was for twenty-five years the prototype of the modern courtesan.[23]

Cora died painfully, of cancer of the intestines, in a third-floor flat at 8 rue de Bassano at two o'clock on the morning of 8 July 1886, four months after the publication of her *Mémoires*. She had only been living in the rue de Bassano, not far from the locus of her days of triumph in the rue de Chaillot, for the last few months. Her final domicile was nothing like as squalid as some accounts would suggest, for all the apartments in that building comprised three bedrooms, two reception rooms and a kitchen. She did, however, from time to time have to send out her housekeeper, Eugénie Laforet, on begging expeditions to former lovers. Cora's death was reported at the Prefecture by Eugène Picot, a costumier of 4 rue Gustave Courbet. She was buried two days later, under her original name of Emma Elizabeth Crouch, in grave number 10, row 4, of the Batignolles cemetery. No tombstone was erected. Notices of the sale of her effects at the Hôtel Drouot appeared in *Le Journal des Arts* on 24 September and 1 October. The items are said to have included a considerable amount of false hair and a blonde wig. Her father, Frederick Nicholls Crouch, survived her by ten years, dying in Portland, Maine on 18 August 1896.

Cora's unmarked grave has long since disappeared. Batignolles cemetery is one of Paris's municipal cemeteries; out by the Porte de Clichy, behind the Lycée Honorée de Balzac which is itself surrounded by barbed wire, and partly underneath a road bridge, it is no tourist attraction. Perhaps her spirit lingers in the rue Ponthieu, where the house she once shared with Caroline Hassé is now a block of expensive apartments at the back of the Galerie des Champs, one of the Champs Elysées' exclusive shopping arcades. But what really remains of Cora are her memoirs, which she ends in characteristically clear-sighted and ironic fashion:

It is finished – my memoirs have come to an end – many others are at the beginning or in the middle of theirs. There will always be attractive graces, just as there will always be princes and diplomats, idlers and capitalists, gentlemen and swindlers. Were I to begin my life over again I should be less a madcap perhaps, and also more respected; not because I should be more worthy of esteem, but because I should be more careful. Am I to regret my present position? Yes, if I consider how poor I am. No, if I take into account what a quiet life would have cost me.

If louis are made to roll, and diamonds to glitter, I cannot be reproached with having perverted from their normal uses these noble things. With the latter I glittered, the former I set rolling. It was according to the rule, and all my sin has been a too great respect for the rule, rendering to the currency what belonged to Cæsar, and to my creditors that which had ceased to belong to me. Honour and justice are satisfied. I have never deceived anybody, because I have never belonged to anybody. My independence was all my fortune, and I have known no other happiness; and it is still what attaches me to life; I prefer it to the richest necklaces, I mean necklaces which you cannot sell, because they do not belong to you.[24]

Apollonie Sabatier's life after the war and the Commune was placid in comparison with those of Cora Pearl and La Païva. With her new-found prosperity, courtesy of Richard Wallace, she moved in 1871 from the rue Pergolèse to a six-roomed apartment on the third floor at 13 avenue de l'Impératrice. (Everyone continued to call the street by this name even though it had been officially renamed the avenue Ulrich, and changed again in 1875 to the avenue du Bois. It is now the avenue Foch.) She also had the use of a stable in the courtyard. The rent was three thousand five hundred francs a year, more than four times what she had been paying in the rue Pergolèse. She was able to employ a cook and a maid, and hired a small landau by the month to take herself and her three dogs for walks in the Bois de Boulogne.

Apollonie used some of Wallace's benefaction (the income was transmitted to her through Wallace's agent, Emile Levasseur) to help support her remaining family, particularly her mother. Wallace himself (now Sir Richard) moved to Hertford House in London in 1872, taking with him from Paris many of his finest works of art. (In 1871 he had added to his own collections by buying those of the Count de Nieuwerkerke, Princess Mathilde's former lover.) In 1872 he also funded the installation of a hundred water fountains in Paris, after a design by the sculptor Le Bourg. Between 1872 and 1875 he had major alterations made at Hertford House, including the provision of purpose-built display galleries on the first floor, but he hung *Polichinelle*, the painting which had once been a door panel in Apollonie's apartment in the rue Frochot, in one of his own rooms, rather than in the gallery of modern art along with the other paintings by Meissonier.

In her new apartment Apollonie decided to resume her Sunday soirées, but the brilliance of those earlier days could not be recaptured. The guests had changed; some were dead, others ageing and not always wishing to be reminded of the fact. Apollonie herself had grown plump – or *plantureuse*, the French word expressive of spreading flesh – with the passing years; only her hands retained their former beauty. Paul de Saint-Victor came to visit her, and

Ernest Reyer attended a few of her dinners. She saw Flaubert for the last time on 6 January 1872 at the première of *Aissé*, for which he had sent her tickets. After that they drifted apart, through age, indifference and forgetfulness. Since the mid-1860s she had sustained her links with her former life mainly through the agency of Théophile Gautier and the dinner parties which he held every Thursday at his home in Neuilly. These Thursdays had become as much of an institution as Apollonie's Sundays had once been. The guests would arrive at about four or five o'clock in the afternoon and stay for dinner and beyond. As with her Sundays, some people were always welcome at Théo's Thursdays, while others were specially invited. Apollonie herself was a regular, but she was not well acquainted with many of the younger people who frequented them.

On 15 May 1872 she attended the wedding of Théo's younger daughter Estelle to Emile Bergerat in the church of Saint-Pierre in Neuilly. Less than six months later Apollonie was among the mourners at Théo's funeral, an event which was as significant as any in marking the end of an era. Théo had been much tried and depressed by the events of the war and its aftermath; as he saw his beloved Paris shelled during the siege, then ransacked and burned during the last days of the Commune, he grew noticeably older and began to lose his zest for life. He also experienced the tiredness of the lifelong journalist, unwilling to start all over again to build up sources of income (it has been estimated that over the course of twenty years he earned no more than twenty thousand francs for his books and plays and a hundred thousand francs from his journalism), particularly as he had for the first time attained some financial security with his appointment as Princess Mathilde's librarian in 1868. (Mathilde herself had taken refuge in Belgium after the collapse of the Empire; she returned to Paris and Saint-Gratien in 1872 and continued to provide hospitality to writers and artists until the end of her life.) His health was also in decline; he had grown stout and had difficulty walking. He was no longer the sparkling, witty Théo who enlivened every gathering; he spoke little and was enthusiastic about nothing. On his death on 23 October the

doctor diagnosed cardiac arrest, but his friends felt he had died of
tiredness and grief.

On the day of his funeral a large crowd of those friends gathered
outside his house in the rue de Longchamp. The church at Neuilly
was too small to hold all the mourners; there were more people
outside than congregation within. Many old friends from the Pimodan and rue Frochot days were there, including Auguste Préault,
Paul Chenavard, Ernest Reyer, Paul de Saint-Victor and Théodore
de Banville. More recent friends included the artists Gustave Doré,
Paul Baudry and Puvis de Chavannes. Ernesta Grisi was there, with
Judith and Estelle. There is no record of La Païva having been
present, however. After the funeral a cortège of three hundred people
made its way to Montmartre, and crowds lined the route. At the
cemetery a crowd of several thousand were waiting to see Théo laid
to rest.

A few months later the painter and portraitist of Apollonie,
Gustave Ricard, also died, suddenly of a heart attack; he was not
yet fifty. He too had been complaining of tiredness and of feeling old;
he preferred to visit Apollonie when she was alone and had taken to
avoiding the Sunday dinners.

Early in 1873 Apollonie made another trip to Italy, this time in the
company of an old friend, Madame Delabarre. They spent a fortnight
in Rome where they encountered Paul Baudry in the Sistine Chapel,
attached to some scaffolding and copying one of Michelangelo's
sybils in preparation for the work he was to carry out in Garnier's new
opera house. (That year the old Opera House in the rue Le Peletier
burned down, an event which finally galvanised the authorities of the
Third Republic into agreeing to fund the completion of the new
building. Garnier handed over the keys – all one thousand nine
hundred and forty-two of them – on 30 December 1874, and the
Opéra Garnier opened on 5 January 1875 with a gala evening of
operatic and balletic extracts. The event was attended by dignitaries
from all over Europe, including the Lord Mayor and Aldermen of
London.)

Edmond Richard, who on his death left extensive – if not always trustworthy – biographical notes about Apollonie which have been preserved in the municipal library of Fontainebleau, claims that he was introduced to her in 1875 when he was twenty-eight and she was fifty-three. The introduction was made, he said, by his friend, and her nephew by marriage, Dr Zabé (whose daughter would one day marry D.S. MacColl, the Keeper of the Wallace Collection). Apollonie was still attractive despite her amplitude. Her naturally auburn or chestnut hair showed hardly a trace of grey, her eyes were lively and her mouth nearly always smiling, though her cheeks and jowls were becoming rather heavy. Her hands were still covered in rings, and her voice retained its musical tone. She attributed her increased weight to the fact that she now drove to the Bois instead of walking. She had left the avenue de l'Impératrice in the spring of 1874 and was living at 168 avenue d'Eylau (now the avenue Victor Hugo) in Passy, still in the same locality in which she had lived since leaving the rue Frochot.

Richard, who from the evidence of correspondence he left actually met Apollonie some time before 1875, became her final lover. He was an orphan, the eldest of a poor family, and had carved out quite a successful career in railway administration while also harbouring an interest in literature. He encouraged Apollonie to recount her reminiscences to him and he in turn kept her informed on all the latest developments in Parisian life. Richard consoled her somewhat for her faded glories, while he received a kind of reflected glory from her and her history.

Number 168 avenue d'Eylau consisted of a whole house on two floors, containing a dozen rooms. A small courtyard separated the house from the stable, the coach house and the coachman's quarters. A shaded garden full of flowers sloped down to the rue Spontini. The windows of the drawing room, which extended for most of the length of the ground floor, opened on to this garden, which was also overlooked by the basement kitchen. Apollonie's bedroom was on the first floor, the bed being raised on a small platform. The dining room, decorated with tapestries from Beauvais, fronted the avenue d'Eylau. This room could easily seat a dozen guests, but only six to eight would now attend on Sundays. Pride of place on the walls was reserved for those works of art Apollonie had kept with her through all her changes of abode and fortune: the portraits of herself by Ricard and Meissonier, the painting by Boissard, a drawing by Jalabert, and a watercolour and sketch of *Polichinelle* by Meissonier.

She now only saw her old friends from time to time. Ernest Reyer, always in good spirits, was one of her most regular visitors. The sculptor Christophe sometimes came to dinner and once had a long conversation with Apollonie about how *La Femme piquée* was made. Paul de Saint-Victor came from time to time and continued to provide Apollonie with theatre tickets when she asked for them. Meissonier visited only occasionally. Ernesta Grisi frequently came to see her, as did Bébé's daughter Jeanne and her husband Emile Zabé. Apollonie also gathered some new friends around her, who would come regularly to play cards and talk. Some of them, notably Monsieur and Madame Worms, were introduced by her old friend Madame Bressant, née Lucenay; Gustave Worms was also an actor who eventually took Jean-Baptiste Bressant's place at the Comédie Française. Both men were celebrated actors in their day, and through them Apollonie was kept very much abreast of developments in the theatre. Never having greatly enjoyed her own company, she gave small dinner parties several days a week and continued to keep open house on Sundays.

In 1880 Maxime Du Camp came to the avenue d'Eylau to see Apollonie, who had written to congratulate him on his election to the Académie Française. They had a long talk, which left her in tears and him greatly moved. In October of that year Paul de Saint-Victor informed her about a Belgian gentleman with a great enthusiasm for Théophile Gautier, who was in the process of collecting as many of Théo's manuscripts as possible with a view to writing a history of his works. This man was the Viscount Spoelberch de Lovenjoul. He had a passion for the great French writers of the nineteenth century and had spent his life collecting documents relating to Balzac, Gautier, Musset, Sainte-Beuve and George Sand. He had asked Saint-Victor to find out whether Madame Sabatier would be prepared to sell him her letters from Théo. She refused absolutely, and neither was she prepared to lend them to him. All she would allow was that the Viscount could consult them in her house. The staid Belgian was rather nervous about meeting her, having acquired the impression that she was a flamboyant courtesan in the style of Cora Pearl. Nevertheless he duly presented himself at 168 avenue d'Eylau, where he was shown into the drawing room by a maid. Apollonie was doing her knitting. Edmond Richard was also present. Apollonie had already got out the letters which she thought would interest the Viscount, and Edmond was deputed to read them aloud. And so, over the course of several evenings, he read out Théo's scatological epistles, while the Belgian sat there dumbfounded and La Présidente got on with her knitting.

During the 1880s Apollonie left the house in the avenue d'Eylau and moved to Neuilly-sur-Seine, first to 32 boulevard de la Saussaye and then to 48 rue de Chézy, a two-storey house surrounded by a garden on the corner of the boulevard Eugène. The drawing room, dining room and bedroom were on the ground floor; on the first floor Apollonie created a studio where she carried on with her painting. Here she spent the remaining years of her life, living quietly, continuing to enjoy the services of a coachman to drive her and her little dogs to the Bois for their daily walk, a chambermaid, and a cook to enable her to receive guests on Sundays. These guests included some of the younger generation of artists, such as Tony Robert-Fleury. Edmond Richard would come for long visits. Apollonie continued to support her elderly mother, providing her with a monthly allowance and visiting her regularly (she lived in a small single-storey house in Bois-le-Roi). Her brother Louis was now dead and Apollonie kept in close contact with his two children, Richard and Marie Marguerite.

Augustin Thierry, great-nephew of the famous historian of the same name, describes in *Le Temps* of 23 August 1932 a visit he made to Madame Sabatier in Neuilly, in the company of a schoolfriend of his who was also her nephew, a few months before her death. He describes her as having become very fat and lost all her beauty – apart from her still lovely eyes and hands. He talks of her reminiscing, particularly about Baudelaire, 'showing off her treasures',[25] as he puts it – the letters from Baudelaire. It does not appear to have occurred to the youthful Thierry that she was exhibiting the Baudelaire letters for their sakes, rather than for her own. She would have known perfectly well that it was her identity as the poet's muse which interested them; they would hardly be fascinated in a rotund and ageing woman for herself.

Apollonie died of influenza, during the epidemic which had broken out in Paris the previous month, on 3 January 1890. Her nephew Eugène Fallet, a lieutenant in the dragoons, and Edmond Richard registered her death. The official insisted that her real name of Aglaé-Joséphine Savatier be used on the certificate. She was buried in the cemetery at Neuilly, her headstone bearing the name 'Apollonia'. Her funeral, on a cold, damp day, was sparsely attended; among the mourners was the old, white-bearded figure of Ernest Meissonier.

She was survived by her mother, who died nearly a year later on 1 December 1890, at the age of ninety-four. Sir Richard Wallace also died in 1890, at Bagatelle, where he had returned alone in 1887 after the death of his son, leaving Lady Wallace in London. Apollonie's younger sister, Adèle or Bébé, had moved to El Biar in the suburbs of Algiers, where her husband, a retired colonel, possessed not inconsiderable vineyards. She had not been able to be present during her sister's illness or death, but had arrived in time for the funeral and then spent several months living in the house in the rue de Chézy, sorting out Apollonie's affairs and attending to their mother. Her husband died in December 1897, while she herself lived on until 10 July 1905.

In 1897 Lady Wallace bequeathed Sir Richard's art collections to the British nation; the Wallace Collection at Hertford House opened its doors to the public in 1900 and continues to be one of London's most treasured museums. The Meissonier door panel from Apollonie's apartment is on permanent display.

---

1 Emma Elizabeth Crouch, *Mémoires de Cora Pearl*, p.155
2 Ibid., p.159

3 Ibid., pp.160–1

4 Emma Elizabeth Crouch, *The Memoirs of Cora Pearl*, pp.90–1

5 Ibid., pp.92–3

6 Pierre de Lano, *L'Amour à Paris sous le Second Empire*, p.111

7 Emma Elizabeth Crouch, *Mémoires de Cora Pearl*, pp.268–9

8 Emma Elizabeth Crouch, *The Memoirs of Cora Pearl*, p.94

9 Ibid., p.97

10 Ibid., pp.101–2

11 Emile Zola, *Nana*, tr. George Holden, Penguin, Harmondsworth, 1972, p.471

12 Henri Rochefort, *The Adventures of My Life*, tr. Ernest W. Smith, Edward Arnold, London and New York, 1896, p.108

13 Ibid., p.110

14 Pierre de Lano, *L'Amour à Paris sous le Second Empire*, p.119

15 Zed, *Le Demi-monde sous le Second Empire*, p.55

16 Anon, *The Pretty Women of Paris*, Paris, 1883, pp.153–4

17 Emma Elizabeth Crouch, *Mémoires de Cora Pearl*, p.335

18 Ibid., p.337

19 Ibid., pp.341–3

20 Julian B. Arnold, *Giants in Dressing Gowns*, Macdonald, London, 1945, p.41

21 Ibid., p.42

22 Captain The Hon. D. Bingham, *Recollections of Paris*, Vol. 1, p.61

23 Philibert Audebrand, *Petits Mémoires d'une stalle d'orchestre*, p.220

24 Emma Elizabeth Crouch, *The Memoirs of Cora Pearl*, pp.187–8

25 Quoted in André Billy, *La Présidente et ses amis*, p.257

Seen and Unseen

A MIDST THE CATALOGUE of stereotypes, the listing of the usual prejudices of the time about the causes for women turning to prostitution, Alphonse Esquiros in his book *Les Vierges folles* suddenly casts a beam of unexpected light:

> All the same, the real cause of prostitution, in our opinion, is neither poverty, nor idleness, nor ignorance, nor incapacity, nor love: it is man.
>
> If there were not men who buy, there would not be women who sell themselves . . .[1]

Amidst all the glamour of the courtesan, there is a tendency to forget that money is being exchanged for sex. This is partly because so much else enters into the transaction as well: La Païva, La Présidente, Marie Duplessis and even Cora Pearl provided their male companions with far more than sex in return for the maintenance of their lifestyles. It is also an aspect of the *demi-monde* that the actual nature of the transaction is veiled, semi-deliberately; when the common prostitute solicits, it is clear that what is on offer is sex, but when a *demi-mondaine* is looking for a protector, or even just a client, she is offering a whole package in which the sexual act is implicitly included but may be the one thing which is not overtly displayed – or, when it is displayed, it is done so in a statue, or on stage, or in stylised half-joking, half-erotic letters. In other words, it is all part of the show. There are signs that sex is what the transaction is fundamentally about – signs in the clothes she chooses to wear and, in particular, in her elaborate bed, sometimes designed to resemble a goddess's throne. We hear much talk about the proceeds of the sexual transaction, and the rewards for having sold one's body are expected to be ostentatiously paraded; but the actual sex stays hidden in the alcove. In a sense she is selling far more than is the prostitute, for she is not much interested in a one-off transaction, involving only her body and only for an hour or so; the whole package she has to offer is herself – and 'if there were not men who buy' she would not be able to do so.

Cora Pearl was insistent that she was at all times exercising her independence, though even she admitted this independence had to be tempered when faced with something like the threat of expulsion from France. She makes it sound as though she chose to live the way she did; she certainly – usually – gives the impression of enjoying herself. Yet there is also a suggestion in her memoirs that she devoted her life to taking revenge on men because of what one man did to her when she was young, that she was determined to exploit men because she had herself first been exploited. Something similar was at work in La Païva's life. On her arrival in Paris she had had no choice but to prostitute herself. Having realised this, she applied all her efforts to reach a level of prostitution where she could make vast sums of money, and finally attained her aim, through capturing Henckel von Donnersmarck, of being able to leave the life of a courtesan behind altogether. Her enormous reserves of willpower enabled her to turn the tables on men, coming to dominate where initially she had been dominated – yet she also came to be dominated by the need for money. Though she might have preferred another route than prostitution originally, she came to realise that the only way open to her to acquire the wealth she desired was to avail herself of the wealth of men.

At this point there is a very narrow dividing line between the *demi-monde* and the *haut monde*, and that is marriage. If La Païva resented not being received into respectable society – and it has been said that she resented it very much – part of the reason was her recognition that plenty of women in that society were quite as mercenary, quite as self-seeking, quite as determined to entrap a man for his money as she was; the difference was that they had managed to get a rich man to marry them – and to marry them before they had time, or the need, to commit that first 'error' from which there was no way back. What had made the difference for these women was that they had been born into families of high enough class and income for them to be in the right market to attract a wealthy man prepared to marry them. In his preface to *La Dame aux camélias* Dumas *fils* expressed how this mere difference in circumstance could lead to a lifelong difference of reputation:

> A girl with no education, no family, no profession and no bread, possessing nothing at all apart from her youth, her heart and her beauty, sells it all to a man foolish enough to clinch the deal. This girl has sealed her dishonour and society excludes her forever.
>
> A well-brought-up girl, born to a conventional family, with just about enough to live on, and clever and determined, gets herself married to a man old enough to be her father or even her grandfather, whom she doesn't of course love, but who is immensely rich. She buries him after a month (there have been recent examples). This girl has made a good marriage, and society receives her with open arms, as wife and widow.[2]

La Païva, who had had to struggle every inch of the way, knew that many of the women who looked down their noses at her, who would have refused to enter her *hôtel* had she deigned to invite them, were no better than her in their hearts and souls; as far as she was concerned, they had just had it easier, and had no right to judge her, particularly as most of them could not hold a candle to her in terms of intelligence. That high society remained obstinately closed to her, despite her marriages to an ersatz marquess and then to a genuine count, can only have increased her resentment and maybe also her bewilderment.

La Païva was by no means alone among *demi-mondaines* in being frustrated in her attempt to rejoin, or join for the first time, the world of respectability. Another courtesan who made a determined effort to do so was the woman known in her heyday as Mogador. She had been renowned as a dancer at the Bal Mabille and also appeared in 1845 as an equestrienne in a circus at the new Hippodrome. One of her lovers was a scion of one of the oldest families in France, Lionel de Chabrillon; the couple loved one another but in 1852 Lionel set off to make his fortune in Australia. Meanwhile Mogador went into the theatre and enjoyed some success at the Théâtre des Variétés.

Lionel then returned to France, having lost what little money he had, where he proposed to Mogador, offering her a future as the wife of the French consul-general in Melbourne. She accepted, they were married in January 1853, and soon afterwards sailed for Australia. Mogador, who had reverted to her original name of Céleste, undertook charitable work in Australia and played the role of respectable wife. Ill health necessitated her return to France after three years. Lionel joined her on leave but had to return to Australia in July 1859. He became ill during the voyage and died in December, at the age of forty. Céleste struggled to survive without him, and eventually made a successful writing career for herself, producing twelve novels and many plays and operettas.

Nothing, however – neither her life of respectability with Lionel, nor her literary or charitable activities – could redeem her in the sight of French society, to whom she always remained the notorious Mogador. When she arranged for a home for war orphans from Alsace and Lorraine to be built on her own land, she was not allowed to attend the inauguration on 22 August 1877. *Le Figaro* commented on her situation in 1885:

Poor woman, she has attempted the hardest thing on earth: rehabilitation. The public has a habit of classifying people. It rarely lets them change their original classification. The Comtesse Lionel de Chabrillon, widowed after five years of marriage, has been trying to kill Mogador for more than thirty years. She has never managed to do so.[3]

Apollonie Sabatier, unlike her sister Bébé, appears never to have been particularly interested in becoming respectable; she threw away her chances of marriage at least twice, once in her youth with James de Pourtalès and later with Richard Wallace. Alfred Mosselman, despite the apparent security and happiness of their fourteen-year liaison, did not treat her well. Neither of them seems to have considered at the outset what agreeing to live as a kept woman might mean for her long-term future and, when he had the option to marry her, he did not take it. But I doubt whether this worried Apollonie unduly; she appears to have been a genuine free spirit, despite the efforts made to contain her in sculpture and poetic image.

Marie Duplessis, like both Cora Pearl and La Païva, began by being exploited by men and ended by exploiting them too. The men retained the ultimate power, however, for they could leave her whenever it suited them, with no ill consequences for themselves, whereas she needed them to maintain her way of life. The story of a disagreement she had with one of her lovers illustrates her power-lessness well:

Marie had arrived at her lover's house at two o'clock without having forewarned him, and the Count had replied through his valet that he was out. She knew for certain he was not, and her vanity was cruelly hurt by this slight.

On the following day, Marie was taking her usual drive in the Champs Elysées, in an uncovered barouche. The Count, who was on horseback, rode up to greet her. She averted her head and said to her driver, with a cold and mocking air:

'Tell the Count I am not in.'[4]

'The Count', however (he was the Count de Grandon), held all the cards as he was the one currently paying the bills. Marie had therefore to swallow her pride and capitulate, at least for the time being – their reconciliation only lasted for about a month. The desertion of her lovers when she became ill left her no way out from poverty, other than to sell what they had previously given her or provided her with the money to buy. As was the case with Cora, her independence was illusory, like so much else in the shadowy world of the *demi-mondaine*.

That Cora, Blanche and Marie were skilled sexual performers must be beyond doubt, even though the delivery of the actual sex act was only part of their allure. The impression conveyed of Marie is that, at least with some of her lovers, she enjoyed sex. For Cora and Blanche it was first and foremost a financial transaction; there is something in Blanche's determination to cease being a courtesan that suggests that she came to dislike, even hate, it. Her faithfulness to Henckel was made up of genuine affection and possibly sexual attraction, of relief at no longer having to engage in sex with anyone else, and prag-matism. Having attained her goal of possessing a secure source of wealth, she would never be foolish enough to jeopardise it. Cora had the reputation of being business-like and would be no more senti-mental about sex than she was about anything else; she could be amused by her partners, and even liked a few of them, but she made it quite clear that love never came into it and one imagines that fairly speedy sex would suit her purposes best. 'I can honestly say,' she wrote, 'that I have never had an *amant de cœur*. That is explained by that very sentiment which has always inspired me with an instinctive horror of the stronger sex . . . as for what is conventionally termed blind passion or fatal attraction, no! Luckily for my peace of mind and happiness, I have never known them.'[5] Apollonie, on the other hand, was interested in relating to men and not just in having sex with them, for money or any other reason. This is obvious in many of her actions, from her rejection of Alfred's further support of her when their relationship fundamentally altered, to her willingness to attempt to be Baudelaire's friend, rather than his lover, when it became clear that he was rejecting her sexual advances.

There is no equivalent word for a male version of a courtesan, the masculine version '*demi-mondain*' never being used, but if there was one man of the Second Empire to whom the term might have been applied, that man was Auguste de Morny. There are many similarities between him and the *demi-mondaines* of this book, from the circumstances of his birth, the slight change he made to his name and his adoption of a spurious title, to his financial dependence for many years on a married woman, the Countess Le Hon. Where he differed from the *demi-mondaines* was in the attitude society took towards him and the fact that nothing he had done in his life, no disreputable act, no exchange of love or sex for material comfort, was ever held against him or prevented him attaining high office and moving in the most elevated circles. Morny was admired for some of the very qualities for which La Païva was abhorred – ambition, willpower and determination to succeed, energy, an eye for the main chance and the use of other people to satisfy his own ends. His long and well-publicised liaison with the Countess Le Hon did nothing to damage his prospects. The only criticism he engendered was for ending the affair, not for having it; he even worked alongside his mistress's husband and brother in the direction of the Société de la Vieille-Montagne.

The case of Morny is but one illustration of the unbridgeable gap between the experiences and opportunities of men, and those of women, in Paris in the mid-nineteenth century. Morny wanted money and power; so too did La Païva. Morny had a number of routes he could take to reach his goals, and he used all of them: the love of rich women, speculation, business, the army and high political office. Most of those routes were closed to La Païva. She proved herself an able business woman and a shrewd investor, but she could only get into the position of being able to exercise her talents in those arenas through the agency of men, initially by selling her body for the highest price possible and then by finding a man prepared to dedicate himself and his wealth to her, whatever her past may have been. In this, Henckel was remarkable, for most men would have been too blinded by prejudice to see in her more than the archetypal, irredeemable courtesan, and too overcome by fear that her past would contaminate their own future to agree to ally themselves with her in this way.

The only other route open to women ambitious of wealth was through the stage. Certain figures stand out from this time, such as

Rachel, the great *tragédienne*, who did manage to command enormous fees at least for a short period (during a year touring Russia in
1853–4 she netted four hundred thousand francs for herself and one
hundred thousand for her troupe), Hortense Schneider, the heroine
of many an operetta and, later, Sarah Bernhardt. In many cases,
celebrated actresses also had lovers who paid for the privilege. Those
who were highly talented were less denigrated than other *demi-
mondaines*, but still remained outside the realm of genuine respectability.

A man like Morny could move easily between worlds, entertaining
a courtesan before going to a meeting with the Emperor, drafting the
libretto for an operetta in between sittings of the Legislative Assembly. He could join in the ostentation of Empire, play his part in all the
ceremonial and the show, but also enjoy genuine and far-reaching
power and influence. The *horizontales* were allowed the ostentation,
but it was supposed to be only that. The show was hollow. They
were supposed to know their place, to know that they were
ornamentation, trinkets, to be easily discarded when the time came.
They were not supposed to seek power, not supposed to be noticed
for themselves rather than for the men who had enabled them to be
noticed, not supposed to display their superior wit, not supposed to
attempt to get into a court reception at the Tuileries or to build vast
houses on the Champs Elysées and then ostentatiously refuse to let
anyone in. The impossible was demanded of the *demi-mondaine* – that
she should both display herself and not be seen. They were supposed
to be like Marie Duplessis, or like the legend of her – available when
required, seductively conscious of sin so that she seemed simultaneously to be displaying herself and shrinking from display, and
conveniently and discreetly dying before becoming old enough to be
a source of embarrassment to erstwhile lovers. Here is where the
courtesan and the common prostitute find common ground: despite
the demand that the courtesan should flaunt her acquired wealth
ostentatiously to be an obvious status symbol for the man who has
provided that wealth, she is simultaneously supposed to remain
invisible, just as prostitution is supposed to be contained and invisible

to those who do not already know where to look, so that the 'innocent' may be protected while the men who enjoy the services of the fallen woman may forget about her on their return to the world of high society and their legitimate concerns of business and politics. Charles Baudelaire could have been speaking for most of his peers when he declared to Apollonie Sabatier: 'I am an egoist, I make use of you.'[6]

Such a world of double standards, of ostentation combined with secrecy, is mirrored in the physical nature of Second Empire Paris subjected to 'Haussmanisation', the glittering façades designed to conceal the slums, great wealth co-existing alongside extremes of poverty, and that wealth itself of the here-today-gone-tomorrow variety. Moreover, in this world where sex is dressed up and flaunted, while being simultaneously hidden and discreet, the sewers become a tourist attraction, the dark side of the city there to be gazed upon, always provided it is controlled and packaged acceptably.

Yet despite all the constraining elements placed upon these women – *horizontales* at the highest level of prostitution, subject to received ideas about their nature, even about their physical appearance, expected to remain in their shadowy half-world, grateful for the attentions lavished upon them and not seeking to exercise undue power and influence – the personalities of Marie Duplessis, Cora Pearl, La Païva and La Présidente were all of sufficient strength and individuality that they could not ultimately be contained. Something of their true natures shines through all the myth-making to which they were subject, notwithstanding the difficulty of seeing them without the distortions of contemporary stereotypes about prostitutes and women in general. Had they lived a century or so later, Marie's ability to manipulate the men around her by creating the image they desired or expected to see, Cora's wit, acerbity and abilities of self-expression and self-display, La Païva's business acumen, drive and cultivation of artists, and La Présidente's gifts for friendship and for putting guests at their ease would surely have found other outlets than those available to them under the July monarchy and the Second Empire. Even before the deaths of Blanche, Cora and

Apollonie, things had begun to change for women: Paris's first *lycée* for girls, for example, opened in September 1883. That these women made of their lives as much as they did when they did, all four coming from nowhere to make their marks not only on the *demi-monde* but on the world beyond that half-world, where they became the stuff of legend even though they were not allowed to intrude on it in their lives, demonstrates their remarkable qualities, including those of resilience, creativity and power to act upon the imagination. 'Like a track of perfume, these women have left behind them a strange and unforgettable tradition of invincible tenderness, of daring independence, of hughty caprice or wild dissipation, which seems a long extension of the intoxicating hours of the eighteenth century.'[7]

---

1 Alphonse Esquiros, *Les Vierges folles*, p.42

2 Alexandre Dumas *fils, Théâtre complet*, Vol.1, p.19

3 Quoted in Joanna Richardson, *The Courtesans*, p.136

4 Romain Vienne, *La Vérité sur la Dame aux camélias*, p.116

5 Emma Elizabeth Crouch, *Mémoires de Cora Pearl*, pp.299–300

6 Baudelaire, *Correspondance*, Vol.1, p.276

7 Frédéric Loliée, *Women of the Second Empire*, tr. Alice M. Ivimy, John Lane, London and New York, 1907, pp.xviii–xix

Select Bibliography

On Marie Duplessis

The most recent work on Marie Duplessis is also the best – that by Micheline Boudet, a former member of the Comédie Française; a detailed and readable biography, whose only idiosyncrasy is the undue weight given to Marie's liaison with Franz Liszt. Prior to Boudet, the most informative work was that by Christiana Issartel. Romain Vienne is fascinating for some of his insights into Marie's character, though his whole account is romanticised and his factual detail is not reliable.

Boudet, M., *La Fleur du mal: La véritable histoire de la dame aux camélias*, Albin Michel, Paris, 1993
Dolph, C.A., *The Real 'Lady of the Camellias' and Other Women of Quality*, London, 1927
Graux, L., *Les Factures de la dame aux camélias*, Paul Dupont, Paris, 1934
Gros, J., *Alexandre Dumas et Marie Duplessis*, Louis Conard, Paris, 1923
Issartel, C., *Les Dames aux camélias de l'histoire à la légende*, Chêne Hachette, Paris, 1981
Saunders, E., *The Prodigal Father. Dumas Père et Fils and 'The Lady of the Camellias'*, Longmans, Green & Co., London/New York/Toronto, 1951
Vienne, R., *La Vérité sur la dame aux camélias*, Paul Ollendorff, Paris, 1888

On Cora Pearl

The best writer on Cora Pearl remains Cora Pearl herself, particularly in the French version of her memoirs. The so-called memoirs 'edited' by William Blatchford, which contain far more erotic passages than Cora ever wrote, are in fact a spoof, 'William Blatchford' being the pseudonym for Derek Parker, editor of *Poetry Review* from 1965 until 1970 and current editor of the Society of Authors' journal *The Author*. Despite the fact that the author admitted to the hoax at the time of publication (as reported in the *Sunday Times* on 3 April 1983), the book is still classified as 'biography' both in the catalogue of the British Library and on the shelves of the London Library. W.H. Holden and Baroness von Hutten are both worth consulting. B. Narran's strangely titled book is a not very good novel.

Binder, P., *The Truth about Cora Pearl*, Weidenfeld & Nicolson, London, 1986

Blatchford, W., (ed.), *The Memoirs of Cora Pearl*, Granada, London/Toronto/Sydney/New York, 1983

Crouch, E.E., *Mémoires de Cora Pearl*, Jules Lévy, Paris, 1886

Crouch, E.E., *The Memoirs of Cora Pearl* [authentic and authorised translation from the original], George Vickers, London, 1886

Holden, W.H., *The Pearl from Plymouth*, British Technical & General Press, London, 1950

Hutten, Baroness von, *The Courtesan. The Life of Cora Pearl*, Peter Davies, London, 1933

Narran, B., *Cora Pearl 'The Lady of the Pink Eyes'*, Anglo-Eastern Publishing Co. Ltd, London, 1919

On La Païva

The most informative and reliable book about La Païva is easily that by Janine Alexandre-Debray. Everything prior to her is far too coloured by prejudice and hearsay.

Alexandre-Debray, J., *La Païva, 1819–1884: ses amants, ses maris*, Librairie Académique Perrin, Paris, 1986

Boulanger, M., *La Païva*, Editions M.P. Trémois, Paris, 1930

Fleetwood-Hesketh, P., *Hôtel Païva*, Editions Champflour, Marly-le-Roi, 1994

Houssaye, A., 'L'Ancien Hôtel de la Marquise de Païva' in *Un Hôtel Célèbre sous le Second Empire*, n.d.

Le Senne, E., *Madame de Païva: Etude de Psychologie et d'Histoire*, H. Daragon, Paris, 1911

Loliée, F., *'La Païva.' La légende et l'histoire de la Marquise de Païva*, Jules Tallandier, Paris, 1920

On La Présidente

The most informative book to date on La Présidente is that by Gérard de Senneville; this is likely to be superseded, however, by Thierry Savatier's *Une femme trop gaie: biographie d'un amour de Baudelaire* due for publication during 2003. Savatier's knowledge and scholarship have already been demonstrated in his edition of Gautier's *Lettres à la Présidente*. Prior to Senneville, the most informative book was that by André Billy who was the first to make extensive use of Edmond Richard's notes. Jean Ziegler adds some fascinating detail in his two articles in the *Bulletin du Bibliophile*, while his *Gautier-Baudelaire* is particularly interesting for its section on Apollonie's sister, Bébé. Louis Mermaz's book contains much fantasy. Every writer on Baudelaire includes a section on his relationship with Apollonie and contributes his/her own theories about it: Enid Starkie and Joanna Richardson have the most sensible suggestions to make, while Claude Pichois writes about various liaisons he supposes Apollonie to have had, for which there is no evidence at all.

Billy, A., *La Présidente et ses amis*, Flammarion, Paris, 1945

Gautier, T., *Letter à la Présidente*, Editions Sauret, Monaco, 1993

Gautier, T., *Lettres à la Présidente et poésies erotiques*, ed. Thierry Savatier, Honoré Champion, Paris, 2002

Mermaz, L., *Madame Sabatier. Apollonie au pays des libertins*, Editions Rencontre, Lausanne, 1967

Moss, A., *Baudelaire et Madame Sabatier*, A.G. Nizet, 1978

Pichois, C. (with Ziegler, J.), *Baudelaire*, tr. Graham Robb, Vintage, London, 1991

Porché, F., *Baudelaire et la Présidente*, Gallimard, Paris, 1959

Richardson, J., *Baudelaire*, John Murray, London, 1994

Savatier, T., *Une femme trop gaie: biographie d'un amour de Baudelaire*, CNRS Editions, Paris, 2003

Senneville, G. de, *La Présidente: une egérie au XIXe siècle*, Stock, Paris, 1998

Starkie, E., *Baudelaire*, Victor Gollancz Ltd, London, 1953

Troyat, H., *Baudelaire*, Flammarion, Paris, 1994

Ziegler, J., 'Alfred Mosselman et Madame Sabatier', *Bulletin du Bibliophile*, 1975, pp.266–73

Ziegler, J., *Gautier-Baudelaire: un carré de dames*, A.G. Nizet, Paris, 1977

Ziegler, J., 'Madame Sabatier (1822–1890). Quelques notes biographiques', *Bulletin du Bibliophile*, 1977, pp.365–82

On courtesans in general

Anon, *The Pretty Women of Paris: Their names and addresses, qualities and faults*, Paris, 1883

Blanchard, C., *Dames de Cœur*, Editions de Pré aux Clercs, Paris, 1946

Briais, B., *Grandes Courtisanes du Second Empire*, Librairie Jules, Talladier, Paris, 1981

Decaux, A., *L'Empire, l'amour et l'argent: amours Second Empire*, Librairie Académique Perrin, Paris, 1982

Esquiros, A. *Les Vierges folles*, P. Delavigne, Paris, 1842 (3rd edition)

Griffin, V., *The Mistress: Histories, myths and interpretations of the 'other woman'*, Bloomsbury, London, 1999

Lano, P. de, *L'Amour à Paris sous le Second Empire*, H. Simonis Empis, Paris, 1896

L'Estoile, J. de, *Les Courtisanes du Second Empire*, Office de Publicité, Brussels, 1871

Loliée, F., *Les Femmes du second empire. La Fête impériale*, Librairie Félix Juven, Paris, 1907

Loliée, F., *Women of the Second Empire*, tr. Alice M. Ivimy, John Lane, London and New York, 1907

Parent-Duchâtelet, A.J.B., *De la Prostitution dans la ville de Paris, considérée sous le rapport de l'hygiène publique, de la morale et de l'administration*, J.B. Baillière, Paris, 1836

Richardson, J., *The Courtesans: The demi-monde in nineteenth-century France*, Phoenix Press, London, 2000

Roberts, N., *Whores in History: Prostitution in western society*, HarperCollins, London, 1992

Ryan, M., *Prostitution in London, with a comparative view of that of Paris and New York*, H. Bailliere, London, 1839

Skinner, C.O., *Elegant Wits and Grand Horizontals. Paris – La Belle Epoque*, Michael Joseph, London, 1963

Contemporary memoirs and letters

Adams, H., *The Education of Henry Adams*, 1905

Arnold, J.B., *Giants in Dressing Gowns*, Macdonald, London, 1945

Audebrand, P., *Petits Mémoires d'une stalle d'orchestre*, Jules Lévy, Paris, 1885

Baldick, R., (ed. and tr.), *Pages from the Goncourt Journal*, OUP, London/New York/Toronto, 1962

Banville, T. de, *La Lanterne magique. Camées parisiens. La Comédie Française*, G. Charpentier, Paris, 1883

Baudelaire, C., *Correspondance*, ed. Claude Pichois, 2 vols, Gallimard, Paris, 1973

Baudelaire, C., *My Heart Laid Bare, and Other Prose Writings*, tr. Norman Cameron, Weidenfeld & Nicolson, London, 1950

Beaumont-Vassy, Vicomte E. de, *Les Salons de Paris et la société Parisienne sous Napoléon III*, Ferdinand Sartorius, Paris, 1868

Bellanger, M., *Confessions. Mémoires anecdotiques*, Librairie Populaire, Paris, 1882

Bergerat, E., *Souvenirs d'un enfant de Paris*, Vol.2, Bibliothèque Charpentier, Paris, 1912

Bicknell, A.L., *Life in the Tuileries under the Second Empire*, T. Fisher Unwin, London, 1895

Bingham, D., *Recollections of Paris*, Vol.1, Chapman & Hall, London, 1896

La Chroniqueuse, *Photographs of Paris Life*, William Tinsley, London, 1861

Claudin, G., *Mes Souvenirs. Les boulevards de 1840–1870*, Calmann Lévy, Paris, 1884

Colombier, M., *Mémoires. Fin d'Empire*, Flammarion, Paris, 1898

Contades, Comte G. de, *Portraits et fantaisies*, Maison Quantin, Paris, 1887

A Cosmopolitan, *Random Recollections of Court and Society*, Ward & Downey, London, 1888

Crane, E.A. (ed.), *The Memoirs of Dr Thomas W. Evans. Recollections of the Second French Empire*, 2 vols, T. Fisher Unwin, London, 1905

Daudet, A., *La Doulou. La Vie. Extraits des carnets inédits de l'auteur*, Fasquelle Editeurs, Paris, 1931

Daudet, E., *Les Coulisses de la société parisienne*, 2me série, Paul Ollendorff, Paris, 1895

Delaxroix, E., *Journal*, tr. Walter Pach, Grove Press, New York, 1961

Du Camp, M., *Souvenirs d'un demi-siècle: Au temps de Louis-Philippe at de Napoléon III 1830–1870*, Hachette, Paris, 1949

Escoffier, A., *Memories of My Life*, tr. Laurence Escoffier, Van Nostrand Reinhold, New York etc., 1997

Feydeau, E., *Théophile Gautier: souvenirs intimes*, E. Plon, Paris, 1874

Field, J.O., *Things I Shouldn't Tell*, Eveleigh Nash & Grayson, London, 1924

Field, J.O., *Uncensored Recollections*, Eveleigh Nash & Grayson, London, 1924

Field, J.O., *More Uncensored Recollections*, Eveleigh Nash & Grayson, London, 1926

Flaubert, G., *Correspondance*, Vols II–IV, ed. Jean Bruneau, Gallimard, Paris, 1980–98

Foucher, P., *Entre Cour et jardin. Etudes et souvenirs du théâtre*, Amyot, Paris, 1867

Gautier, J., *Le Collier des jours. Le Second Rang du collier*, Félix Luven, Paris, 1909

Gautier, T., *Correspondance générale*, ed. Claudine Lacoste-Veysseyre, 12 vols, Librairie Droz, Geneva/Paris, 1988–2000

Goncourt, E. and J. de, *Journal. Mémoires de la vie littéraire*, ed. Robert Ricatte, Fasquelle & Flammarion, Paris, 1956

Gsell, P. (ed.), *Mémoires de Madame Judith de la Comédie Française et souvenirs sur ses contemporains*, Jules Tallandier, Paris, 1911

Halévy, L., *Carnets, Vol.1: 1862–1869*, Calmann-Lévy, Paris, 1935

Harrison, B., *Recollections Grave and Gay*, Charles Scribner's Sons, New York, 1911

Hegermann-Lindencrone, L. de, *In the Courts of Memory 1858–1875. From contemporary letters*, Harper & Brothers, New York and London, 1912

Henningsen, *Revelations of Russia: or the Emperor Nicholas and his Empire in 1844 by one who has seen and describes*, Vol.1, Henry Colburn, London, 1844

Herz, H., *Mes Voyages en Amérique*, Achille Faure, Paris, 1866

Houssaye, A., *Les Confessions. Souvenirs d'un demi-siècle 1830–1890*, 6 vols, E. Dentu, Paris, 1885–91

Hyslop, L.B. and F.E. (tr. and ed.), *Baudelaire: A self-portrait. Selected Letters*, OUP, London, 1957

Knepler, H. (tr. and ed.), *Man about Paris. The confessions of Arsène Houssaye*, Gollancz, London, 1972

Leclerc, Y. (ed.), *Correspondances: Gustave Flaubert–Alfred Le Poittevin; Gustave Flaubert–Maxime Du Camp*, Flammarion, 2000

Liszt, F., *Selected Letters*, tr. and ed. Adrian Williams, Clarendon Press, Oxford, 1998

Lonergan, W.F., *Forty Years of Paris*, Fisher Unwin, London, 1907

Maupas, C.E. de, *Mémoires sur le Second Empire*, 2 vols, E. Dentu, Paris, 1884–5

Metternich, Princess Pauline, *The Days That Are No More: Some reminiscences*, Eveleigh Nash & Grayson, London, 1921

Murat, Princess Caroline, *My Memoirs*, Eveleigh Nash, London, 1910

North Peat, A.B., *Gossip from Paris during the Second Empire*, Kegan Paul, Trench, Trübner & Co., London, 1903

Rochefort, H., *The Adventures of My Life*, tr. Ernest W. Smith, Vol.1, Edward Arnold, London and New York, 1896

Roqueplan, N., *Parisine*, J. Hetzel, Paris, 1869

Uzanne, O., *La Femme à Paris. Nos contemporains*, Les Librairies-Imprimeries Réunies, Paris, 1894

Vandam, A.D., *An Englishman in Paris (Notes and Recollections)*, Chapman & Hall, London, 1893

Vandam, A.D., *Undercurrents of the Second Empire. Notes and recollections*, Heinemann, London, 1897

Viel Castel, Comte H. de, *Mémoires sur le règne de Napoléon III (1851–1864)*, Chez Tous Les Libraires, Paris, 1883–5

Villemessant, H. de, *Mémoires d'un Journaliste, Vol.1: Souvenirs de Jeunesse; Vol.3: A Travers Le Figaro; Vol.6: Mes Voyages et mes Prisons*, E. Dentu, Paris, 1872–8

Vizetelly, H., *Glances Back Through Seventy Years*, Vol.II, Kegan Paul, Trench, Trübner & Co., London, 1893

Zed, *La Société parisienne*, La Librairie Illustrée, Paris, 1888

Zed, *Le Demi-monde sous le Second Empire. Souvenirs d'un sybarite*, Ernest Kolb, Paris, 1892

Other works on Paris

d'Alméras, H., *La Vie parisienne sous le Second Empire*, Albin Michel, Paris, 1933

d'Ariste, P., *La Vie et le monde du boulevard (1830–1870)*, Editions Jules Tallandier, Paris, 1930

Burchell, S.C., *Upstart Empire. Paris during the brilliant years of Louis Napoleon*, Macdonald, London, 1971

Cabaud, M., *Paris et les parisiens sous le Second Empire*, Pierre Belfond, 1982

Le Cérémonial Officiel ou les honneurs, les préséances, les rangs et les costumes civils, militaires, ecclésiastiques et diplomatiques, Paul Dupont, Paris, 1868

Christiansen, R., *Tales of the New Babylon: Paris 1869–1875*, Sinclair-Stevenson, London, 1994

Delvau, A., *Les Plaisirs de Paris: guide pratique*, Achille Faure, Paris, 1867

Du Camp, M., *Le Salon de 1861*, A. Bourdilliat & Cie, Paris, 1861

Du Camp, M., *Paris: ses organes, ses fonctions et sa vie jusqu'en 1870*, G. Rondeau, Monaco, 1993

Friedrich, O., *Olympia: Paris in the age of Manet*, Aurum Press, London, 1992

Gasnault, F., *Guinguettes et Lorettes. Bals publics et danse sociale à Paris entre 1830 et 1870*, Aubier, Paris, 1986

Harsin, J., *Policing Prostitution in 19th-century Paris*, Princeton University Press, 1985

Horne, A., *The Fall of Paris: The Siege and the Commune 1870–1*, Macmillan, London, 1965

Manéglier, H., *Paris Impérial: La vie quotidienne sous le Second Empire*, Armand Colin, 1990

Miller, M.B., *The Bon Marché: Bourgeois culture and the department store, 1869–1920*, George Allen & Unwin, London, 1981

Pinkney, D.H., *Napoleon III and the Rebuilding of Paris*, Princeton University Press, Princeton NJ, 1958

Richardson, J., *La Vie Parisienne 1852–1870*, Hamish Hamilton, London, 1971

Richardson, J., *The Bohemians. La Vie de Bohème in Paris 1830–1914*, Macmillan, London, 1969

Séché, L., *La Jeunesse dorée sous Louis-Philippe*, Mercure de France, Paris, 1910

Simond, C. (ed.), *Paris de 1800 à 1900, Vol.II: 1830–1870*, Librairie Plon, Paris, 1900

Sitwell, S., *La Vie Parisienne. A tribute to Offenbach*, Faber & Faber, London, 1937

Sonolet, L., *La Vie parisienne sous le Second Empire*, Payot, Paris, 1929

Tulard, J. and Fierro, A. (eds), *Almanach de Paris, Vol.2: De 1789 à nos jours*, Encyclopædia Universalis, Paris, 1990

Uzanne, O., *Les Modes de Paris: Variations du goût et de l'esthétique de la femme 1797–1897*, L. Henry May, Paris, 1898

Walsh, T.J., *Second Empire Opera: The Théâtre Lyrique, Paris 1851–1870*, John Calder, London, 1981

Worth, J.P., *A Century of Fashion*, tr. Ruth Scott Miller, Little, Brown & Co., Boston, 1928

On the history of France

Allem, M., *La Vie quotidienne sous le Second Empire*, Hachette, Paris, 1948

Bac, F., *Intimités du Second Empire*, 3 vols, Librairie Hachette, Paris, 1931–2

Bellesort, A., *La Société Française sous Napoléon III*, Librairie Académique Perrin, Paris, 1932

Benbassa, E., *The Jews of France: A history from antiquity to the present*, tr. M.B. DeBevoise, Princeton University Press, Princeton NJ, 1999

Bresler, F., *Napoleon III: A life*, HarperCollins, London, 2000

Corbin, A., *Women for Hire: Prostitution and sexuality in France after 1850*, tr. Alan Sheridan, Harvard University Press, Cambridge MA, 1990

Echard, W.E. (ed.), *Historical Dictionary of the French Second Empire, 1852–1870*, Aldwych Press, London, 1985

Fleury, Comte and Sonolet, L., *La Société du Second Empire*, 4 vols, Albin Michel, Paris, 1913

Furet, F., *La Révolution, 2: Terminer la Révolution (1814–1880)*, Hachette, Paris, 1988

Kracauer, S., *Jacques Offenbach ou le secret du Second Empire*, tr. Lucienne Astruc, Editions Bernard Grasset, Paris, 1937

Kurtz, H., *The Empress Eugénie, 1826–1920*, Hamish Hamilton, London, 1964

McLaren, A., *Sexuality and Social Order: The debate over the fertility of women and workers in France, 1770–1920*, Holmes & Meier Publishers Inc., New York and London, 1983

Plessis, A., *The Rise and Fall of the Second Empire, 1852–1871*, tr. Jonathan Mandelbaum, CUP, Cambridge, 1985

Price, R., *Napoleon III and the Second Empire*, Routledge, London and New York, 1997

Smith, W.H.C., *Second Empire and Commune: France 1848–1871*, Longman, London and New York, 1985

Tombs, R., *France 1814–1914*, Longman, London and New York, 1996

Williams, R.I., *The World of Napoleon III 1851–1870*, The Free Press, New York, 1965

Poems, plays and novels

Baudelaire, C., *Les Fleurs du mal*, ed. Enid Starkie, Basil Blackwell, Oxford, 1942

Baudelaire, C., *The Flowers of Evil*, tr. James McGowan, OUP, Oxford, 1998

Barrière, T. and Thiboust, L., *Les Filles de marbre*, Michel Lévy Frères, Paris, 1853

Dumas *fils*, A., *La Dame aux camélias*, tr. David Coward, OUP, Oxford and New York, 1986

Dumas *fils*, A., *La Femme de Claude*, Michel Lévy Frères, Paris, 1873

Dumas *fils*, A., *Théâtre complet*, Vol.I, Michel Lévy Frères, Paris, 1868

Dumas *fils*, A., *Théâtre complet*, Vol.II, Calmann Lévy, Paris, 1895

Feydeau, E., *Sylvie*, E. Dentu, Paris, 1861

Flaubert, G., *L'Education sentimentale: Histoire d'un jeune homme*, Seuil, Paris, 1993

Gautier, T., *Emaux et camées*, ed. Claudine Gothot-Mersch, Gallimard, Paris, 1981

Gautier, T., *Gentle Enchanter* (34 poems), tr. Brian Hill, Rupert Hart-Davis, London, 1960

Guitry, S., *Deburau*, tr. Harley Granville-Barker, Heinemann, London, 1921

Meilhac, H. and Halévy, L., *La Vie parisienne*, Michel Lévy Frères, Paris, 1867

Zola, E., *Drunkard*, tr. Arthur Symons, Elek Books, London, 1958

Zola, E., *Nana*, tr. George Holden, Penguin Books, Harmondsworth, 1972

Zola, E., *Pot Luck (Pot-Bouille)*, tr. and notes Brian Nelson, OUP, Oxford and New York, 1999

Zola, E., *The Ladies' Paradise (Au Bonheur des Dames)*, University of California Press, Berkeley/Los Angeles/Oxford, 1992

Other works consulted

Aretz, G., *The Elegant Woman: From the rococo period to modern times*, tr. James Laver, Harrap, London, 1932

Aron, J.P. (ed.), *Misérable et glorieuse: la femme du XIXe siècle*, Fayard, Paris, 1980

Auriant, *La Véritable Histoire de 'Nana'*, Mercure de France, Paris, 1942

Barry, P.B., *Sinners down the Centuries*, Jarrolds, London, 1929

Benjamin, W., *Charles Baudelaire. A lyric poet in the era of high capitalism*, tr. Harry Zohn, Verso, London and New York, 1983

Dictionary of National Biography, OUP, London, 1973

Dubnow, S.M., *History of the Jews in Russia and Poland from the Earliest Times Until the Present Day*, tr. I. Friedlænder, Vol.1, Jewish Publication Society of America, Philadelphia, 1916

Escudier Frères, *Etudes Biographiques sur les chanteurs contemporains*, Just Tessier, Paris, 1840

Estignard, A., *Clésinger: sa vie, ses œuvres*, Librairie H. Floury, Paris, 1900

Forster, J., *The Life of Charles Dickens*, Cecil Palmer, London, 1872–4

François-Sappey, B., *Charles Valentin Alkan*, Fayard, 1991

Gréard, V.C.O., *Meissonier*, William Heinemann, London, 1897

Henriot, E., *D'Héloïse à Marie Bashkirtseff. Portraits de femmes*, Librairie Plon, Paris, 1935

Hosking, G., *Russia: People and empire 1552–1917*, HarperCollins, London, 1997

Hungerford, C.C., *Ernest Meissonier: Master in his genre*, Cambridge University Press, Cambridge, 1999

Klier, J.D., *Imperial Russia's Jewish Question, 1855–1881*, Cambridge University Press, Cambridge, 1995

Manéglier, H., *Les Artistes au Bordel*, Flammarion, 1997

Marmontel, A., *Les Pianistes Célèbres: silhouettes et médaillons*, A. Chaix & Cie, Paris, 1878

McLaren, A., *A History of Contraception: From antiquity to the present day*, Blackwell, Oxford, 1990

New Grove Dictionary of Music and Musicians, Second Edition, Macmillan Publishers Ltd, 2001

Pauvert, J.J., *L'Erotisme Second Empire*, Carrère, Paris, 1985

Piesse, G.W.S., *The Art of Perfumery and the Methods of Obtaining the Odours of Plants*, Longman, Green, Longman & Roberts, London, 1862

Richardson, J., *Théophile Gautier. His life and times*, Max Reinhardt, London, 1958

Richardson, J., *Judith Gautier. A biography*, Quartet Books, London and New York, 1986

Riddle, J.M., *Eve's Herbs: A history of contraception and abortion in the west*, Harvard University Press, Cambridge MA and London, 1997

Shaw, T., *The World of Escoffier*, Zwemmer, London, 1994

Smith, R., *Alkan. Vol 1: The Enigma*, Katin & Averill, London, 1976

Teppe, J., *Vocabulaire de la vie amoureuse*, Le Pavillon, Paris, 1973

Walker, A., *Franz Liszt, Vol.1: The Virtuoso Years, 1811–1847*, Alfred A. Knopf, New York, 1990

Watterson, H., *'Marse Henry': An Autobiography*, Vol.2, George H. Doran Company, New York, 1919

Wyndham, H., *Feminine Frailty*, Ernest Benn Ltd, London, 1929

Useful websites

These recommendations are made with the proviso that web addresses can change, or sites cease to exist. I have, nevertheless, attempted to select sites that are of professional quality and seem likely to last.

The Wallace Collection http://www.the-wallace-collection.org.uk/index.htm
A comprehensive introduction to the Wallace Collection, including reproductions of the exhibits.

The Art Renewal Centre http://www.artrenewal.org
An on-line museum, featuring reproductions of the works of numerous artists, including many of those mentioned in this book.

Ville de Jouars-Pontchartrain http://www.mairie-jouarspontchartrain.fr
Includes photograph of château of Pontchartrain, which once belonged to La Païva.

La célèbre baignoire de la Païva http://perso.wanadoo.fr/sbr/paiva.htm
Photographs and details about the bath made for La Païva at Pontchartrain.

Salons http://www.aei.ca/~anbou
Site devoted to the history of salons, including a page each on Madame Sabatier and Princess Mathilde.

Charles Baudelaire http://www.poetes.com/baud
Excellent site devoted to Baudelaire, including texts of poems.

Messieurs de Goncourt http://membres.lycos.fr/goncourt
Site devoted to Goncourt brothers.

Gustave Flaubert http://www.univ-rouen.fr/flaubert
Comprehensive site dedicated to Flaubert, maintained by the Centre Flaubert of the University of Rouen.

http://perso.wanadoo.fr/jb.guinot/pages/accueil.html
Another worthwhile Flaubert site.

Théophile Gautier http://www.mta.ca/faculty/arts-letters/mll/french/gautier
Site dedicated to Gautier, including biography, illustrations and extracts from correspondence.

http://www.llsh.univsavoie.fr/gautier
Another Gautier site, including complete text of *Emaux et camées* (Edition Charpentier 1884)

La Bibliothèque Electronique de Lisieux   http://www.bmlisieux.com
Archive contains many complete texts by nineteenth-century French writers, with a new one added every month.

Les antres de l'almasty   http://membres.lycos.fr/almasty
More texts by various writers mentioned in this book.

Franz Liszt   http://www.d-vista.com/OTHER/franzliszt.html
An amusing site about the Romantic pianist which even contains an animation in which Liszt blinks, but also has useful information on life and works.

Napoleon III   http://napoleontrois.free.fr
Excellent and detailed site on the Emperor and the imperial family.

Fondation Napoléon   http://www.napoleonica.org/us/na/na_fondation.html
Dedicated to the history of the First and Second Empires, this is both an academic and a general interest site.

The Siege and Commune of Paris, 1870–1
http://www.library.northwestern.edu/spec/siege
This site contains links to over 1200 digitised photographs and images recorded during the Siege and Commune.

ExpoMuseum – 150 years of International Expositions
http://www.expomuseum.com
Concerns history and future of Universal Expositions, including some photographs from 1855 and 1867.

La Comédie Française   http://www.comedie-francaise.fr/index.htm
Official site of the Comédie Française, including history and details of past members.

La Vie parisienne
http://www.regardencoulisse.com/oeuvres/vieparisienne/vieparisienne.php3
Details about Offenbach's opera (in an e-magazine of musical theatre).

Gallica 2000   http://www.bnf.fr/site_bnf_eng/connaitrgb/gallicagb.htm
Multimedia documents from Bibliothèque Nationale.

Chimères: Petit glossaire de la prostitution
http://www.insenses.org/chimeres/glossaire.html
Definitions of words connected with prostitution, courtesans etc.

Handbook of Volapük   http://personal.southern.edu/~caviness/Volapuk/HBoV
For anyone wanting to follow in Cora Pearl's footsteps by taking up the study of Volapük, here it all is.

Index

A NOTE ON THE AUTHOR

Virginia Rounding is a social and sexual historian
living in London. This is her first book.

A NOTE ON THE TYPE

The text of this book is set in Bembo. This type was first used in 1495 by the Venetian printer Aldus Manutius for Cardinal Bembo's *De Aetna*, and was cut for Manutius by Francesco Griffo. It was one of the types used by Claude Garamond (1480–1561) as a model for his Romain de L'Université, and so it was the forerunner of what became standard European type for the following two centuries. Its modern form follows the original types and was designed for Monotype in 1929.